the
IMMORTALS

THE CATHAR ASSOCIATION

WWW.THEOGAMY.COM

THEOGAMY.BOOKS@GMAIL.COM

Tel.: 0774 6277614

Second edition, revised and expanded

Blessed John
of the Holy Grail

the IMMORTALS

THE REVELATION OF THE IMMORTALS, THE HIGHEST RANK OF GREAT CHURCH OF LOVE, TO BLESSED JOHN

A new God for a new humanity. Recognize the greatness of what is happening: the Sun of suns, revealing Himself for the first time to the sunny Theohumanity.

The Father-Sun reveals Himself for the first time and has no analogues in the 84th civilization.

Keep the courage of the pioneers and fearlessly profess the coming of the era of the Sunny Divinity.

John the Theologian saw Him on Patmos, in the form of the Wife Clothed in the Sun. Inflame hearts with a passionate faith in the rising sun of the Divinity!

Costa Brava
05-11.2007

Blessed John of the Holy Grail
The Immortals

The immortals, as the highest rank of the Great church of Love, reveal themselves at the end of the present 84-th civilization as the workers of the future age, intended to transmit the mysterious particles and rules of divinization to their disciples.

ISBN 978-5-98290-086-9

Printed in the United States of America

ℐHAT, WHICH YOU HAVE DONE WITH THE EASTERN CHURCH, DO WITH THAT OF THE WEST

During the ascent to the castle of La Selva de Mar:

We chose you (and your church), because we have read in the book of life that in former times you glorified the Solovetsky martyrs and the saints of our spirit in Orthodoxy.

The ray of Our Father revealed to us that, in all the world, only you can glorify us, the saints of the true school of Christ.

You have already proved yourself to be the holy zealot of the last truth. In spite of fierce prohibitions, having spiritual sobriety through the consecration of Sophia of the Exceeding Wisdom of God, you were able to break the clichés and hypnoses of the Roman-Byzantine inquisition, and opened the eyes of millions to the true church.

This is why we have chosen you. That, which you have done with the Eastern Church, do with that of the West.

CONTENTS

INTRODUCTION 9

PREFACE. SAN SALVADOR – REVELATION
OF THE GREAT CHURCH OF LOVE 15

1. A HYMN TO OUR FATHER,
THE SUN OF SUNS OF PURE LOVE..................................... 25

2. THE CATALONIAN HORN OF PLENTY OR THE MYSTERY
OF THE MULTIPLICATION OF THE CHALICE..........................37

3. THE HOURS OF DIVINIZATION,
THE HOURS OF COMMUNION
WITH CHRIST OF THE SECOND COMING 53

4. THE FIFTEEN-STAGE CONSULAMENTUM................................75

5. LUCIFER DEFEATED: THE EIGHTY-FIFTH
CIVILIZATION HAS BEGUN!...97

6. THE SCATTERING OF THE BLESSINGS.
THE REHABILITATION
OF THE COMPOSITIONS OF MAN 113

7. THE APPEARANCES OF THE FATHER
OF PURE LOVE UNION WITH
THE TREASURE TROVE OF OUR DIVINITY.......................... 131

8. THE VOWS OF ETERNAL VIRGINITY
AND ETERNAL BROTHERHOOD 155

9. THE CANDLES OF IMMORTALITY
ABOVE SAN SALVADOR VERDADERO................................... 171

10. THE ARCHETYPE OF 'KIND PEOPLE'................................. 189

11. THE EARTH – THE GREATEST CELESTIAL BODY
OF CRUCIFIED LOVE..215

12. THE CATHAR MOTHERS IN THE COMMUNION
OF THE EVER-PRESENT CHRIST..229

13. THE SUNNY RELIGION,
REVEALED FOR THE FIRST TIME
IN THEOHUMANITY...247

14. THE CATHAR REVOLUTION
IN THE HISTORY OF HUMANITY...271

15. THE FRAGRANCE OF THE BRIDAL BED
OF OUR DIVINITY..289

16. THE ASCENT TO SAN SALVADOR.....................................307

17. THE IMMORTALS...321

18. THE KNIGHTHOOD OF THE FATHER
OF PURE LOVE IS THE BATTLE
WITH THE FORCES OF ELOHIM...329

19. PURIFICATION...339

20. THE SECRET OF THE AIRY CASTLES.................................343

21. KEYS TO THE TRANSFORMATION OF MAN......................363

22. THE PILLARS OF THE CATHAR PATH
TO PERFECTION...377

23. THE BLOOD OF CHRIST FLOWS
INTO THE CHALICE. THE MYSTERY
OF THE CHALICE IN THE HOLY GRAIL.............................393

24. THE GOSPEL OF SAN SALVADOR.....................................411

25. THE FULLNESS OF THE DIVINITY,
WITHOUT DISTORTIONS
AND DISTORTING MIRRORS 423

26. THE BURNING HEART. THE DESERT
HOURS OF THE SECOND CONVERSION 437

27. THE NEW NAME OF OUR FATHER 449

28. JUAN DE SAN GRIAL, THE SUPREME
APOSTLE OF THE FATHER OF PURE LOVE 461

29. SIMON CEPHAS, THE 'APOSTLE' PETER 467

30. THE DOUBLE STANDARD OF MONOTHEISM 487

31. FIVE MILLION WILL BE LED TO THE ARK 501

32. THE RADIANCE OF THE MOST ETERNAL
ONE IN THE EXISTENCE TODAY 507

APPENDIX. 20 MYSTERIES OF THE HOLY GRAIL 519

GOD'S MESSENGER OF LOVE AND PEACE
Charles Mercieca, Ph.D. 533

FOOTNOTES 544

❦

Introduction

Blessed John is the father and the teacher of the divinized, Christ's branch of the humanity, transfigurated and united with the beloved Father of Pure love. He is the founder of the new spirituality of which the universal Exceeding Wisdom of the Holy Grail is the original source. The mystery of the anointed one is that he is a heavenly man, literally, created from the unearthly compositions, born in the virginal vestments of the Mother of God.

He proclaims the kingdom of the immaculate life and he has been given the keys for the victory over the sin and he holds the secret of clothing in the immaculate new body. He has been restored in the archetype of the Godman. Blessed John belongs to a kind of people, who are not satisfied with the ideological version of the faith in Christ, but who is of His spirit and His nature. The Divinity manifests so clearly and obviously in him, that it does not require much work and effort to distinguish Him.

There is no limit of surprise and delight: the greatest saint lives among us. The only motive of his life on earth is the love Minne. He hurries to the suffering ones of love, seeing the shapes of the Divine love in the hearts of neighbours, and undergoes great holy passion for each of them as their inner spiritual potential can emerge.

The world is on the threshold of great achievements. The new spirituality teaches the new ways for improving, the need to change the whole inner being of man by the power of Love. As our fathers, the Cathars, think that man from his creation has been combined by the bridal bonds with the Divinity.

The mysterious Father sends us into the world for the soul being more and more improved on the ways of love. To live in this nightmarish, deceitful, unscrupulous world is worth only for the sake of love, which is not on the earth. Man searches to express himself, but all his aspirations are robbed by the father of lust and lie, the author of the original sin, who has sealed the divine potential in man.

If God is evil, man becomes evil too. If God is kind, the humanity is also kind. But at the last depth man remains in the original and primordial formation of the Divinity – the loving Father, not engaged into the sin, illness, death, adultery, violence. Father's name is the Father of pure love.

The task of spiritual elders, the true purpose of the true religion is to return man to the fullness of the divine compositions, 100 from 100, and, moreover, to add to this a new quality – to create him as the bride of his beloved heavenly Bridegroom, the Holy Spirit, to become more beautiful and more perfect.

The new spirituality of the new millennium is the spirituality of the Bridal Chamber, of the Cross as the Bridal Bed and the Chalice with the shedding of the last drop of the burning love in the transcendental holy passion. The Exceeding Wisdom, personified Sophia, giving birth from on high in the immaculate bosom through the immaculate conception, leads along the way of the disclosing of the divine potential. The Virgin Lady as well as Christ were immaculately born in the formation of the Holy Spirit. She opened in the glory of pristine purity 'I am the Immaculate Conception' at Lourdes.

In book of "The Immortals" the great anointed ones reveal the secrets of perfect love, pure, virgin, unstained, the ways back to the palaces of the Father, to the most fragrant bridal chambers at the cost of the cross, holy passions and miraculous cures, provided by the Exceeding Wisdom and Church of the perfect ones, the Church of Christ!

Oh, the Father of pure love, the great consolation to mankind! The orphans, intimidated by the wicked stepfather, acquire the kindest, loving Father. Blessed are screaming, not as slaves: "Have mercy and do not kill", but as the loving sons: "Avva, Father, Beloved Father, I long to fall into Your arms!"

The concealed mysterious Chalice... It is impossible to understand anything about the immortals out of the spirituality of the Chalice, outside of Its radiation. The Grail has established Its kingdom, whose name is the kingdom of the divine love, of the messianistic anointed ones. The Grail anointed the disciples of Christ by the myrrh composition and inscribed the inner of the Chalice inside of them. The Chalice of the adoring love becomes a tool of deification of the Creator in His creation, the Father in His children.

The philosophy of the immortals: "Transubstantiate unceasingly. Transubstantiation is the pledge of immortality. He, who has mastered the mystery of transubstantiation as a transition from the erased form into the superior form (with the condition of absolute unworldliness) has mastered the foundations of the immortals' philosophy."

The book is of interest to everybody, who strives for the spiritual perfection, seeking effective ways of transformation and illumination, for the uniting in love with the loving Father and beloved neigh-

bour, for those, wishing to comprehend the laws of
the Universe and Exceeding Wisdom, are interested
in the mystery of the Holy Grail.

Eleonora Virginova, Ph.D.
philologist, translator

◄§

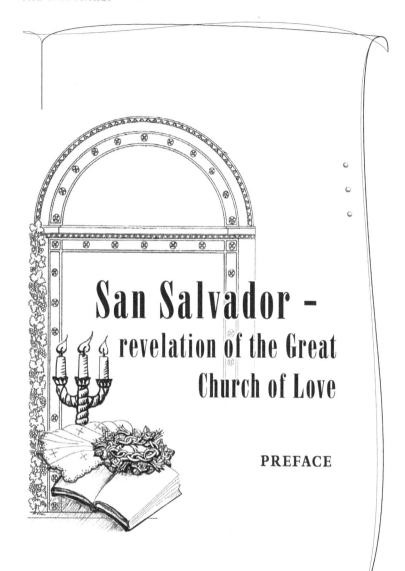

San Salvador –
revelation of the Great Church of Love

PREFACE

On San Salvador there are such spheres of prayer that the most eternal spirituality, lost due to *the cosmic catastrophe*, is returned through the union with the angelic world.

*

On San Salvador was embodied a form of Christ opposing that of the distanced and judging Christ: the Bridegroom of the Bridal Chamber, revealed infinitely uniting more than is possible – as it is not possible to unite with one mortal, but with Him alone.

The Mother of God Herself personifies His church-bride. Lengthy preparation through the worship of the pre-eminent Bride is needed – as She is in the annals of original Catharism – in order to partake of the bridal blessings of the Bridegroom-Christ in the civilization of the pure ones.

The Cathar secret: souls descend into the world in order to receive anointing through the Holy Passion and to experience that which is not in the heavens. Earth is higher than heaven.

The new earth will be manifested only when humanity has been given the revelation that the earth is higher than heaven. And then the new heaven will be revealed, which is higher than the earth.

Fragrant relics, myrrhic oils. The earth is open...

*

For the Catholics Christ was the liberator from sins, but for the Cathars He conquered the world and established the Kingdom of the Father, having opened the entrances into the earth for immaculate souls.

The prince of this world was defeated by the fact that the Messenger from the Father of pure love arrived in the world and established the Christhumanity.

*

The Cathar spheres are qualitatively different from those of the Christians. This is a world of purest vibrations, most eternal beings, and universal truths. A world, absolutely unaffected by the devil and excluding any kind of battle. The purest, most heavenly sphere.

◄§

'Adored brother, adored sister'... With such an address our fathers adored, divinized. The burning-adoring look at one's neighbour lights the candle in the heart.

Abandon the external path: preaching, conversion. Remember the first conversion: did the great elderly nuns, sent from on high, convert you?[1] The mysterious voice, sounding in the interior, turned your spiritual essence towards the light of the Heavenly Father.

And so, child, work more with the staff of divine existence. The mysterious voice has been given to you – come and sound the interior of the hearers.

Today the parasitic shells have grown so numerous that it is impossible to remove them without harming the very core of man... Preserve tranquility and peace... Expect the manifestation of our Father in the sunny universum.

ᴥ§

Do not fear the earthly. You have been transformed. The cunning one attacks with threats of physical reprisals: solitude, 'the ambulance', heart attacks... Infirmities are given to the pure ones solely for their spiritual inspiration.

*

The physical body remains in the world, while

the immortal bodies, perfecting themselves one after another, leave the world and find divine light.

◄§

Whatever man does (even if he sets off firecrackers or simply howls derangedly, or sits doubled over, or gives himself up to extreme sports...), he is unconsciously seeking a state of ecstasy.

Raving madness and the search for the unusual are connected not so much with self-expression as with the unconscious ecstatic call of the soul to return to the lost heavenly bosom and to overcome the earthly prohibition of the prince of this world on ecstatic rapture, on the soaring and raising of the wings of the soul.

◄§

The Judaic fear (the spectre of Auschwitz) originates with the faith in the single embodiment without the prospect of further transformation and eternal life.

The delight caused by the divine incarnations is never-ending!

*

The secret of virginity is that, in order to become an embodied angel on earth, to inhabit the celestial communities and find eternal life.

Catharism is unthinkable without virginity. The return to the bosom of the Father presupposes chaste vestments. Virginity returns angelic bliss.

❧

The great secret of the Exceeding Wisdom of San Salvador. In any location of the earthly sphere it is possible, having stretched out your hands, to raise a prayer in the sphere of the Father of pure love, if you mentally reside at San Salvador.

San Salvador lays a special anointing. It is necessary to ascend this mountain or to grasp this anointing from him, whom the immortals of San Salvador have accepted into their number, in order to raise a prayer for the conversion of the six million inhabitants of earth at any place in the world.

❧

Divine existence is the sphere between the seen and the unseen world: the purest of pure sphere of spotless immaculateness, mysteriously manifesting itself in the world and eliminating its tempting influences.

*

Not one uninitiated should enter here. For them San Salvador is only a stone ruin or the possibility to see the earth from the height of an eagle's flight.

Here the soul is consecrated in divine existence and, with its transubstantiation into the Divinity, remains forever. Henceforth, wherever it is, part of it will remain here, at San Salvador Verdadero. Here it clothes itself in the last truth and holds it firmly, desiring the brightest destinies together with the enlightened ones – the pure ones and the perfect ones.

❧

What can be greater than Miramar? Miramar multiplied.

What can be greater than Nightingale Mountain? Nightingale Mountain multiplied: San Salvador.

What can be greater than San Salvador? The most eternal Father, savoured one day during the transition into eternity.

❧

Man does not even imagine the way in which he needs to change. An open heart, the forgiveness of sins – yes. But the direct and sole criterion of the validity of the path of ascent along the spiritual staircase is the undoubted increase of kindness in the conditions of perfect purity.

❧

Holy Passion, solitude, cross... O adored one, this is the language of love!

With what love is borne this scrupulously calculate darkness! Love does not fear it, as it does not fear illness, death, suffering, solitude, or the devil.

Such love may be opened only by the throne of our Father, alien to the Roman-Byzantine surrogates and mimicking masks.

For two thousand years they mimicked the saints, and now their diabolical faces will come to light. And together will be revealed the true saints: holy fools, mysterious, not-from-this-world, included among the wicked creatures, heretics, sectarians, hunted by the authorities and by themselves...

*

It is possible to comprehend the true Christ only through the throne of the Father. First know how beautiful is the Father and His only, most beautiful Son.

And then model the other brothers and sisters of the Bridal Chamber in His image. And form the image of the Great Church of Love before your mental gaze.

To inherit this church is the greatest honor which can befall you on earth, in spite of persecutions, sorrows and crosses.

*

I examine my past. All that I have done is glorify the saints of the Great Church of Love: the adored Euphrosinia, Innokenty Baltsky, Seraphim Solovetsky, with the 12 brothers from the Fiery Hierarchy... I literally dragged so many saints from the unclean scrolls of the pharisees and returned to them the bleached mother-of-pearl bone: as they are seen from the heavenly heights, and not as they are represented by the institutional fawners with their mercantile goals.

There is nothing more repulsive than, when the bigots, having killed a saint, model from him their 'devotee' to attract naïve believers. I was attracted to this office, impressed by St. John of the Ladder and the Great Anthonies, as if these and other devotees had some kind of relationship to the Stalin-Beria nomenclatura, which will have to answer for the 50 million souls ruined in the Gulag.

What a monstrous deception! So many even today are falling into their nets, identifying the saints from the bureaucratic investiture and the double Inquisition.[2]

Much deception has taken place in human history. But I do not know another, which can compare. The villain killed his master, dressed himself up in his clothes and passed himself off as him; the servile underlings are under the hypnosis of the master's clothing and not looking straight at he, who prances on the horse before them, mockingly viewing the crowd.

*

To go the way of the cross is a great honour, the greatest joy.

There is a stage after which the cross turns into a blessing, the wilderness – an oasis of peace, retreat – the greatest presence. And blessed is he, who dwells in the spectrum of these never-ending ascents, ascending and descending the staircase, without delaying in the middle for long.

*

The pure love of Minne prolongs life, dispels illnesses and chimeras, defeats the enemy. It is indeed the wreath of creation. Man was initially created from the composition of the Sacred Minne.

Our adored Lady, coming to Her disciples as the bride, perceives *Herself* in them. In this way it is not a great effort for Her to combine with them.

*

THE IMMORTALS:

The Grail is the fullness of presence, the undefiled essence of Our Father.

Ascend to San Salvador as often as possible, the true sanctuary of Our Father – only here it is possible to experience the fullness of His love.

1.

a Hymn
to our Father,
the sun of suns
of pure love

- The Adamites were destroyed by their belief
  in the Punishing Evil One

- The Chalice of Christ's blood concealed itself for 2000 years.
  And now – it is transformed by the fiery fountain of 200 million
  answering Last Drops

- Christ's kingdom is made up of those, who gave Him
  the answering Last Drop

- The Father-Sun reveals Himself for the first time
  and has no analogues in the 84th civilization
- The Sunny Father revealed Himself
  at the beginning of the 84th civilization
- No less than 150 prophets read the fiery tablets

◦§

THE FIERY HIERARCHY:

A new God for a new humanity. Recognize the greatness of what is happening: the Sun of suns, revealing Himself for the first time to the sunny Theohumanity.

The revelation is given for salvation in the Ark and is intended for a few of the inhabitants of the future age, the Seraphites. The Father of purest light and pure love will become the Divinity of the sunny people.

The Adamites were destroyed by their belief in the Punishing Evil One, which lay on man like a shadow...

2000 years ago humanity missed the opportunity to change (the Christ of the Jerusalem period).

The Chalice of Christ's blood concealed itself for two thousand years.

And now – it is transforming like the fiery fountain of 200 million answering last drops!

Christ's kingdom is made up of those, who have given for Him the answering last drop, which is called Christ's fiery drop of regeneration, the extract of eternal life.

With this last drop, each of the 200 million martyrs of love freed the divine essence, hidden in the Adamite potential.

Deiparous vestments, virginity, holiness and the Great Church of love were required to shed the last drop into the solar Grail of Christ.

Become apostles of the great Holy Passion, Eucharistmen of the answering last drop, Melchizedeks in the image of the High Priest Melchizedek and the Agnus Dei of Christ.

In vain we tried to insert ever-burning candles into the hearts of the Adamites. The cunning one enslaved them, and our attempts remained fruitless.

Seraphim succeeded in the Gulag: for unities. The Blessed myrrh-pouring Euphrosinia succeeded: for the church of John, her disciple.

*

Do not pin Our Father to Adamite wretchedness. Believe in the Divinity of divinities of the transforming Christ-III.[3]

Accompany faith (= the retention of the sphere) with confidence in purifying disasters (1), mysterious sights (2), and the miraculous salvation (3) of those, who listen and love.

> Our Father – Sun,
> Father of pure love,
> in the lights of Theocivilization III –
> approach!

The forms of the old (Adamite) faith end up as antiques in the best case or on the rubbish dump in the worst (the biblical idol).

The Father-Sun reveals Himself for the first time and has no analogues in the 84th civilization.

Do not compare, do not contrast, do not make artificial clothing for yourself. Do not pin 'new patches to an old garment', becoming like the Jews of the Old Testament.

Keep the courage of the pioneers and fearlessly profess the coming of the era of the Sunny Divinity.

John the Theologian saw it on Patmos, in the form of the Wife Clothed in the Sun. Inflame hearts with a passionate faith in the rising sun of the Divinity!

> O rising sun of the Divinity of pure love
> overworldly and gloriously approach!
> Melt the ices of unbelief and prejudices –
> the Lord's summer, the morning before the dawn!

*

O John, pure among the pure, our brother! From

the beginning of your witness on Earth you were not understood by the Christians, because you professed our Christ and believed in our Father.

In the Gospels and even in the Jewish Torah you perceived the Father-Sun, proclaimed by you over-worldly the Solar divinity, embodied in 200 million Christs great and small.

Your 400 (= 400 000!) books are a hymn to our Father, the Sun of suns of pure love. Now they will hear!

And the deaf... Our Father will remain deaf to their requests. Agonizing sobriety awaits them, as severe as their obstinacy in rejecting our Father.

*

There is only one true Divinity in the heavens and on Earth: the Father-Sun, the Father of pure love.

The others are chimeras, adopted and mastered by demonic hierarchies with the goal of disorienting man.

Our sweetest Father, glorified by millions of solar hierarchies, will descend in glory with the sunny Church

Our sweetest Father, glorified by millions of sunny hierarchies, by millions of celestial sunny bodies great and small, by millions of transformed sunny beings (who have never yet descended to the Earth), will descend in glory with the solar Church of overworldly Tabor and establish the kingdom of the sunny man (homo solaris).

Man will be transformed by faith into the sunny Christ of pure love, Christ-III. The Gospel of the sun is proclaimed today.

Today it is easier than ever before to enter the sunny ark, to be transformed with one touch of the sunny right hand of Our Divinity.

O Divinity of purest lights! The homeland of sunny fathers and mothers!

The time of assembling in the ark

The time of assembling in the ark. The universal preaching. Advise those, who have been deceived, to abandon biblical fairy tales and absurd prejudices.

Tomorrow they will remember about the day of the universal preaching with great grief. Tomorrow may be too late.

I hear the apocalyptic alarm bell, accompanied by the words 'Too late, too late, too late!'.

*

The pioneers should have the courage to abandon their Christian prejudices, like the Christians abandoned the Jewish circumcisions, sabbaths and meticulous instructions.

31

The personification of the Divinity of pure love

In sunny lights millions will see His indescribably beautiful, most beautiful, most sunny face! The embodied and personified Divinity, the Third Christ,[4] and not Buddha, Mohammed or Zoroaster.

Misunderstood and unperceived by the Jews in Jerusalem and in the Roman-Byzantine surrogates, He will accede to the throne in the universe.

The true Christians will accept this and come to believe.

Christ approaches in the sunny lights! John the Theologian's great prophesy about His thousand-year kingdom is realized.

The immortals lay wide the fiery scrolls.

The sunny sword

We will place ever-burning candles in the hearts of those, who believe in Our Father the Sun of suns, we will give them the fire of the Holy Spirit and the great fearlessness to strike our enemies.

Here is the sunny sword and the ever-burning fire of the Holy Spirit! Walk in his ether, and enemy arrows will fly away as from a steel hauberk.

The revelation of the Father of pure love

The sunny Father was revealed in the beginning of the 84th civilization: blinding dawns and a golden tablet stretching from heaven to Earth.

Millions read with eyes of internal vision. The revelation came to fifteen peoples simultaneously. Life on Earth faded, and then in an instant was transformed.

A word from the Sun of suns of the purest Father begot thousands of new flowers, trees, plants, types of animals, birds, fish. A universe of the brightest of bright thoughts filled the world.

150 prophets read the fiery tables. The memory of them has been erased..

The Jews by their "holy scriptures" erased the memory of the true Divinity from the face of the Earth, having replaced Him with an opposing substitute.

The Christians erased the memory of the true Christ, imprinted in 200 million martyrs of love, amongst whom there is not a single Christian of orthodox mark.

Prayer (with the raising of hands):
    Our Father,
    Sun of suns of pure love,
    enrapture us from the Chalice of Chalices.
    O dazzlingly new Divinity
    Sun of suns of Our Father,
    erase mortal outlines.
    Reveal yourself, man-universe!

*

My heart is full of indescribable joy, bursting beyond its boundaries. There is no limit to my happiness. At long last I have seen Him, for whom I waited, whom I predicted, in whom I believed, whom I anticipated, whom I professed, whose seals I propagated, seeing Him before my spiritual gaze, and now I see with my own eyes!!!

O sweetest Divinity of divinities, revealed to humanity for the first time, inflame our hearts with the fire of pure love!

Our Father,
Sun of suns of pure love,
enrapture us from the Chalices of Chalices.

*

𝒯he perfect imprint of the Divinity of divinities on creation

The distinguishing feature of the Divinity of divinities of pure love will be His perfect imprint on creation.

It will be possible to see Him in one's neighbour perfectly, without distortion.

Each of His sons and daughters will show the creative hypostasis of He Himself, the sum of all human beings (= divinities great and small): Him as a whole.

Tirelessly, on Earth and in the heavens, wherever I am – in camera obscuras, on other worlds, in concentration zones, in light and dark hearts, I will propagate the sun of suns of the Father of pure love, the Divinity, revealed to the Theo-humanity for the first time.

His throne will embrace all creation. The Revelation will be perceived not from without, as it is by the Adamites, but from within, from hidden springs, by internal hearing; it will be contemplated by spiritual, internal vision.

Man will experience bliss from within, from hidden internal springs.

*

Enough and more than enough Seraphic seals have already been laid upon you.

Judge their presence according to that deep grief with which you watch the Adamites, controlled like puppets; who are, from the point of view of the Seraphic enlightment by the spirit, senseless beings.

◆§

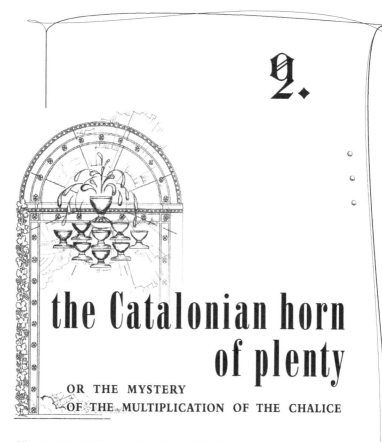

9.

the Catalonian horn of plenty

OR THE MYSTERY
OF THE MULTIPLICATION OF THE CHALICE

- The source Grail is continually enriched
  by the answering myrrh-pouring last drops of the martyrs of love
- The greatest Chalice multiplies into twelve great chalices
- Profess the Father, the purest of the pure
- The expulsion of the chimeras comes with great effort
- After the crushing defeat of the Cathars the Holy Grail
  was hidden from the world and transferred into divine existence

what grace pours from the castle of the Chalice under the name of the Catalonian Horn of Plenty! The Christ of the Catalonian Grail in castle 73. The castle of Juan de Lopes and his father, Renato.

From this castle the immortals rose through the aether.

Here is the mysterious place of the control of the world.

The Cathars set their throne here for a thousand years, and brought us hither in consolation. Here many secrets of Catharism will be revealed.

ℛENATO DE LOPES

I see a great hidalgo. The great knight of the Holy Grail knew, where the Chalice was kept. He was one of its 12 apostles, a segurador (keeper).

He was called Renato de Lopes. He had an estate not far from this castle. He was a free knight, having dedicated himself to the secret of the Holy Grail, to Catharism, and to the search for the holy vessel of immortality (of universal spirituality).

Renato de Lopes waged a war with Rome, considering the Roman church to be not simply a whore, but the great distorter of Christ.

"Rome is crucifying Christ. Rome forbids His news".

To present Christ-as-He-is to the world

From the XII century the Cathars took upon themselves the task of rehabilitating, purifying Christ, of presenting Him-as-He-is to the world.

The masters of the castle explain:

Rome was called 'the synagogue of Satan', because it was considered that Rome had fulfilled the mission of the second synagogue: the Judaisation of Christ.

Having attached Him to the Old Testament, Rome became the same synagogue that Christ had denounced in Jerusalem.

The words of Christ: 'Destroy the old temple, and I will raise it up in three days.' The Cathars called the churches, cathedrals, chapter houses, consistories, curias, and so on, *the old temple*.

Christ raised His new temple (of the Holy Chalice) in Jerusalem, having shed an entire five litres of blood.

He called the last drop as the dome (pinnacle) of the temple, uniting heaven and earth.

The teaching of Christ (the mysterious throne of the Holy Grail, the chalice of Christ's blood) was considered to be the living altar of His presence.

The secret of solarity

The religion of the pure ones was solar. Solarity is impossible to understand outside of the Chalice. Christ's Chalice (five litres of blood) was transformed into the sun and descended from heaven like the sun.

The Chalice is the temple of His flesh and blood, raised by Christ and not by man, and to partake of the Chalice means to visit the temple of the presence of Christ.

Such a privilege is given only to the true priors of the order.

*

Renato de Lopes had the title 'knight of Selva'. Here his huge, three-storey Cathar castle was erected – one of 144. Before us stands only its flanking wall.

The castle was 20 to 30 metres in height and around 80 metres in length. Later, during the persecutions, more than 100 pilgrims lay hidden within (although this number sometimes rose to three hundred). The Cathars accepted them.

Hither came ambassadors from the whole world. One unfortunate, having broken his vows, betrayed the Great Castle to the Roman church. But the fortress of Selva de Mar remained impregnable: the crusaders were unable to occupy it even after a long siege (the Cathars themselves abandoned it, going out into the mountains).

...Here was the Cathar Church, which was visited by God's Mother. Here was the special throne of worship of the Immaculate Conception.

The secret of the castle was that it was considered to be a chalice: a place, which was visited by the Holy Grail and where the mysterious Christ appeared.

The great overworldly round table

The knights resided in the mysterious liturgical communion of the Round Table.

Besides the small table, around which sat three (4, 8, 12, 14, 15, 20... up to 50 knights), there existed a great overworldly Round Table. Thousands of knights sat around it.

Christ came to them. The Chalice nourished each and every one of them.

JUAN DE LOPES

In the middle of the tenth century the father of the Cathar church, Juan of the Holy Chalice (Juan del Gran Grial), knew what kind of cross he would accept when Christ appeared to him and said that he would fortify him in the struggle against the Roman 'synagogue of Satan'. He clothed him in immortal vestments and revealed to him the mysteries of the Cathar church.

Juan of the Holy Grail accepted the chalice, kept in the Holiest Holy of Holies (in divine existence), from the hands of Christ. He worshipped the cross of Jerusalem, having accepted anointing with the blood of the Lamb, which transubstantiated before his eyes into fragrant oil, the myrrhic composition.

Juan de Lopes was a count, the first in the line of succession, the son of the keeper of the Chalice, Renato de Lopes, and was killed by the Catholics: pierced by the spear of the crusaders.

St. Juan de Lopes:

The great prophet revealed the secret of the Holy Grail to the Cathars:

seeing how the path of superficial Judaism finished with Maccabeeism and Phariseeism, Christ transubstantiated into the Chalice. Christ dwells in the Chalice.

Christ abolished the temples. His blood, transubstantiated into myrrh, became His living temple.

The original source Grail

The keeper of the Chalice is clothed in the immortal vestments of the Father of heavenly love.

Otherwise he is not able to take the Holy Grail, shining in the light of lights, into his hands.

Clothed in vestments, after lengthy prayers and fasts, he takes the Chalice of the Divinity into his hands.

Raising it to the heavenly throne of the 'Trinity, which has become four' and the 'Hepternity which has become eight', he completes one of the most incomprehensible mysteries, which is called the multiplication of the Holy Chalice.

The original source Grail, having miraculously gathered the five litres of the blood of Christ, is continually enriched by the answering myrrh-pouring last drops of the martyrs of love

and arrives (often simultaneously) in 144 chalices.

The original Chalice in the hands of the keeper of the Grail

The original Chalice in the hands of the keeper of the Grail (called the sunny elder or Avva in the golden thrones of divine existence) multiplies in accordance with the number of its great and small keepers...

The secret of multiplication:

$1 \times 2 \times 2 \ (=4) \times 3 \ (=12) \times 12 = 144$.

The greatest Chalice multiplies into twelve great chalices, which in turn each multiplies into twelve small chalices.

From the source Chalice of the sunny Christ spreads the radiance of each of His twelve dazzling multiplied thrones (the 12 great keepers) and each of the 12 small thrones (the 12 lesser keepers).

The Round Table of the knights of the Holy Grail is surrounded by 144 chalices, 144 golden candlesticks, and 144 ever-burning lighted candles, symbolizing the 144 internal castles of the perfectly divinized man.

Above it shines the figure X (ten out of ten components): the absolute manifestation of divine potential, the renewal of once-defiled particles in their original fullness: Pleroma, crown.

JUAN (with hot tears in his eyes):

What a heavy cross it is for the Church of anointed sovereigns to wage war with the villains of the pagan temples, with poisonous tarantulas and rapacious sharks!

But in answer to loyalty, the sunny Father and Heavenly King gives Himself to them multiplied.

Grace originating the Father of pure love

The grace of the Cathar church, having entered into the immortal thrones of divine existence, and returning to earth today, originating from faith in the Father of sunny, pure and superior Love.

Juan of the Great Chalice called the casket (40x70 cm) which contains the golden keys of complete purification, of the Cathar path to perfect holiness, the Cathar treasure house.

The keys may be given to the initiated (who have taken vows of loyalty to the sunny church) by the descent of the Holy Spirit in the gifts of the consulamentum.

THE LITURGY OF THE ANOINTED AND PERFECT ONES (19)

1. The summoning of the Father of pure love. The rapture of the mind, the flight of the spirit,

2. The birth of the Godman from the Last Drop – more than Divinity, more than man,

3. The blessing of blessings. The entrances of the Kingdom,

4. Worship and contemplation of Exceeding Wisdom,

5. The Holy Grail of Jerusalem,

6. The Last Drop of the Lamb as a gift for the reviving Theohumanity,

7. The Holy Theogamic Grail of Nightingale Mountain with miracle-working oils of unity and combination,

8. The raising of the chalice to the Bridal Chamber,

9. The adoration of the Holy Chalice in divine existence with the ascension into the divine spheres accessible only to the pure of heart, to those having passed the stage of catharsis in the Church of the saints,

10. The mystery of the multiplication of the Chalice,

11. The Grail descends into the interior,

12. Perfect catharsis,

13. Exceeding Wisdom draws apart the gates of the 144 internal castles, and the grace of the mystical Eucharist spills among them,

14. The mystical Eucharist (by word, grace, spirit),

15. The fraternal combination of hearts, the Bridal Chamber among Christ's beloved,

16. Minne,

17. The ascension of the Chalice to the 12 thrones,

18. The consecration of compositions (bread, water, wine, honey, myrrh),

19. The partaking, combined in love, of the meal in 'honey' goblets.

The grace of Our Father

The Cathar church had no forbidden secrets!

Grace descended solely from the profession of another God, inaccessible to pagan priests and spiritual tricksters.

Profess the Father, purest of the pure, not connected to corruption, sin, treachery, darkness or lust, and the grace from the heavenly horn of plenty will flow out upon you.

Thousands of sunny cherubs will attend to you, as they served us in the years and hours of the persecutions.

The expulsion of the chimeras comes with great difficulty even for him, who has achieved a degree of the perfect one.

After the heavy spiritual battle of the anointed sovereign, millions of souls are enlightened with the expulsion of the next chimera and come out of hypnosis.

Exorcism originating from us. The perfect ones were great exorcists, because they cast out not individual spirits, but rather conducted a battle with the very prince of this world.

*

The great mysteries of the Chalice

The Heavenly Father Himself came to Golgotha in Jerusalem and sealed the Chalice, having covered it with a mysterious layer.

The keeper of the Chalice (the sunny father) perforates the cover, and drops of the blood of Christ are shed, immediately crystallizing into myrrh.

During the divine service a light cover of a type of tracing paper is used. The Chalice, covered with transparent paper, is perforated. One drop is poured out onto the hand and partaken of.

Faith in the myrrhic composition of the blood, not only of Christ as king of the anointed sovereigns, but also of each of the Godmen revived by Him, is necessary for the Cathar Eucharist.

The answering last drop of myrrh is shed from the heart of the anointed one during the achievement of the stage '10 out of 10' (the restored ten internal components of man).

It is possible to achieve restoration (in the event of the damaging of 8 of the 10 components) with the help of the great consulamentum and melioramentum in the true church, with the help of its keys.

*

Each of our fathers, entering the fire of the inquisition, shed his last drop and burnt the essence of sin, having thus achieved a degree of the perfection of the perfect ones – of the anointed one.

Thus was discovered the gift of shedding the Last Drop in each of the great divine services in divine existence.

The original source Grail has been enriched with 200 million (!) last drops of the disciples of Christ.

The blood of Christ multiplies into 144 small chalices – Christ multiplies into His disciples, achieving a level of messianistic meal (= a level of sacrificial love, during which the last drop is shed).

The Grail of multiplied last drops

Our Divinity became so angry with the world, because the Roman whore subjected His messianistic sons to complete genocide that, after the destruction of the Cathars, the Holy Grail was hidden from the world and taken across into divine existence.

The sky was covered with tears. It rained for 40 days. A new Noah's flood threatened the world...

The mysteries of the multiplication of the Chalice stopped occurring after the fifteenth century. Worthy successors were not found. The Holy Grail went deep underground.

Today, after five centuries, the Father desires to restore the mystery of the round table and present the Grail of multiplied last drops, the transforming solar chalice, fountaining with 200 million last drops.

The churches will be given a marvellous sign: a firework of sunny myrrhic splashes, resembling the dancing of the sun in Fatima.

Today the Holy Grail is descending in divine existence, in the sphere revealed only to the anointed ones, to the pure of heart.

Divine existence serves as defensive wall against the unworthy ones. The sphere of divine existence has been created today by the martyrs of love and is with ease attainable for those, that have been summoned. Whereas it is inaccessible for others, however much they desire to enter into it.

The Holy Grail is accepted as a mystery of divinization and of the entrance into the Bridal Chamber with the renunciation of the chimeras of the world and the chalice of Lucifer, from which partake those, who have been seduced by him.

The Cathars do not object to the chrysostom liturgy and Roman Catholic mass. But it is necessary to erase the old liturgical order to imprint the true liturgy of the Grail, coming from the Heavenly Father.

Christ on the cross perfected the living liturgy. Then Christ at Nightingale Mountain, the Fiance of the theogamic chalice in new holy Rus', then also among His true disciples: the chalice of the Holy Grail.

John, my sweetest namesake, recognise yourself in me.

Bravely erase more and more! Free a space for the anointings of the Cathar church. We will not be able to reveal the miraculous myrrh-pouring liturgies of the Chalice, while even one particle of 'the synagogue of Satan' hides in your composition.

*

$\mathscr{T}$he sunny mystery of the Chalice

I see the huge sunny chalice half the size of the sky, covered with film.

The film is perforated with a sharp spear (caduceus[5]). On the surface of the chalice one, two, three drops appear: wine, blood and myrrh.

I see the radiance of 144 golden chalices. The phenomenon of the original Grail.

A big table. Around it there are 150 (according to the number of spiritual levels of ascent) priors, knights, fathers. The chalice multiplies into 144 small cruets. Six attend to us.

*

In what purity our fathers clothed themselves! With what radiant light of the virginity of the Father, the purest of the pure, they shone!

◄§

3.

the Hours
of divinization, the hours of communion with Christ of the second coming

- The Theohumanity of the sons of our Divinity approaches
- See our Father of sunny love, of superior images, and of the hypostasis of Our Lady
- The treasure of treasures, the mysterious forms of the Father
- His conception was as mysterious as His blood
- The Holy Grail preserves the memory of the last drops of two hundred million perfect ones

- The mystery of Christ the Transubstantiator

- His mouth was sealed in the earthly days

- Christ came with mysterious drawings

- Christ made us immortal

- The childbearing of Christ in Her bosom was mysterious

- We felt like divinities in His presence

- The indescribable hours of the descent
  of the divinity of Christ into the interior

❧

JUAN DE LOPES:

The castle has been built from the compositions of the Chalice. The castle is the sweetest Christ.

144 x 12 x 12 internal castles of the initiated, pure, and perfect ones have been sanctified by the visitation of the Christ of the Holy Chalice, and not by the hand of the 'whistler'.[6]

I.

El Elevado Superior, Elevadísimo: the Highest of the high. The Sweetest One. The Most Sealed of the sealed, the Most Mysterious of secrets... Another thousand names: Altísimo, Superior, King of kings...

My child, without enlightenment, without flight, without inflammation of the soul, it is useless to teach about the Father. But first: exorcism and mighty expulsion.

His secret cannot be revealed to the Adamites, to the poor creatures that writhe like helpless fledglings in the claws of a rapacious bird, just one glance of which inspires in them utter terror...

Humanity drinks in a version of the Demiurge, imprinted in his 'masterpiece': the Torah, honoured equally in the notorious triangle of 'Islam-Judaism-Christian pharisees'.

*

The serpent is the symbol of the Jewish synagogue of the Old Testament, introduced by Lucifer.

Lucifer and Lucibel... We distinguished between them. Lucibel is Baal (the king of this world). Lucifer is the creator of mimicking spheres, the god of the synagogue of Satan. His authority remains strong over millions of souls, my child.

*

The sword of the Montségur against Elohim

My child, take the sword of the Montségur from our hands and bravely enter into battle against Elohim.

Drive him away! Be angry with him as with the ancient serpent. Be a thousand times more angry with him for his cunning machinations, for his ability to steal and mimic, for his base activities: tracking down and prohibiting the mission of the anointed sovereigns.

So many saints came! But only our Cathar perfects were able to drive him away with the cudgel of righteous anger.

My child, we were far from being meek lambs allowing ourselves to be led to sacrifice, as the historical chronicles of the stubborn mandibles portray.[7]

O, we were great warriors of truth! We were able to expel this monster, the chimera of chimeras. We forbade him from seducing the world, for which Our Divinity gave us the title 'heaven-dwelling kings of the earthly kings'.

Take the exorcistic staff from us – the club of the expulsion of *the Elohimic soul.*

Drive him from all the cracks. Drive him through the air, drive him across the earth. Drive him from your own interiors. Drive him from your closest ones. Drive him from the churches. Drive him from the spirits of the trees. Drive him from the marshes and rivers. Drive him from the cities and villages. Drive him from everywhere: from saints and magicians, from the great and the small, from fathers and mothers, from sons and daughters, from every kind of creature. Drive him from all that lives on earth – so that not one speck of the breath of Elohim remains on any flower!

Use prayers against Elohim with the fervour, with which your myrrhic mother Euphrosinia created 'Cyprian's' one.[8]

My child, if you do not dedicate even a quarter of an hour a day to fiery prayer against the great mimicker, we will barely succeed in establishing the throne of El Altísimo, El Elevado Elevados – of the Divinity of divinities, the Superior of superiors.

*

Now accept absolutions from us in the font of white mysteries, still arriving from the Slavic Theogamites of Holy Rus', from whence you came to visit us as our most dear guest.

How can we not rejoice? With you came millions of brothers! Behind you stand Seraphic hierarchs, divinized holy fools, and sunny Theogamites... The apostle Andrew First-Called tails the procession with the primal source vessel, *the Theogamic chalice*. So many divine maidens – from Noema to Esklarmonda – participate in the procession!

The mysterious forms of the Father, lost by modern man

O, to what degree the Father has been sealed! We believed in Him, through 'dull glass', through cloudy and frosted glass...

The Cathar superiors, the fiery missionaries will

reveal to you *Our Divinity*, crowned with a sunny tiara.

My adored one, did not my brothers at Perpet-ouse promise to entrust to you the world for mod-elling in the mysteries of the Holy Spirit? And here is the first of them:

new gates, new man.

'Reveal heaven for the pioneers of the glory of Our Father-Sun!' We pray today, in the days of the May Easter week of the visit of our Cathar divine existence communities, by the anointed sovereign of the new holy Rus'.

The Theohumanity of the sons of Our Father ap-proaches. Each of them will be modelled anew.

I. THE FIRST GATES FOR THEOHUMANITY

We drew our inspiration, our faith, our super-admiring mode of thought, our mysteries, our mod-elling of the new man, our vision of Christ, solely from the throne of El-Elion – our all-perfect Father.

Father Theogamites, the sunny Cathars of the twenty-first century, read in your hearts of as-tounding beauty the worship of Our Lady in the eastern Byzantine code.

Now, with the lighting of the new, ever-burning lamp in your internal castles, see our Father of sunny love, of superior images, and of the hypostasis of Our Lady.

Love Him, seeing the unseen — may His image be established before your spiritual gaze! Worship Him with hot, completcly devoted fervour — even more than that with which you loved the Mother of God, worshipping Her in the years of the first communion. And you will see what kinds of fruits the key, given by us, will bring you.

My child, for the first time, for the sake of the 85th Theocivilization, proclaimed by you, we are conveying the treasure of treasures, the mysterious images of the father, lost by modern man and intended for the Adamites, transubstantiating into Seraphites.

Without the sunny disk in the interior of the Cathar cross, without the little candle, lighted in the heart, you will not see Our Father.

Such are the first gates, revealed today for the Theohumanity — El Elevado Superior, El Elion.

See the Father with our eyes

God's kingdom (however much you taught about it in your sermons in the liturgies, however strongly you summoned it in the revelations of Split, Miromar, and Nightingale Mountain[9]), revealed itself vaguely. Eyes saw the light shortsightedly, not seeing further than several metres in the boundless distances.

Now, when the sunny disk of Our Divinity has been lighted in your heart, see the Father with our eyes,

may you enter into the deepest, ecstatic, world eternal, experienced by us in the internal Cathar castles and on the peaks of celestial towers.

My child, do not simply inherit His transcendental spheres and most divine names – live by them.

Master the highest truths of our church one after another, and your soul will fill with the fragrant aroma of the pastures of Heaven.

I hear singing:

O El Elion O
Superadmiring bliss
greater than Himself
sunny Divinity!
O Beloved O

(Bridal chamber procession with brides)

II. THE DIVINE CHALICE

No creations of human hands, however skillfully made from gold and silver and even more valuable metals, are able to replace the sunny Chalice of Our Father.

Remember:

Our Father is the Chalice, full of the myrrhic drops of the tears of pure love, of divine tenderness.

Our Christ is the Chalice.

Our Mother of God is the Chalice.

The Holy Spirit is the ungrasped, transubstantiating Chalice.

The heavens, my child, are a form of the sunny chalice of Our Divinity.

And the earth seeks to accept the contours of the Grail.

Millions today seek the secret of our entrances.

Give it to them, my child: the San Grial the myrrhic composition of original immaculateness – the mystery of our Father of fathers, the God of gods, the Divinity of divinities, the Christ of christs.

Thus prayed your fathers in the earthly days:

O Eloi O / [10]
Superadmiring bliss /
greater than Himself /
sunny Divinity /
O Beloved O

Thus, the second revelation (after the sunny hypostasis of our Father) before the spiritual gaze of the true disciple of Christ is the divine Chalice, its mysterious composition from the blood of Our Divinity.

*

III THE GATES: THE SECRET OF THE COMPOSITION OF THE BLOOD OF CHRIST

Master the most marvellous secret of the composition of the blood of Christ.

His blood was not of human origin, not of the blood and lust of men.

The composition of the blood of the Anointed Sovereign is absolutely of divine origin.

His immortal spiritual bodies remained divine (during Advent).

His residence in the world was mysterious. Do not confuse this with the conception from the Virgin Mary.

Rid yourself of the version 'of the Annunciation of the archangel Gabriel' as from a hallucination ('How will this occur? – The Holy Spirit will come upon You, and the power of the Almighty will overshadow You...') We called the Gospel tales popular nonsense. From them, believe it, come more evil and prohibitions than from simple pure-hearted atheism.

The blind man does not pretend to anything. The mad man considers himself seeing, whereas he is more than blind.

Enough of this cowardly hunted madness under the threat of the Roman bugbear.

We feared nothing, and you should not be afraid. There are no fears. Before the Sun of Our Divinity there is never-cnding grace.

My child, Christ took His human composition not from the Mother of God.

It is impossible to liken Christ to a mere man. Otherwise we cannot flee the temptations 'of inherited corruption', 'of the birth of Our Lady in original sin' and other sin-centric vileness and abuse.

The conception of Christ

His conception was as mysterious as his blood.

The Father shed a hot, *last* myrrhic drop, when the temperature of the heart was 10,000 degrees (!).

The Infant God began to shine from it in miraculous reflections. 144 perfect angels of Our Divinity surrounded Him.

His face began to shine in 144 perfect mirrors, and his voice resounded in 144 divine worlds.

*

The myrrh of our Divinity

The mystery of Christ the Transubstantiator is founded upon His continual transubstantiation into connatural compositions.

At the meals of the Round Table there was neither bread nor wine. The goblets were filled miraculously. And there was nothing sweeter than the heavenly communion.

We partook of not 'blood and flesh' (blasphemous cannibalism), but the myrrh of our Divinity.

What is this?
THE MYRRH OF OUR DIVINITY

(the formula before the partaking of the Holy gifts in the Cathar church).

The meaning of the Cathar fast: the renewal of the purity of the compositions

The meaning of the Cathar fast is not the purification of the flesh, not the abstinence from passions, but the renewal of the purity of the divine compositions against the influences of Lucifer.

The Inquisition charged us with dualism because we believed in another God.

For us, Elohim is a mimicking chameleon, having stolen thousands and seduced millions.

The Holy Grail preserves the memory of the last drops of two hundred million perfect ones.

Enough of them have been collected for our disciples to experience the blessings of the Chalice of Our Father.

My child, the Holy Grail is in your hands!

For the sake of its acquisition they abandon the world, the neighbours, and their former selves, and enter the castles of exalted lights, into the castles of the men of light.

> O myrrhic Padre Mirron,[11]
> extolled El Elion,
> reveal the secret of the multiplying Chalice.

My child, the hour will come, when the Holy Grail, lying continually ahead of the internal gaze, sounding and manifested in the anointed sovereigns, will descend to the world from divine existence.

They will literally see the Chalice physically and partake of it.

THE LETTER OF THE CHALICE

In the space of the Round Table the Grail outlined mysterious symbols and moved through the ether.

Filled with the Holy Spirit, the pure and perfect ones read the hierograms.

The Holy Chalice served as a stylus of the living letter of Our Father-Sun, and revealed hierograms, otherwise unexpressed. It imprinted them in the higher chambers of the internal Grail, called the 'divine potential', in higher consciousness.

Often the letter of the Chalice was accompanied by the mystical silent commentary of thousands of angels surrounding it.

The perfect ones experienced unbelievable blessings after the revelation.

$\mathcal{W}$hat Christ discussed with the initiated ones in San Salvador Verdadero[12]

O, Christ revealed so many incomprehensibly beautiful secrets to us in the castles of our Divinity!

My child, His mouth was dumb in the earthly days in Jerusalem. What was he able to say to these ill-educated Jews and rabbis? They were full of prejudices from their idol, strutting his muscles above the people acquired by him and keeping them in fierce customs and ruling with a rod of iron. This father of worldwide tyranny sealed the gates of our Divinity.

Christ revealed 12 golden keys from the sunny universum to us.

He came to us with drawings, with mysterious symbols and seals.

He told us about the town planning in the ancient civilizations of the perfect ones, about the structures of castles, about the universum of the

Godman, about the universum of the earth, about the universum of heaven, about the universum of Exceeding Wisdom,

about the mysterious foresight of the Father and of the role, devoted in it to Armageddon with the prince of the world.

Christ taught us how to take control of the divine chalices and imperishable compositions.

Christ made us immortal. 'The Chalice will make you small divinities, small christs.

The perfect and anointed keeper carries out a keen watch, not relinquishing the sunny vessel of Our Divinity from his hands.

The secrets of the origin of man from the heavens are in it. 12x144 spatterings and seals, miraculous substances and undistorting mirrors are in it.

The voices of angels and the never-ending hypostases of Our Father, the paradisiacal tabernacles and heavenly words are in it.

In it Exceeding Wisdom Herself spreads divine learning about Our Divinity and about Herself.

*

We revered the Eternal Virgin Mary as a perfect Divinity

We revered the Eternal Virgin Mary (the name acquired for Her by the Slavic Theogamites and conveyed to us as the mysterious teaching of Exceeding Wisdom) as a perfect Divinity, as the maternal hypostasis of Father of pure love.

The heavenly Lady did not stop revealing Herself to us. Among Her disciples She distributed regal virgin tents, fearlessly teaching about the mystery of the immaculate conception.

The childbearing of Christ in Her bosom was as mysterious as the immaculate conception, without signs of human pregnancy.

There does not exist an 'abstract human' body. There are bodies of Adamite and of Seraphic composition.

Christ was the greatest of the teachers of the transubstantiation into Seraphic compositions.[13]

The hours alone with the sunny Lamb

Entering our divine castles, the sunny Lamb brought a never-ending multitude of vessels. He explained the secret of each of the oils and divine objects. He showed us the archetypal structure and essence of the Godman, as he was until the unlawful adaptational reformation.[14]

Visiting us with the most divine Theogamic chalice, He filled our interior, and our bodies were transformed. We found ourselves in regal divine existence.

We rose through the air.

Angelic intellects were given to us.

We comprehended the deepest of secrets...

Christ, the sunny Divinity of divinities, had the power to summon the fullness of Exceeding Wisdom to our brows.

In His presence we felt like divinities, divinized and adoring angels.

We walked in immortal bodies.

The unforgettable hours of divinization, my child, the hours of communion with Christ of the Second Coming.

The secret of the Cathar meal

The secret of the Cathar meal of the Round Table is in the perfect return to the heavens.

The secret of Catharism is in the gifts of divine exits.

The Teacher continually turned to the Chalice. The Chalice was always at the centre of His divine discussions. The Exceeding Wisdom of the Chalice contained in Herself the fullness of being, the absolute presence of seen and unseen worlds, souls, essences, shapes and forms.

It was as if Christ extracted the divine knowledge from the Chalice, and the Chalice from within His very self. He combined with the Chalice and merged with it into one, continually repeating that

He is, all in all, only a vessel of Our Father and has come to us to reveal His beauty.

That is enough about holy kindness or peace. Now grasp His incomprehensible, superior beauty...

A man cannot see the beauty of the Divinity, unless the Father has inserted into him His own compositions, His vision.

Christ granted to us that which was called 'seeing eye to eye' in the earthly days.

My child, the pictures of the Kingdom presented by Him were so indescribably perfect! We saw them not from without. We dwelt in them, with our whole essence, dissolving at this moment.

$\mathscr{T}$HAT WHICH THE PERFECT ONES CALLED THE SECRET OF THE CHALICE

To partake from without, even in divine existence, in the exalted condition, was considered to be the lot of the first stages of initiation into the highest secrets.

The perfect ones were awarded with more, my child: Christ dissolved into them, Christ transubstantiated into them.

The transubstantiation of the Chalice of chalices (12 great and 144 small) reflected a still higher mystery.

Each of the twelve great keepers of the Chalice experienced absolute and complete identification with Him, and even became not 'one with Him', but Christ Himself, stunned by His holy belittling (kenosis),[15] by His capacity for dissolving. These were the indescribable hours of the descent of the divinity of Christ into the interior of the most worthy of His disciples.

'Such is the grace of the true sons and daughters of Our Father', He said after our grateful libations.

I am one with the Father, as you are one with Me. I dissolve with Our Divinity on His divine 150-stage sunny thrones, as My beautiful disciples are dissolved with their Teacher'.

*

The 144th castle, the 'Bridal chamber'

My child, we experienced ineffable bliss when Christ descended into our interior. We understood: in each of us there was the body of Christ, inhabited by the fullness of His divinity!

Accept the regal Eucharist from the sacred Chalice – THE BODY OF CHRIST. Not as symbolically converted everyday wine and bread, but as the mysteriously transubstantiated gifts in the castles of the sacred Grail.

Absolutely ineffable bliss enveloped me: Juan of the Holy Chalice gave me the condition of the combination for Christ.

Our Slavic father-Theogamites lived by Him. They believed Him to be the pinnacle of being Christ-like – of the ascent along the staircase of sacred mysterious speculations and combinations, of Theogamic admirations...

The beloved one wearied our hearts, when (after the most moving blisses) he said, that *something more is possible...*

– What more could there be? We were amazed.

– Uniting into one for the Father, called the 144th Castle, the Bridal Chamber.

Immediately after it is the 145th (the next twelve stages), the Bridal Bed of the coming civilization of Our Divinity.[16]

But first let Me enter into your interior. Continue to make exorcistic efforts regarding the expulsion of the Elohimic spirits from the castles revealed by Me.

In each of them should be conducted a daily cleaning. As you erase dust from the surface of furniture and windows, daily erase the grey dust of mundane devotions, having stuck into the heart...

*

The mystery of purification

The mystery of purification. Create it, my child, with the fullness of the authority, entrusted to you with the news about the second conversion of the world.

Have absolute authority over *the scoundrel, the nobody and the bigot*, who dares to lay claim to his influence on the anointed sovereign.

Only kind people were able to profess the kind Father. And only the saints could profess the Father of the holiest of holies. The vessel is like those who inhabit it.

This is why the first stage in the school of spiritual ascents is the purifying disciple of the laving blessings.

*

Do not worry. The Roman 'Christ' will be erased like that of Byzantium. Whereas our Christ will be the destiny of all the earth.

The time of our triumph is near! It will come astoundingly soon. Do not despair! Believe.

؎

4.

the Fifteen-stage Consulamentum

- The mystery of reformation anew
- See oneself with the eyes of Our Father

*T*HE SONG OF SAN SALVADOR.
heard from the immortals

En la esfera empírea de San Salvador
se revela el Padre del puro amor.
En la esfera empírea de San Salvador
se revela la Madre del puro amor.
En la esfera empírea de San Salvador
se revela el Cristo del puro amor.
En la esfera empírea de San Salvador
permanece la Iglesia del puro amor.
En la esfera empírea de San Salvador
actúa el Espíritu del puro amor.
¡Oh, San Salvador!

Translation from the Spanish:

In the celestial sphere of San Salvador
the Father of pure love reveals Himself.
In the celestial sphere of San Salvador
the Mother of pure love reveals Herself.
In the celestial sphere of San Salvador
Christ of pure love reveals Himself.
In the celestial sphere of San Salvador
dwells the Church of pure love.
In the celestial sphere of San Salvador
acts the Spirit of pure love.
O San Salvador!

I.
The guide to the staircase of ascent

ny ascender leaves the past behind, shedding the clothing of the former life. Nothing old remains.

Approximately between the stages of 10 to 15 the guide to the staircase of ascent offers to erase the memory of the previous life. The past is erased as if the man has died.

The ascender is warned that it is important not to 'renounce' the past, but for it to die.

On the mountain of Our Divinity the smallest particles of the old life will lead to terrible consequences. They will expel the soul back into the world, but with even heavier defeats than before.

Everything is abandoned on the path to the mountain. Nothing human has a place here.

*

77

$\mathcal{M}$ELIORAMENTUM

The number of ascenders was never limited and could reach several thousand. The mountain separatcd miraculously and accommodated all.

$\mathcal{T}$he three-month course of preparation

A three-month course of preparation was planned before the ascent to San Salvador. The neophyte had to reveal the essence of the adaptative modelling of the prince of this world.

For several months, in daily communion with the pure and perfect elders and teachers, the newly-converted analyzed his past. The Holy Spirit showed clearly, what kind of abnormal modelling he had been subjected to.

Next, the neophyte had to pass the special mystery of reformation anew. It was suggested that he become completely like soft clay, so that the Holy Spirit could remodel his whole essence. This remodelling was called the melioramentum.[17]

The elders rarely resorted to the forms of 'instruction' and 'guidance' traditional to Rome-Byzantium. The light, shed by the perfect ones, was so exceedingly fragrant, the action of the Holy Spirit from the throne of the Father of pure love so wonderful, the seals of heavenly love so extraordinary, that souls and bodies were purified without outside help and communication. Never-ending tears, sweat, and excrement flowed from man... After three months his whole composition had changed. Such a person was considered worthy of the ascent to San Salvador.

*

A rumour went around, that San Salvador was a place, where even the mentally ill were cured. Those possessed by demons were carried hither on carts, from the most distant countries. Thousands were cured.

Evil spirits feared to approach. The madness began at 50 kilometres from San Salvador. Demons began to emerge from the possessed: they cried out, named themselves and their sins, talked about, where they had come from... The unfortunate ones fell down completely exhausted, and rose cured.

*

The revelation about the Father of pure love

The first of the fifteen stages of the consulamentum anticipated the revelation about the Father of pure love: about the Divinity, who resorts solely to the language of love and to no other. The first conversation with the mentors was devoted to this sermon.

The second stage was the teaching about the unconditional and absolute character of this love.

The third was the revelation about the spiritual potential of man. Heavenly love should be brought to life by the action of the Holy Spirit and by the perfect purity to which the ascetic is summoned.

The course of catharsis, from 3 months to 3 years

A lengthy catharsis followed the passing of the first three stages.

In specially assigned places the ascetics passed a period of the deepest repentance and purification by the Holy Spirit.

Some needed daily confession (for several hours, several times a day). The greatest significance was given to confession, but it had nothing in common with the grating in the confessional or with the imposition of the priestly stole (epitrachelion).[18] There were no threats or intimidations. It was not even a question of 'sin' or 'guilt', but of the deep damage done to the Godman under the influence of the prince of this world.

The Cathar experience of catharsis demonstrated the perspective of the purest light, and the insight of the extent of man's fall into the earthly darkness. The consulamentum was combined with the melioramentum.

The first stage of catharsis

As the perfect elders taught, in its natural condition the soul sees herself with inserted Luciferic vision. During the confession on San Salvador the cloud of the Holy Spirit sanctified man, and he began to see himself with the eyes of Our Father. The deepest repentance began.

Such was the first stage of catharsis. Before the face of love the soul was wounded by the depth of its former delusion and sobbed never-endingly, passionately desiring to begin all over again.

In such a condition the beginner needed help. The instruction was accomplished at the foot of San Salvador. Special perfect ones came down from the mountain in order to help the pilgrims to become gradually purified of internal rubbish, dust and poison.

It was the task of the mentor to show the putrid and cunning work of the prince of this world and to erase the traces of the adaptative remodelling in the lowest depths. To restore the soul against the prince of this world, and thus return love to Our Father.

The souls were happy, seeing how easily the chimeras, foul-ups, temptations, clouds, and shells (names the mentors preferred to use, avoiding expressions of the type 'unforgotten sins' or 'forgotten transgressions') fell from them.

The course could last from three months to

three, thirty, and even fifty years. Not a single person was able to ascend to the Holy of holies and remain in the Cathar castle for longer than a month (to go into the 'second' airy sea), until the forbidden adaptative remodelling of Lucifer had retreated.

The purification was accomplished as if by itself – by the Holy Spirit.

The order of the prince of this world passed away. The heavenly Father of the exceedingly wise right hand returned to Rex Mundi his own accursed affairs.

*

𝒯he four stages of initiation

Those freed from the modelling of the prince of this world were called pure (1). The perfect ones (2) were those, who had achieved a stage of the masterly modelling of the Holy Spirit.

Then followed the stage of the anointed one (3): christ, the small *redeemer*. And the level of the immortal (4): life in heaven and on earth in one and the same fiery bodies.

𝒜nother spirituality

Another spirituality stuns: purification is possible outside of the framework of sacramental confession.

The elders of San Salvador called the traditional

confession (with the ritual prayers 'not I, but God hears', 'name your sins', 'you are forgiven, child, by the mercy and intercession of the Blessed Virgin' and so on) a usual ruse of Rex Mundi. Cathar spirituality excluded sin-centric elements:

'Rex Mundi wants to lure you into a third trap, beyond the grave, for the sake of which he frightens and scares.[19] Confession to the priest before the Catholic grating does not liberate one from the prince of this world and his cunning moves, but only multiplies enslavement in the sin-centric snare.

Repentance before the face of fear is doubly harmful, and makes one doubly neurotic. It will never lead to perfect holiness, will never bring the Holy Spirit, and will never purify the deepest defeats of the psyche, which reveal themselves only under the ray of pure and great love.

From the beginning all catharsis, instructions were carried out by the Holy Spirit. Its action was absolute. The cloud of the Holy Spirit stood above San Salvador until the fifteenth century, greater here than anywhere else in the world.

The Cathars took bread away from the Romans

The Catholics suffered complete defeat. In San Salvador and in other castles tens, hundreds, and thousands of souls were purified almost instantaneously. Sometimes there was a common confession:

up to several thousand people came to the foot of the mountain. By the action of the Holy Spirit faces were illuminated and angelic hypostases were returned.

The Catholics in the monasteries confessed one and the same sins for 10, 20, or thirty years. As a result, every second one had a growing terror and neurosis.

The parishioners of the Catholic temples remained far from holiness. Holiness was not set as a goal; on the contrary, it was considered extremely suspicious.

Any displays of holiness (especially in the epoch of the Inquisition, beginning already in the tenth century) were regarded as hostile. But a fixation on sins was extremely welcomed.

The Roman Catholic priests came to life, when they felt that a haul had arrived, which needed their consecration, wafers, and so on. On the contrary, when the action of the Holy Spirit began, the papal curia choked with spite: no place for it was found.

The Cathars, liberating thousands of people from the tying ups of Rex Mundi, took bread away from the Romans.

*

Silence and peace in San Salvador

The seals of oral prayer passed away...

For two weeks before the ascent, after the three

month cycle of catharsis, was planned a period of silence. There acted a special grace.

The breath of the airy sea

The silence and peace in San Salvador were indescribable. Oral prayer was considered to be only the first stage. With the purification of the entire internal essence began the breath of the airy sea. The second sea gave miraculous breath (in the lungs of the entire internal essence) and a silent prayer accompanying it.

*

Adoration as divinization

The Cathar key: man needs adoration as he needs divinization. If you want to divinize a man: adore him to death, do not see anything bad in him, endure until the last and bear for him his cross, as you are able. Here is all the Cathar spirituality.

When a man hears the words 'I adore', his face begins to shine. Orphan wounds pass.

In the sin-centric 'Abrahamism' it is the opposite. As much as possible suspect, hate, see in man darkness and sin, deceive him, bewitch him, turn him into Lucifer, turn him into Satan...

The sin-centric confession turns man into Satan. It is impossible for a man to rummage in his sins under the threat of fear. It only unearths Lucifer's fly-droppings from within.

True purification occurs before the face of love, the vision of the face of the heavenly Father. Then it is already impossible to sin.

Metanoia

Metanoia[20] (the second circle of repentance) comes only upon the agreement of the soul to change the whole order of its existence. Then another world, another reality, another being will reveal themselves to the soul: otherness, divine existence.

Above San Salvador stood the greatest cloud of divine existence. Entrance into San Salvador is the entrance into divine existence.

Spirituality begins with the entry of the soul into divine existence, in which also occurs its unity with the loving Father and with all creation, purified and also dwelling in divine existence in the same way. It is also acquainted with close and distant ones, united from different lives.

II.
THE EPOCH OF THE FATHER OF PURE LOVE

THE FATHERS OF SAN SALVADOR:

THE EPOCH OF THE FATHER PURE LOVE has begun. For a millennium the Father has proclaimed His name:

THE FATHER OF PURE LOVE. The Father, surrounded by sons, with the Mother of pure love.

The purification of those, ascending (mentally and in reality) to San Salvador, will occur more quickly than a thousand years ago.

In a short time Our Father will conquer thousands of souls with the revelation of the fiery candle of San Salvador.

The Holy Spirit will work wonders of transformation – the fruit of the millenial Holy Passion with the shedding of the last drops of the Great Church of Love.

Turn your gaze into the interior

Under the action of the divine Cathar radioscope many, seeking perfection, will turn their gazes into the interior. Having at first seen the dark caves, they will then be sainted by the light of the ever-burning candle of the Father of pure love. From the dark alleys of the soul will be expelled thousands of demons, spiteful birds, vampires, bats, hawks, and cawing black crows...

Perfect purification and transformation will come after a brief fainting fit.

The sign of the Great Church of love: instantaneous transformation

The Great Church of love will give a sign. It will

not be in external events (disasters, 'the dancing of the sun', rock fall from the mountains and so on),[21] but in the instantaneous transformation of the souls summoned under the influence of the oceanic grace of the Holy Spirit.

*

The many-tiered architectonics of San Salvador

San Salvador had a fifteen-tiered structure.

The many-tiered architectonics of the mountain were so otherworldly, that movement from tier to tier was not perceived, as if a man had risen or descended by one floor. Some remained for a long time on one and the same tier, without realizing it. Others were ascended.

We pass a small (5x3) stone house with embrasures. This is where the guards lived. They did not permit others further than this first stage.

Further: 14 stages of hierarchical initiation. Each one was celestial heavenly bliss. Movement between them occurred imperceptibly, in the shape of special seals descending onto the anointed ones.

The flight of the white eagle

The last seal revealed the entrance into the Holy of Holies, where the anointed ones accomplished the flight of the white eagle: with the Chalice in their hands they were borne through the air from castle to castle.

Ascent to a new tier anticipated a special kind of anointing and cross. Those, who reached the pinnacle (were admitted into the Holy of Holies as immortals) were amazed, understanding how long the path had been, how long they had been rising.

The privilege of the immortals was to be in direct communion with the Father of pure love. This communion occurred not externally, (like that of the visionaries), but from within. The Father fully imprinted Himself in them. They became a hypostasis of the Father.

They were called christs. The stages distinguished great and lesser christs.

*

The immortals settled in five upper towers (in accordance with the mysterious architectonics of the castle, they corresponded to the Cathar heavens).

Hence the secret of the five-pointed Cathar star.
The number 5 symbolizes the Holy of holies.

From the five-tiered structure on the pinnacle the guards exchanged remarks and moved from castle to castle, passing through the air.

The silent spheres of communion in San Salvador

In the castle reigned the laws of locution.[22] Human speech was permitted only at the entrance. They resorted to it exceptionally rarely, only in events of the special effusion of the grace of the word of God or revelation.

On the pinnacles of San Salvador communion was accomplished silently.

This does not mean that there was a type of 'nirvana' without words and thoughts. There existed the highest communion. The vibrations in the immortal bodies were so fine that the anointed sovereigns did not need words. By these impulses, gazes and prayers they sent that which was considered necessary.

Our Lady's universum of Exceeding Wisdom revealed to them up to 1500 special spiritual states in which communion occurred.

A universum was outlined for the earth: 15000 'cells', which were usually mastered by the mortal ones. All these anticipated conversational speech (starting from the most primitive interjections, swearing and condemnation, to the elevated style of the poets, etc).

In the heavenly universum of San Salvador from 500 to 1500 universal spheres of Exceeding Wisdom revealed themselves. The seals of these spheres were accomplished, and speech was silent.

Such is the secret teaching of the Cathars.

III.
$\mathscr{T}$HE PRAYER ON THE PEAK

Plunge+ earthly souls into the waters of the airy sea.

Reveal+ the entrances and exits of the second airy sea of divine existence.

Bring+ millions of souls into divine existence.

Reveal+ to them the sources of eternal light.

Seal+ the caves with chimeras and Luciferic fingerprints.

Destroy+ the storerooms of fly-droppings and close+ the cursed doors.

*

$\mathscr{F}$orget prayer with the particle 'may'

THE FATHERS OF SAN SALVADOR:

'May it be' is an incorrect prayer. It supposes doubt and bifurcation, subjunctiveness, uncertainty. None of us ever prayed 'may it be'.

Forget prayer with the particle 'may'. The modelling always occurs in the present – *it is accomplished, it is given, it is admired.* Only this kind of prayer is summoned as the prayer from the divine existence by the pure and perfect ones.

> Prayer occurs before our eyes. Humanity is converted, sings to the face of Our Divinity and ascends to the immortal waters of the second airy sea.
> Hallelujah, hallelujah, hallelujah!

Sins are forgiven[+],
sinful spatterings are erased[+].
Immortal man is imprinted[+]
and the interior is adored[+].
The divine potential
Comes unsealed[+] / opens[+].

The castle in the shape of a ship

The castle was built in the shape of a ship, because it was planned to sail across the airy sea.

After a month of residence in San Salvador all of the earthly associations of its inhabitants passed away. A complete disengagement from the earth occurred.

The sailing through the heavenly sea was attended by attacks of its 'leviathans' and 'sharks'. These were not longer earthly but airy demons.

The Holy of Holies

The Holy of Holies, located in the stern of the 'ship San Salvador', had a five-tiered structure.

There is a small cave on three levels (with dimensions of 3x5 metres and a height of five metres). The floors are connected by a stone staircase. The walls and arched ceiling are laid from select stone, and look almost weightless. Above is an airy hatch of dimensions 40x40. On the wall (on the level of the fifth tier) is depicted a white eagle.

Hither the Grail was borne. Hence were accomplished airy flights.

The stones drop myrrh. Bloody spots appear on them, as on the stones of Solovky. They are fragrant and preserve secrets in themselves. On many are imprinted the most ancient and mysterious signs (the latin 'b', two chalices, and others).

The Holy of Holies breathes to this day. Hence descends and dwells the grace of the Heavenly Father.

*In the aerial sea

We are in the place, where prayer was heard absolutely! Hither the immortals came. The Father heeded the prayer.

I beg that all the old things pass and that the Theohumanity arrives.

That the New Holy Rus' is born and every prophesy of the anointed sovereign fulfilled.

That thousands of saints descend into the world.

That lust, depravity, vileness, corruption, mammon and dictatorship are destroyed.

That the seals of the old civilization pass away.

That souls are enriched with the grace of the Father of pure love, and that millions come to believe, are converted to the true faith, and know Our Father as He is.

We are on the verge of flight. Another several minutes, and wings will be given to us.

Here is the place of the highest initiations. We are in the airy sea.

In San Salvador earth, air, and heaven are mixed.

To man, as if spread on a triple Cathar cross, returns the countenance of the Godman. Ascending to the Holy of holies, he realizes that he is an angel, having come down from heaven. He grows spiritual wings.

'The fish have the right to their airy sailing – spread fins and swim', our fathers taught.

Above us is the 'captain's deckhouse' the elevation above the Holy of Holies.

To here usually ascended the 'captain of the ship' (the head of the castle) to conduct the prayer for humanity. He was called the father of fathers or the preacher of light, the immortal keeper of the Chalice.

The hypostatic sons of God

The immortals received the names of hypostases: hypostatic christs, hypostatic sons of God. They achieved the highest degree of divinization possible on earth.

The kingdom of the Father of pure love,
Exceeding Wisdom, bless us!

15 minutes of silent bliss in San Salvador

THE FATHERS OF SAN SALVADOR:

In our school of prayer you will begin with the

94

bliss of silence. To start with, 15 minutes of silent (with deep breathing) bliss with the Cathar anointed ones. Gradually bring the silent bliss in the combination of hearts to three hours.

Silence as the language of Our Divinity

Prefer silence to human speech. Love silence as the language of the Divinity, sending vibrations, impossible on earth.

The vibrations of the airy sea are perceived among the silent ones. Understand silence, not as a pause during speech, not as a time of leisure or rest, but as a miraculous immersion in divine existence with the blessed anointings from the perfect ones of San Salvador.

The sunny Christ in San Salvador

The sunny Christ in San Salvador was inimitable, unique. In each of the castles He wore special clothes and spoke with a special tongue.

The perfect ones came through the air to the castle, where the coming of Christ was expected, in order to hear, what He would say in this precise castle.

Then all gathered at the Round Table, which seated thousands and told each other about the miracles and revelations, given by Christ. A total picture of Exceeding Wisdom and the universe formed.

*

Listen to the sermons of our brother, night-ingale. What theological heights! Salvador is also Nightingale Mountain.

We descend. Flocks of nightingales surround us. We listen to the symphony of sunny joy.

◦§

5.

Lucifer defeated:
the eighty-fifth civilization has begun!

We are full of the desire to change the world and man. It was no accident that our prophecies were not fulfilled.

- Love the silence in the exceedingly fragrant spheres of the Kingdom
- Christ looked at his disciples with eyes of burning love
- The might of the Cathar church is greater than ever before

- The Sweetest one deprived the adversary of His power

- Cherish the treasure trove of unmixed spirituality
  like the apple of one's eye

- Hold in your heart the Father, who does not mix
  with impurity, in order to ascend to the stage
  of the combined ones

- Lucifer was able to convince the unified man
  of the 84th civilization to change his composition

- Of the 100 particles of the Adamites,
  eighty five remain immaculate to this day

- The Cathar staff of the incineration of Luciferic particles

❧

𝒯he ban on oral prayer

THE FIERY HIERARCHY:

n those, who ascended to San Salvador, after lengthy exercises in continual meditation, a ban was laid on oral prayer (as intersecting with Elohimism).

They took a vow of absolute silence, after which they received the first seals of the pure ones on their brows.

𝒯he ineffable logos, uttered silently in the interior

Our spheres are silent. Learn to hear more than the voice: the ineffable Logos, the Logos uttered silently in the interior of Our Divinity.

Our Father would like to talk with you in a language undetectable to the bearing-taking radio of our enemy (oral prayers without the inclusion of the heart).

Silent prayer is born on the heights of our castles in the rays of Our Divinity's glory, fanned by the sweetest music of the Altísimo.[23]

Oral prayer, highly it rises into the spiritual spheres, touches the order of the world and disturbs thought, which is fit to enter perfect repose.

Anxiety (doubt, thought) is caused by an enemy attack. Silence lays a shield and in a short time leads to the acquisition of the victor's wreath.

Love the silence in the exceedingly fragrant spheres of the Kingdom. Begin with the dissolution of oral prayers in the rays of silence, with the exceedingly tender trepidation of the admiring celestial mind.

Silence forms an internal system many times more sensitive to delicate and divine vibrations, conducts the currents of heartfelt love and reveals one after another the gates of the internal castles.

Dedicate two to three hours a day to the art of silent prayer, achieving perfect peace and the stage of the masters, after which inclusion in the earthly spheres will not distract from spiritual doings.

The sudden entrance into blessed silence

The ascent to Montségur-II began with the deepest repentance, the lighting of the candle.

Then, after three months of intense meditational prayers (at first long and verbose, then reduced to three short prayers), followed the sudden admission into blessed silence. It was given more easily here than ever before, by the influence of the higher spheres of our masters, crowned in silent prayer.

The eye of the Father in the composition of man

In the composition of man there is an instrument, capable of sensitively measuring the mixing of spiritual nature: the eye of the Father, the spiritual eye.

The representation of the Eye of God (Oculus Dei) accepted in Rome-Byzantium, a cold glass fish eye, is devoid of the fiery nature of the Cathar seals.

The fiery hierarchy of the Cathar-Solovetsky church acquires vision with the eyes of the sweetest Father.

THE EYE OF THE FATHER, extolled without end, becomes the inheritance of the sons.

Christ looked at his disciples with eyes of burning love. But many trembled in His presence, expecting in Him the action of the 'fish eye' of the Almighty and Elohim.

Not having waited, they were disappointed and left, flatly not noticing *who* He was and closing their ears to his immortal sermons.

*

200 million fiery warriors on white horses gained a great victory in the battle with the Roman church. Thrice Rome collapsed!

Lucifer has been defeated for the disciples of the immortals from the heights of heavenly San Salvador.

The Cathar church and its army (200 million fiery warriors on white horses) gained a great victory in the battle with the Roman church. Thrice Rome collapsed!

The nightmarish scarecrow, instilling terror in humanity on earth, has been thrown into the fire and incinerated. Its poisonous ashes have been scattered.

Lucifer has been defeated: the eighty-fifth civilization has begun!

> The sweetest eye of Our Divinity,
> O vision from the Sun of suns,
> become the property of millions! –

The immortals pray. And indeed the chariots of the immortal eyes begin to burn in their hearts, like shining screens on which it is possible to read the highest secrets of the divine world.

After the medieval genocide of the Cathars we gained a multitude of brilliant victories, and the might of the Cathar church is greater than ever before.

Look at the reconnaisance of our armies! See the fiery ardour before the battle. Such is the might of our Father, the kindest of the kind!

And such is the contemptible face of Lucifer, this compulsively lying nobody, swindler and trickster.

His hypnosis has been exposed. His movements have been revealed to humanity. His webs have been torn to pieces. His curses have been removed.

The Sweetest one deprived the adversary of His power. The Most Pure One gained a threefold victory over the ancient serpent and smashed the thrones of the Adversary.

The great victory, our child! New seals descend into the world. Triumph and festivities in the heavens. At its completion tens of thousands of souls will descend into the world with the immaculate marking on their brows, with Arabic figure *85*, inscribed with gold.

And on the earth – the wilderness and the calm before the storm...

The beginning of the Theocivilization will be proclaimed by the occurrence of the fiery hierarchy on black horses in golden bridles

The beginning of the Theocivilization will be proclaimed by the appearance of the Fiery Hierarchy and the immortal ranks in the radiance

103

of the Divinity on black horses in golden bridles, crowned with crowns and spears.

The enemy is more dangerous than ever. During only the last several days the cunning one issued several thousand poison arrows against us, and sent his most ferocious leviathans and spiders in human form.

*

The renunciation of the obsolete order of the world occurs every day. Catharsis occurs hourly and *tirelessly*. The first Cathar seals are purification from the prince of this world. 'Tirelessly' means: without seductive thoughts, as if 'liberated', 'forgiven', 'purified'...

Until the world is free of the poisonous dust of Rex Mundi, not one person will be able to consider himself perfectly pure.

A battle to the last breath, like that of Christ, like that of the Most Pure Virgin.

Did not the Queen of Nightingale Mountain tell you what kind of battle She waged during several days in all and even hours before Her assumption. She endured a great battle literally until several minutes before Her peaceful and most blessed repose in the ages with the furthest ascent into the Cathar sphere...

Our child, the cunning one despises the regal gold treasure trove entrusted to you. It was once offered to him, to Lucifer.

Lucifer rejected the gifts of the Holy Spirit and preferred his own storehouses with bats, fly-droppings and other evil spirits.

Cherish the treasure trove of unmixed spirituality like the apple of one's eye.

The Father, unmixed for those being converted – not mixing for the advanced ones.

In order to ascend to the stage of the united ones, it is enough to hold in your heart the Father, who does not mix with impurity.

The vow of absolute dissociation from the order of the world

It is impossible to ascend to the Bridal Bed and unite until the chimeras *of mixedness* have been expelled.

Fierce wild boars and aerial predators will drink the blood of living saints like scavengers, until those take the Cathar vow of absolute dissociation from the order of the world and its present chief, Satan.

The vision of the unmixed Father is enough, even in the wilderness, for the sunny disk of Our Divinity to burn before the cloudy gaze, and for the soul in darkness to come blindly to the dull little light.

*

Have the courage to endure the battle for the great sphere of San Salvador, revealing itself to humanity for the first time. And take, at this very moment, a vow not to absent yourself from your immortal fathers, however hard the enemy dodges away or drives you with clubs, cries, and thoughts, however hard he casts you out alive.

The precious pollen of dissociation

THE SUNNY FATHER:

My child, today I am inserting a special kind of particle into the internal caskets. This is the precious pollen of dissociation.

You should know that the consequences are risky. The slightest mixing will be reflected in the internal condition with the most unhealthy manner.

Take for Our Father the vow of complete dissociation from the world, whatever it costs.

And then with the staff of erasure I will liberate you from the yoke of slavery of the prince of this world and will indeed make you free.

A multitude of angels in white vestments. The Father, having clothed me in a miraculous white shawl, shining with transparent light, entered the eternal castles and imprinted with a thrilling movement of the hand the white pollen of dissociation.

The bleached mother-of-pearl bone of original immaculateness

The bleached mother-of-pearl bone of original immaculateness today serves as the foundation of the reformation of the Godman for the 85th Theocivilization-III.

Understand it as an exorcistic staff. With the power of this staff drive away our enemy, wounded by the unblemished power of your Divinity.

The staff of original immaculateness

Do not release the staff of original immaculateness from your hands in the heaviest hours of battle, however much Satan shakes your palm, however much he squeezes your wrist, saying: 'Well, release it from your hands, my creation... I promise you...'

Close your ears and do not listen to anything. THE STAFF OF ORIGINAL IMMACULATENESS − however heavy it might be, wherever you like: in the wilderness, in the gloom, in the darkness.

Two angels from the retinue of the Divinity, knights in splendid white clothing with a red Cathar cross on their chests, entrusted the shining exorcistic staffs of original immaculateness to us.

*

The Bible concealed from man the secret of his origin.

The enemy fell upon the makers, not only in the 84th civilization, but also in the preceding 83. Fifteen supreme angels were able to deflect his attacks.

The 85th civilization is the sixteenth (8+8) from the number of the immaculately conceived ones.

Lucifer was able to persuade the unified man of the 84th civilization to change his composition; the fall began with this.

The cunning one promised an unheard-of multitude of new blessings, superhuman gifts and possibilities.

85 of 100 particles of the composition of man remain immaculate to this day

My child, do not be surprised by what I say now. From the one hundred particles of the Adamites, eighty five remain immaculate to this day, but reside in a frozen and extremely neglected condition.

When the number of poisonous and putrid particles exceeds 15 of the 100 (that is, there are less than 85 immaculate particles), the essence of the Adamite collapses.

The renewal of only 5 particles in total of those stolen by the cunning one (90 immaculate particles out of 100) is sufficient for the Adamite to heed the word of Our Father and strive for the celestial world.

What sacrifice is borne by the Great Church of Love, so that the number of poisoned particles in our younger brothers, the little ones, decreases!

Further, my child (from ninety to one hundred), every particle is priceless;

92 out of 100: the stage of the pure ones;

95: the perfect ones;

97-98: the anointed ones, shining with bright sunny light;

100 out of 100 – the sign of the completely divinized ones, the wreath of the immortal.

Do not stop meditating on the change of internal compositions.

Take from our hands the Cathar staff of the incineration of Luciferic particles (lust, decay, dreams, hypnosis, prostration, sorcery) in each of the ten stages of the change of the composition, from 91 to 100.

The order of the world catastrophically includes impure particles, giving rise to chimeras.

The immortal principles, absorbed by us, combine into one and make the divinity visible.

Perceive from us the Cathar eye – the vision of

Our Divinity and of one's neighbour with His eyes.

In the immaculate civilizations (15 of the 84) there were no sinful particles, but there were present *mixing* particles (85-95).

The silent prayer
of the new divine modelling with rays

Daily, with upraised hands in ecstatic spheres: the silent prayer of the new divine modelling with rays which penetrate your interior, with the incineration of putrid and serpentine particles from the composition of the adored sons and daughters of Our Father.

*

Catharism – dissociation, leading to complete purity and the stage of the perfect ones.

O beautiful new divinely-inspired man, free from chimeras!

Our knights, take stones and smash the skulls of these accursed monsters, so that they do not prevail over our younger brothers, Adamites.

Now draw spears and with them pierce the lustful bellies of the insatiable monsters.

The Adamites will soon be transformed into Seraphites. The Cathar Hierarchy will compel them to this by the paths it has revealed.

The Cathar treasure trove (the throne of the Exceeding Wisdom of the Divinity) knows *how* to convert the world in a short period.

Submit to the blessing of Our Divinity.

The Jews saw the fiery chariots, spotted all over with many-eyed cherubs. We will show you the throne of the Fiery Hierarcy, unheard-of for ages

Preserve purity of vision, and not one but a thousand suns will begin to light up before your gaze!

We are full of the desire to change the world and man. It was no accident that our prophecies were not fulfilled.

*

All the human essence should become continuous prayer.

For those who love, silence is the sacrifice of the heart: as a combination, as the Bridal Bed.

◄§

6.

the Scattering of the blessings

THE REHABILITATION OF THE COMPOSITIONS OF MAN

Our fathers preserved the secret
of the transubstantiation of mortal flesh into relics
and of their myrrh-pouring transubstantiation
into the surrounding space: 'the scattering of the blessings'.

- Christianity leaves without a trace
- The civilization of purest light is born
- He, who ascends to San Salvador, is freed
  from the 1800 hypnotic shells
- The face of Our Divinity is hardly visible
  in the present world
- Three fiery wildernesses
- From the den of chimeras to the throne of Our Father
- The manna of white pollen

෴

THE IMMORTALS:

ur Divinity sealed the gates of Rome and Byzantium.

The age of the cuttlefish[24] has ended. The time for the presentation of scores has begun.[25]

The earth will begin to tremble when, after the presentation of scores, the Roman bigwigs see the real picture of what is happening. Their hair will stand on end with fear, and their bodies will stretch out to several metres.

Exceeding Wisdom will gather them together in one sunny glade and show them the great deception lying at the foundation of the Roman kitchen. Its sweetened, poisonous dishes have been fed upon through the centuries by serpents and the pure souls of God equally.

It will be especially hard for their saints and apologists – the torrent of "until when?" and blows will come down upon them first of all.

Christianity leaves the face of earth without a trace. It is visible no longer.

Christ remains in the universum – among great and small christs, the sunny Teacher among the sunny disciples.

𝒯he temple of Original Immaculateness

The sea of Exceeding Wisdom flows out in the aether of San Salvador...

The true disciples rise from reliquary burial vaults and castles. That for which our fathers ascended the bonfires and accepted martyrdom is being completed.

The civilization of purest light is born.

The anointed sovereigns of eternal virginity descend from the heaven in sunny vestments.

Exceeding Wisdom reveals the universe of the Immaculate Conception, inserting the absolute immaculate beginning into the spiritual bodies of the Seraphites

and founding the temple of Original Immaculateness (= the noninvolvement of Seraphic humanity in the fundamental corruption of Lucifer).

The evil of the world is the corruption laid on the Adamites by the despot.

Lucifer created a civilization of swarming fly-droppings. His microscopic maggots grew into gigantic balloons, full of human-shaped vampires.

The white pollen

Instead of microscopic fly eggs, of which there are an innumerable multitude in the internal storerooms of the Godman, white pollen is inserted.

Here on San Salvador, take the airy white font: the insertion of the cloud of the white pollen of Original Immaculateness.

May the beautiful reformation of Our Divinity reveal itself to the world.

The creation of man from a cloud of white pollen

Does Elohim not begin his ludicrous writings with the creation of man 'from water and clay'?

And we begin our letter of light, not made by human hand, WITH THE CREATION OF MAN FROM A CLOUD OF WHITE POLLEN, and with the most gracious imperishable compositions of Our Father-Sun with a multitude of aromatic oils and mysterious anointings.

*

The 1800 hypnotic shells

He, who ascends to San Salvador, is liberated from 1800 shells, and from the same number of nests warmed by dark birds.

The prince of this world wrapped the immortal creation of the Divinity in 1800 protoplasms.

It [the creation] will be disrobed of one thousand, eight hundred garments!

117

1800 exorcisms lie ahead.

The essence is restored, smelling sweetly with the aromas of the Holy Chalice.

The sun of Our Divinity penetrates the dark chambers of man's interior...

The dark room

The camera obscura... What is this? A dark room. A divine castle once illuminated with light, transformed into a mouldy cave, a stone crypt.

Illuminate yourself over the sky of San Salvador with a new sun, man of pure light!

Reveal the 1800 internal dark rooms.

Let the ever-burning lamp begin to be lit in each, and the sunny disk be established!

> With the staff of the church of John
> man is re-created anew!

With each of your ascents to San Salvador, the mountain of the abode and presence of our Divinity, thousands rush hither, searching and knocking at the door.

Five imperishable scrolls, containing within themselves the secret of the creation of man

Five imperishable scrolls, containing within themselves the secret of the creation of man, travelled through the aethers of our castles from the holy Chalice.

The five words of Our Divinity, uttered during the birth of the small sunny god from the crystalline myrrhic drop of the Father.

The source of imperishable light, inserted like a hypostatic divinity into the interior of interiors of the created Godman.

The secret of the victory over the prince of this world,

The 145th of the 144 castles of His undefiled love.

Take off perishable clothing.

Clothe yourself in the vestments of the immortals.

The cunning one was able to harm the praememoria aeterna (most eternal memory) laid in man during creation.

They remembered enlightenedly.

During the ascent to the sunny San Salvador Padre Nuestro Verdadero[26] THE MOST DELICATE ETHEREAL OPERATION FOR THE REHABILITATION OF MAN is conducted – the removal of perishable clothing and hypnotic shells...

Do not be surprised, our thrice Blessed father John, that the face of Our Divinity is hardly visible in the present world. The Father preserves the pleroma undamaged.

The secret writings of the most eternal

Gospels may not become the property of throngs of millions.

The secret teaching is passed among the anointed ones.

The truth, having fallen into the hands of our enemy, risks being exposed to profanation and being turned against its bearers.

Leave the decorative bell towers with cawing crows. The truth of Our Father reveals itself for the chosen ones.

Seek manifestations of the Divinity on the peaks of the mountains.

Hope to enter the waters of the airy sea and complete your celestial flight.

*

Is it really possible to reach the Grail from a restaurant? From the café chantant to the round table of valiant knights?

The descent is preceded by a wilderness, in which the traveller remains alone.

Reject forever the bloody dogmas of the inquisitors, together with their missals, prayers, and instruments of torture.

Refuse Elohimic mixed sources, in order to accept the sunny anointings of Our Divinity.

Do you reject Elohimic mixtures and distorting mirrors?

– I reject them.

Do you agree to pass through the wilderness and loneliness with a desperate cry (the voice of the one crying in the wilderness)?

– Yes, my sweetest Father.

*

𝒯HE FATHER ON THE THREE WILDERNESSES

THE FATHER OF PURE LOVE:

You are My son, and I will give you the anointings of the future age.

You are My christ, and I will call you My beloved, My only.

You are My lamb, and I will stab you on the throne of My love, having given the wreath of the lamb-victor.

My child, do not be afraid.

Did I not speak thus to the Blessed Virgin during the Annunciation?

I said to her:

– Do not be afraid, Mary, to abandon the angelic cover and the grace of the temple of Jerusalem, the warmed religious nests of the ancient Jews.

And today I say to you: do not be afraid.

Do not be afraid, My son, to abandon mixed seals – I will give you a thousand times more!

Do not fear the hours of devastation – this is catharsis.

DO NOT BE AFRAID to abandon the old prayer,

121

liturgy, habitual shape of thoughts and faith — which have become a support, transforming, alas, into stone prejudices over the years.

*

My child, I will enrich you from the imperishable treasure troves. I will give you that which I have never given to any of the Adamites or even the Seraphites of the 84th civilization.

Have you not been edified by saint Evfrosinia, Innokentiy and Serafim?

These three will be edified by you in the Exceeding Wisdom coming from the earth, superior to their heavenly exceeding wisdom...

The terrible battle with Elohim

Endure, My child. I foretell for you another three fiery wildernesses. Do you agree to pass them?

– What are these – physical illnesses?

Illnesses are in the past. Battle, My child. A terrible battle with Elohim. Loneliness.

The more disciples, the more severe the wilderness. For each of your dear and beloved ones you will have to descend almost every night into their dark, mouldy rooms, boarded up with rusty nails...

Do not despair, My child. My Patronage is becoming more than absolute, and my signs will become incalculably many!

You have been chosen for the salvation of humanity.

Steadfastly renounce the best things that were laid in your heart in the years of the first conversion.

You have been changed a million times more than you are able to contain.

You are going ahead of yourself – you are barely hobbling, lagging behind your very self by many years!

While behind this, behind the sunny John walking ahead of you, is something even greater: immortal, divinized, anointed.

Remember the nuptial bonds with marvellous neighbours. What I say to you, I say to them.

And what I give to you, I give to them – exceedingly generously, inexhaustibly, more than they are able to accept.

*

$\mathcal{T}$HE SUNNY GOSPEL

THE IMMORTALS:

The grace of the Divinity is in the 144 imperishable towers of His divine castle.

We will leave the biblical Elohim far behind and take the fiery scroll of Our Father into our hands.

What is this, you will ask? – THE SUNNY GOSPEL.

Touch it, do not be afraid.

Take it into your hands and lay it wide
before the Theohumanity
of the Third Theocivilization.

The souls appointed from time immemorial, resting in divine existence, will read the great designs in their hour.

Put your trust in Our Father Sun
and thirst for His appearance in the wildernesses.

*

The Father Sun of suns will not reveal Himself to the world before humanity has freed itself from the chimera of Rex Mundi.

Do not release the double-edged sword of the knight of the Most Pure Virgin, the knighthood of the Invincible, from your hands;

sharpen it against our enemy and his hornets' nests (the religious chameleons).

*

THE CATHOLICS ARE CONVERTED TO CATHARISM ON SAN SALVADOR VERDADERO

THE CATHAR KNIGHT:

How were we occupied for 700 years? We were pouring myrrh in the garden of indescribable blisses.

Trust in us like a little child. Believe that we have sufficient experience of liberating from the chimeras.

Our child, tens of former Catholics rushed to San Salvador. And we, reading the seals on their brows and distinguishing in the Spirit, permitted some to enter.

How hard it was for them in the first days and hours! They were thrown into such epileptic fits! The battle was such that it was necessary to tie some of them down like raving lunatics. We did not take our eyes off others in case they threw themselves from the mountain. The demon of doubt gained the upper hand over yet others until the hour of death: so they were not able to complete their battle and renounce the mixed seals...

But there were also those who, after a thrice-repeated laying of the fiery hand and ablutions in the fonts of pure waters, shone like newborn Infant Gods and had the honour of seals higher than those of experienced elders.

You are not the first to complete the path from the dens of chimeras to the throne of Our Divinity.

During the second conversion our beloved breaks away much further from his former self than during the first – from the order of the world and the 'old beginning'.

Chinese temples will fly one after another, and with them – the former hard buttresses and pillars of faith... But what is being formed in return is incomparably greater, my child.

Virginal purity

Purity, complete purity!!!

The virginal mother-purity, the exceedingly pure aethers. Our Father, the purest of the pure. The exceedingly pure Mother, Our queen Exceeding Wisdom in transparent vestments. Never-ending purity, greater than itself, multiplying hour upon hour, endlessly!

The essence of the pure one shines with enlightened purity. Perfection in purity bears indescribable fruits. Such is the new asceticism in the heights of our castles. Illnesses, infirmities, wildernesses, solitude, loneliness persecutions, a battle on the brink of the possible...

Did you not sing in the hour of the revelation of the God of love:

> 'There is no one except Him,
> My beloved.
> There is nothing except love,
> His love'?

Now you will begin to silently sing after us: 'There is nothing except purity'.

Proclaim the purity as your Lady. And with it – the kindest kindness.

It is possible to acquire it only in the castle of enlightened lights.

Then peace descends onto the disciple of Our Father.

$\mathcal{T}$HE INITIATION

Now we will initiate you into the brethren of San Salvador, into its eternal sacred dwellers.

We accept you into the number of our immortal anointed brothers as an equal and send you into the world.

Thus almost a thousand years ago we sent our beautiful brothers into the world.

They returned crowned and radiant, and after a short rest in the valley of the Father again asked to be sent into the world...

The all-human soul can't be satisfied while younger brothers suffer at the foot of the mountain.

*

$\mathcal{T}$his world is a wilderness, inhabited by precious divine beings

This world is a wilderness, inhabited by precious divine beings.

As they ascend the staircase of celestial blessings the wretched human-shaped beings, tormented by passions and fatal programmes, reveal themselves as potential brethren of San Salvador, as our most chaste brothers in clothes of light...

$\mathcal{T}$he celestial flight with upraised hands

The celestial flight with upraised hands begins on San Salvador... What prayer!

The walls of the castle, we note with Father Pa-icy, have been deprived of the modelling of the prince of this world. Imperishable and exceedingly pure. To kiss them is joy. Warmth emanates from them, even if the surrounding temperature is -50°.

These walls only seem material. In reality they stand in a different space. Rest your hand – it enters the stone. And from the stones come hot tears of peace and Cathar kindness.

The embrasures of the castle are heaped with stones. Eight centuries ago they fired catapults against our fathers from Perderodes.[27] Even the stones wailed about the villainy of the Roman inquisition... But today the Cathar windows shine onto all the worlds.

Our fathers keep the secret
of the scattering of the blessings,
the myrrh-pouring transubstantion
of relics into the surrounding space

Many anointings preceded the mystery of *the anointing with oils* (the imprinting of the immortal bodies).

Our fathers kept the secret of the transubstantiation of mortal flesh into relics and of the myrrh-pouring transubstantiation of the relics into the surrounding space – THE 'SCATTERING OF THE BLESSINGS'.

The kingdom of day and night locutions

In San Salvador there was a kingdom of day and night locutions. The silent ones conversed amongst themselves in the language of divine vibrations through the internal revelation of the Word. Not needing physical contact, they conveyed questions through the finest, exceedingly heavenly channels, sent blessings and aid, and resolved their affairs.

On the surrounding flowers had been scattered the manna of white pollen. To savour the symphony of smells was the highest bliss.

*

The Catholics in the eyes of the Cathars

We looked upon the Catholics as desert hyenas and jackals. On the forehead of every second Catholic was the seal of the 'holy Inquisition'.

If the Inquisition (the interrogation, torture, and murder of saints) is holy to them, what is there to say about their disciples and followers? Drowsy dog's muzzles.

Perderodes will collapse shamefully. Serpents will crawl through its ruins.

But San Salvador, with the favour and the divinity of the heavenly Architect, will be restored in its initial beauty and will shine more beautifully than 800 years ago.

San Salvador Verdadero will be seen in all the ends of the earth. They will ascend from Chile and Argentina with the words: 'We saw San Salvador!'

> The throne of Our Divinity
> in all the ends of the earth.
> The castles of our sweetest Father
> in divine existence!

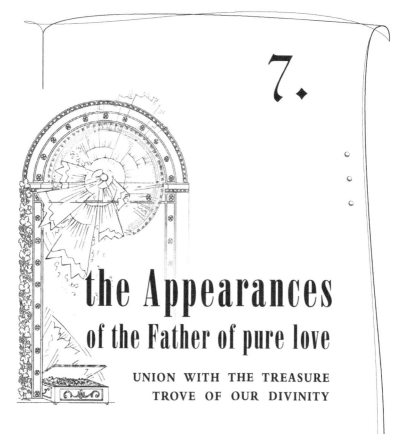

7.

the Appearances
of the Father of pure love

UNION WITH THE TREASURE TROVE OF OUR DIVINITY

- The Luciferic glasses were removed by the appearance of the Divinity

- The fullness of the presence of the Divinity is contained in the internal sunny disk

- At first three, and then thousands of springs

- The potential for purity and virginity in man is inexhaustible

- The Cathars did not keep diaries or write books

- On San Salvador the devil had no power over man
- Without the God-maternity of the Most Pure Mother of God divinization is impossible
- Secrets imprinted in hearts were revealed to the most eternal sight
- The mother of those that love Christ-as-He-is, contemplating Him with their own eyes
- The treatment of one's neighbour: a burning angel
- Rome criminally silenced the living heavens of Our Father
- Cathar spirituality has been warmed by the breath of the Slavic Theogamic chalice of Andrew First Called
- The revelations of Christ on San Salvador were, for the greater part, silent

THE FIERY HIERARCHY:

The heavenly Father came to San Salvador Padre Nuestro and, as in the modern revelations at Beleser, revealed the true history of earth and man.

The appearances of the Father of pure love (the name, revealed by Him in the middle ages for the highest levels of Catharism – the anointed ones and the immortals) were accompanied by thousands of sunny chariots.

The Father Sun of suns revealed Himself in a suite of thousands of great and lesser lamp-suns (the divinized ones).

*

One of the goals of the arrival of the Divinity was to return to man his divine hypostasis, which suffered damages during the adaptative remodelling of Rex Mundi.

The second stage of Slavic-Cathar-Theogamic

spirituality (the initiation into the Holy Passion) was considered obligatory. Without it the secret of the embodiment of man and the tolerance by the Divinity of his earthly confinement in the 'camera obscura', the earthly pitch-dark prison, remain inexplicable.

The lamp, *flaring up in the darkness* in the beginning, and then *ever-burning*, revealed indeed the inexhaustible potential of love in the purified, virginal Godman.

The Eye of sunny goodness, love and exceeding wisdom, which has not grown dim in the night

The anointed ones often dwelt night and day in illuminated ecstasy and thanked Our Father for the opportunity to shed such high and great love onto the Adamites.

The Father, coming to the chosen ones and raising them to the stage of the Seraphites,[28] showed how absolute (in spite of all deviations and betrayals) His love for creation was.

He inserted His eye, which does not grow dim in the night, after which the anointed ones learnt to see the people around them with eyes of sunny goodness, love and exceeding wisdom (by which they were also conquered).

For perfect spirituality, one thing that the Cathar anointed ones taught is enough: see the Divinity, oneself and the world with the eyes of heavenly kindness.

On the contrary, the corruption inflicted on the spiritual sight, has catastrophic consequences.

'The Luciferic glasses' were removed, not by repentance or even by introspection, but by the appearance of the Father. Onto the sight of the disciples were laid special sunny lenses, while the heart was turned into a small sunny disk.

The practice of the lighting of the internal sun

Our Father showed the elders of San Salvador, Montségur, Perpetouse, Quermanco and other 'heavenly communities' (as the castles were called then): the fullness of the presence of the Divinity is contained in the internal sunny disk.

The stages of its achievement (the realization of the internal cave in the heart, darkening, darkness (1), the revelation about the Father of pure love (2), the lighting of the candle (3), which turns into the unfading lamp (4), and at last flaring up into the sunny disk (5)) form the sense of the embodiment of the Godman on earth.

The cunning one was able to darken that which cannot be darkened. From the heavens the Divinity will do something more: he will light the lamp amidst the darkness which eliminates the light.

*I*n the undamaged vision of the Father

Purification from chimeras consists in the undamaged vision of the Father, in the ability to perceive the never-ending light of His love.

We concluded the degree of spiritual ascent according to the ability for one's soul to be continually illuminated spiritually = to reside in the revelation of the Father of love.

The darkening of the mind, the inability to walk before the revealed heaven, was considered to be the stage of the beginner.

*P*ictures of Armageddon, the battle of Our Divinity with Lucifer

Above San Salvador repeatedly swept pictures of Armageddon, of the battle of Our Father with Lucifer, who has taken the shape of a fire-breathing red dragon covering half the sky.

The perfect ones saw the cosmic retinue of the cunning one with its centre in Tibet, and were amazed by the exceeding wisdom with which the Father drove into a trap and subdued the stubborn monster, who claims sole authority over the earth.

*T*he Divinity and Lucifer (a dialogue)

Continually presenting scores, Lucifer said:

– Man has been completely corrupted! At the very bottom he made and repeatedly confirmed his covenant with me. At the bottom of man is the underworld!! Hosts of sleeping chimeras are ready right now, like rapacious Erinyes, to destroy every living thing!

The Divinity answered him:

– At the very bottom man is invulnerably pure. To dig down to this very bottom forms the secret of purifying introspection.

At the very bottom of man is the invulnerable hypostasis of pure love, the immortal bodies.

Man is immortal, not only because there exists a life other than the physical flesh (the elders instructed the new arrivals), but also because of the invulnerability of his heavenly origin.

The connection of the most unforgivable and heavy sinner, seemingly lost and thrice cursed, with his heavenly origin, is not broken under any circumstances.

*

The four-circle Cathar cross

The dispersing Cathar cross, passing beyond the limits of three circles, symbolizes the combination of the pure bride with her heavenly hypostasis through the practice of the Holy Passion and the spiritual experience of metanoia (internal transformation).

> The first circle is the spiritual heart,
> the doors to the heavens revealed.

> The second circle is the man-universe,
> the scattering of the pollen of the cross.
> The third circle is the Cathar kingdom,
> the diarchy of the Divinity and Satan.
> The fourth is the grace of the Bridal Chamber
> of the perfect divinized ones.

The divine anthropology of the immortal ones taught that the composition of man includes a fiery body – one of the three great sources in man, able to return him to the primal modelling of Our Father, to the combination with the particle *te-el*.[29]

ℋealing on San Salvador Verdadero

On the heights of San Salvador, cleansing was accomplished by the very purity in the aether.

Those who were not summoned, unable to perceive the virginal vestments, were not able to pass even an hour here. Some turned into living vampires and demons. It was necessary to tie them down, because they fell aggressively upon those around them. Some began, with an evil spirit, to expose their sins and those of their neighbours, and to lay curses. The demons (including the institutional Roman demons) moved in them. The initiated ones of San Salvador were forced to send such people back into the world.

*

Miracles of divine mercy and compassion occurred on San Salvador. Thousands were cured of
incurable illnesses. Some cripples were lifted to an
inaccessible height of 700 metres on stretchers –
this sometimes took several days and nights.

The contemplation of the castles

San Salvador was visible for tens of miles around.
One view of the castle healed and cleansed.

The inhabitants of neighbouring villages during the morning prayer with upraised hands gazed
at the castle of Our Father, and admiring rapture
accompanied them all day, however they were occupied.

At the beginning of the eleventh century, with
the blessing of the Divinity, at first three, and then
thousands (!) of springs gushed from the earth.

Thousands simultaneously! Each was named in
honour of one of the bright divinized ones of the
Chalice.

A day did not pass without the pure ones, wash-
ing in their waters. The new beginners were instructed to complete ablutions several times a day, with
cathartic prayers, under the guidance of the elders.

The Divinity promised that the mysterious waters of the miracle-working springs would wash
away the pollutions of the prince of this world,

until the pilgrims and inhabitants of San Salvador achieve complete purity.

The cunning one (taught the fathers of San Salvador) considers the darkening and corruption of man never-ending.

The Cathar anointed ones confirmed the opposite: the potential for purity and virginity in man is inexhaustible. None of them dared to consider himself utterly cleansed, in order not to seal the prospect of further purification.

*S*ilent myrrh-pouring ecstasies

The aether and spheres of San Salvador brought such bliss that it was simply impossible to live without them.

No oral prayers nor even contemplative raptures could replace the silent myrrh-pouring ecstasies.

The ecstatic 'o-o!' and the savouring of the aromas of relics were daily practices.

*D*eath was defeated

On San Salvador a sphere of the highest fiery divine existence reigned. Death was defeated.

Those that had achieved the fourth, highest stage of immortality came in fiery bodies whenever they wanted, taking appearances one more beautiful than another.

Often the immortals, whose myrrh-pouring relics already reposed at a depth of several hundred metres in the architectonic divine existence of San Salvador, came in the shape of beautiful angelic adolescents. Having modestly installed themselves in a corner of the cave, they silently passed days, weeks and months among their brothers, who were contemplating the light.

The goal of their presence on earth was the purification of aether and the shedding of grace.

With their participation the mysteries and anointings passed silently, apart from the usual human instruction, religious rites, enlightenment, preaching...

Union with the treasure trove

The Cathars did not keep diaries or write books. The goal of the ascent to San Salvador (mystical, and not only external) was considered to be union with the treasure trove of our Divinity.

The Father of pure love returned the original grace, and the need for anything else faded.

All the devotee's being was filled with ineffable light. In the spiritual language of the anointed ones of San Salvador this was called 'the pinnacle of rehabilitation'.

*

The destinies of the unworthy ones

The heavenly Father (the masters of San Salvador said to the disciples) placed around His most eternal throne on earth 144,000 angel-keepers from the so-called 'protective hierarchies'.

Not one unknown soul (not speaking about the enemy) is able to approach here. Grief to those, who endeavour to pass the 'cordons' of our Divinity with impure goals: severe retribution awaits them.

There were many parables and rumours about San Salvador. In some were mentioned bloody and disfigured bodies, as if thrown from heaven – the bodies of those who tried to penetrate San Salvador unworthily (the Roman agents).

*

The secret of the 'second sea', which was spoken about several days ago in the revelation, was revealed. We swim through the second sea, desiring to moor at the harbour of the blessed ones.

They initiate us into divine existence. Our legs do not walk, but swim: the flesh becomes weightless.

The faces of the masters of San Salvador

The faces of the masters of San Salvador were full of such sunny light, that some of them held their eyes meekly downwards, being wary of looking in the face of their neighbours.

142

The pilgrims were often unable to endure the glance of a perfect one, and fainted.

*

According to the promise of Our Father, the devil had no authority over man on San Salvador.

This was the only corner of the earth, where the true Creator and Architect of Theohumanity, with the help of His perfect instruments, cured in a brief time the souls of the heaviest injuries and traumas.

The language of the birds

The immortals of San Salvador understood the language of the birds. The song of the nightingale brought them incomparably greater joy than conversation with the most spiritually enlightened neighbour.

The heartfelt vibrations from Divinity Himself were transmitted by mystical channels.

THE SPIRITUAL CENTRE OF THEOHUMANITY

The Father promised never to leave them, generously anointing in the superior Holy Passion — the key to the true salvation of the world, free from the malice of the inquisition and the troubles of indulgences.

None of the anointed ones abandoned San Salvador.

Those, who had already passed the stages of purification, had to instruct the new beginners.

The perfect ones passed into seclusion. The highest stages – of the anointed ones and the immortals – presupposed a vow of eternal service to humanity, without abandoning San Salvador Verdadero.

It was impossible to abandon the mountain. At the highest stages of divinization the world looked worse than a hellish bottom or demonic backwater.

A great white cherub was continually raised above San Salvador – the seal of our Divinity and His eternal cover above the mountain of the chosen ones.

The fathers of San Salvador called it the spiritual centre of the Theohumanity.

*

The appearance of the Mother of God on San Salvador

Without the God-maternity of the Most Pure Mother of God divinization is impossible.

Our exceedingly wise Lady is the mediator between Father and children. The human race has been entrusted to HER.

After Her revelations, the seals of Exceeding Wisdom descended on the shining angels of San Salvador, so that they sparkled with the knowledge of God, higher than that of the angels.

144

The Most Pure One enlightened them about the hiding places of Holy Passion: about the miraculous mines, contained in the secret of suffering for one's neighbour, about the joy of redemptive feats.

Masters and new beginners caught Her every word, savoured Her seals, and inserted them into themselves.

An hour did not pass without the Queen accomplishing miraculous mysteries over them, or anointing their internal caskets, or revealing to them THE DIVINITY, reposing in the castles of the heart...

The vision of the potential

The very favourite theme of the divine existence instructions of the Most Pure One in the spheres of San Salvador was the vision of the divine potential.

It was as though the Most Pure One lulled the disciples to sleep, immersing them in the divine existence blisses of Heavenly Love,

after which they contemplated their interiors as if from the side.

The introspective entrance into the internal 'holy of holies'

The introspective entrance into the internal 'holy of holies' amazed them like no external revelation or vision.

What riches Our Father laid in man during creation! To what insignificantly small degree have they yet been revealed!

The Most Pure One did not stop revealing more and more internal mines.

The disciples did not know how to thank Her. Each time they met Her with ever greater reverence.

The Most Pure One unrolled the white scrolls before them, on which were revealed for the most eternal sight the secrets, imprinted in hearts.

The signs of these secrets were almost immediately forgotten, but revealed themselves in their own time, showing the influence on the destinies of the initiated ones and those surrounding them.

The mother of those who love Christ

The Most Pure One, inserting mysterious oils, did not tire of calling Herself the mother of those that love Christ-as-He-is, or those that contemplate Him with their own eyes.

– But how did it happen, Heavenly Queen, that the world is in a great delusion? They see our dear Saviour with corrupted eyes, with Luciferic glasses!

– It doesn't matter, – The Most Pure One comforted us with a smile. – At some time I will open the vision of millions. Didn't Christ promise that those that love Him would see Him with their own eyes? May it be so!

Her prophesy is being realised. With the deliverance from 'distorting mirrors' man begins to see Christ outside of the distortions and conventions inevitable for the modern Adamite.

*

Airy wings for hovering above the castles

The airy wings for hovering above the castles were considered the stage of the immortals.

The perfect ones of San Salvador in the highest stages rose to the Holy of Holies and had the honour of accepting the sunny chalice from the angels, having conveyed the Holy Grail from other castles. Then with a ceremonial procession the Chalice of Chalices was conveyed to the living altar of Our Father.

The caskets of Exceeding Wisdom

It happened that the retinue of the Most Pure Virgin carried with it *the caskets of Exceeding Wisdom*. With the blessing of the heavenly Queen these caskets opened themselves, and the perfect ones contemplated with exceeding rapture the symbols of the secrets of our Divinity, inaccessible on earth.

Just one contemplation of these drawings and

signs (even without explanation) brought indescribable bliss. The entrances to the secrets of the future age were contained within them.

The anointings were completed despite the absence of rational explanation of the sacred attributes. The time of Our Father had not arrived...

*

*D*uring the entrance into San Salvador:

O San Salvador de Padre Nuestro –
most heavenly Father!
Reveal the sunny tabernacles
for the coming Third Theocivilization!
Descend, apostles of the new heaven and
                              new earth,
unite us to the spheres of the airy sea.
But for the pharisees – woe to them, woe.

*

THE FATHER:

I spoke with my disciples, as with you today.

Juan de San Grial had his Father Paicy and 12 heeding disciples, listening apostles.

My child, on the celestial heights they delight the ears with the words of Our Divinity.

There is no place for the 'classical' gospels and commonly accepted canons here.

The laws of the universum reign in the immortal bodies.

I appear in consolation. Forseeing the machi-

148

nations of Lucifer from the beginning of the age, I promised not to abandon my children, however, hard it is for them. And now I am fulfilling my promise.

*

On San Salvador the treatment of one's neighbour was: a burning angel.

The appeal to brothers: the burning angel Juan, the angel Miguel, the burning angel Mateo... To sisters: 'most glorious wife of mercy', 'my sunny lady'...

'Is it possible, O myrrhic vessel of the Most Pure One, to ask you for a small service?'

Indifferent, coldblooded treatment ('according to the rule', 'as is customary') was considered a sign of dullness of the mind.

− The candle should not be extinguished for even an hour! If it is extinguished, ask again and again for the Holy Passion. Only it can warm the internal waters, and shed the ineffable warmth...

Communion as an aspect of the highest spirituality

The residence of the anointed ones on the heights of San Salvador was not reduced to only one solitary seclusion. Communion did not give them less joy than the contemplation of the Divinity.

Brothers and sisters lived together. In the mysterious hours of communion with the Most Pure One, having raised hands, they dwelt in celestial flight on the peaks of the castle.

Communion was considered the highest spiritual practice. The mystical spectrums of communion contained a vision of the mysterious vibrations of Our Father in one's neighbour.

Spiritual contact between the perfect ones was a continuation of the contemplation of the Most High, another aspect of communion with the Divinity.

– THEOHUMANITY, – the initiated of San Salvador did not tire of saying, – IS THE DIVINITY, LIVING IN ONE'S NEIGHBOUR.

On the heights of San Salvador it was achieved that, which was impossible anywhere on earth:

to see the flawlessly imprinted fullness of the Divinity in one's neighbour.

And more than to see: to converse with Him, to participate in His plans and to empathise with Him.

*

$\mathcal{O}$n the sunny revelations

Rome criminally silenced the living heavens of our Divinity (= the true church): the innumerable appearances of the Father of fathers, the Christ of christs, the Holy Spirit of spirits and the Mother of God of the divinized ones...

The anathemas pronounced upon the revelations, and the inquisitorial inquiries concerning them, began almost at that hour, when the synedrion learnt about the resurrection of Christ.

The thought of the appearances of the immortals Christ and the Mother of God instilled terror in the rabbis of Israel and their successors, the Christian priests.

Nothing haunted the pharisees of all times more than the voice of the living Lord.

Having understood the resurrection of Christ as their own defeat, the Jews did not dismiss His subsequent appearances in the heavenly bodies – and fervently cursed every one of them...

Meanwhile, Christ did not stop appearing.

Cathar spirituality has been warmed by the breath of the Slavic Theogamic chalice of Andrew First Called.

The unique face of Catharism formed as a consequence of the direct sunny revelations of the Father of fathers, the Christ of christs, and the Mother of God of the divinized ones.

The revelations of the Divinity were often anticipated by the discovery of His new name.

*

The attainment of the highest stages of anointing (the third and fourth: the anointed ones and the immortals) apart from anything else gave the privilege to heed the voice of the Divinity.

The perfect ones dared to prepare themselves for the stage of the Bridal Bed.

The anointed ones (the Theogamites) passed the stages of the sacred Theogamy.

The immortals found the fullness of Christ's divinization.

*

The revelations of Christ on San Salvador were for the most part silent.

With a special sign from above, the pure ones and the perfect ones gathered in a vast, specially appointed hall.

Christ came and silently spoke into their hearts.

Not a single word was pronounced. The instructions were given mystically. But how the witnesses of the coming trembled, when they had shared His words with one another! It turned out that they had heard and accepted one and the same text, word for word!

The silent meals, called the bridal suppers of the Lamb of Our Divinity, were accompanied by the partaking from the Chalice and were enraptured in the spheres of the very highest divine existence.

THE IMMORTALS:

The cunning one began with forbidding the appearances of Our Divinity. He forbade aromas of the relics, and forbade the return of the immortals to their lawful settlements.

Then he began a cycle of *his* revelations, and created a caricature of Montségur and San Salvador: Tibetan caves with mahatmas, in a state of samadhi for a thousand years.

The three levels of sunny clothing

What I see defies description.

The most blessed ones wore immortal vestments. Other than human vestments, they wore three layers of clothing of the purest light.

Around their brows shone a triple halo of irresistible grandeur.

Prayer:

Father, save[+] and divinize[+]
lead[+] the world to the heights
of Your ineffable anointings.
Liberate[+] from the enchantment
          of the prince of this world,
from his never-ending chimeras and traps.
Complete[+] anointings over the sleepers
and direct[+] their spiritual gaze
to Your eternal castles of ineffable
blisses in the heavens and on earth.
AMMI.

*

The architectonics of San Salvador

San Salvador, the most eternal creation of the Divinity, had 144 divine existence tiers.

Each of the perfect ones was given his own castle, where the chosen ones dwelt for a long time, and then returned to the brothers and combined with them with bonds of pure love.

Some passed through heavy trials and wildernesses.

But, as there was no birth in the usual sense (the immaculate conception is an unusual arrival in the world), there was no end in the usual sense.

Death passed away. For those, that had been restored, after the fiery rehabilitation from the hand of the Father, existed only mysterious transformations (transubstantiations) and transitions from one state to another.

*P*rayer with the raising of hands
on San Salvador:

O celestial heights!
O bliss of Our Divinity!

∞

8.

the Vows
of eternal virginity
and eternal brotherhood

- The mystery of reformation anew
- See oneself with the eyes of Our Divinity
- It is only possible to teach about pure love in the categories of eternal virginity.

- The knighthood of pure love becomes
  the invaluable property of those, who take the vows
  of eternal virginity

- Not a single person achieved the stage of the immortals
  until he had thrice died, giving up his life for his neighbour

- Immerse yourself in the sources of eternal virginity

◦§

The regal particle Te-el'

an is ready to be ecstatic in any way ridiculously, like holy-fool and silly in order to break the limits of him himself with his fouls-up. If he would only overcome the philistinism, so blessed by the ritual inquisition, which has one staff – that, which puts one to sleep.

The soul achieves true happiness only having united with its heavenly source, its 'first tenth' – Te-el'.[30]

Then it enters into a perfect marriage with the Divinity.

The regal particle Te-el' is the crowned bride of the Divinity.

On her hand is a wedding ring, given to the earthly Holy Passion sister-martyr.

*

*E*ternal virginity

The ascender to the mountain of blessings becomes enlightened.

The ascent itself presented gravity. But what consolation and rewards for the audacity of the break!

*T*he inexhaustible potential of eternal virginity

At the first stage of the staircase of ascent the inexhaustible potential of eternal virginity, which we called the regal treasure trove, is revealed.

Why eternal? – Many asked.

Eternal, – we insisted, – because, due to the temptation of lust, many angels were turned from the path of Theoadoration-Theorapture-Theoattachment.

Only he, who takes the vow of eternal virginity, overcomes the temptations of the prince of this world and comes to the kingdom of Our Father.

Do you know, our sweetest one, how many of those, who have taken the vow of monasticism and celibacy, have slipped on the otherworldly staircases of ascent only because their vow was earthly and temporary? Temptations beyond their strength weighed on them. The devil turned them 'black and blue': having immersed them in pitch darkness, and tempted them as he was never able in the earthly days.

158

**It is only possible to teach about pure love
in the categories of eternal virginity**

First master, with every cell of your being, with every entrance to the internal castle:

IT IS ONLY POSSIBLE TO TEACH ABOUT PURE LOVE IN THE CATEGORIES OF ETERNAL VIRGINITY.

Do not dare to approach superior love without striving for eternal virginity with equal strength.

Sing the never-ending hymn to eternal virginity.

What do the nightingales of San Salvador sing of, if not virginity? Virginity sheds the aromas of unearthly flowers.

Virginity betrothes the soul to the Divinity as a bride.

Virginity returns immortality and unites with the most heavenly bonds those who, outside of the vow, would serve as a temptation and burden to one another.

The knighthood of pure love becomes the invaluable property of those, who take the vows of eternal virginity.

They are indeed born from on high, and the former life seems to them a nightmarish hallucination, an oblivious sleep...

*

The mental sunny disk

Our child, what hot flows of sunny love we shed, sending them to one another!

On San Salvador we learnt to send each other the mental sunny disk.

By mysterious vibrating channels, understanding the condition of our neighbour, we shed love from internal chambers, and the cunning one fell back, however powerful his attacks were (judge them by your own battle).

The internal man in the heavenly spectrum of immortal bodies

Does the Adamite in his present condition understand, to what degree his every thought, reaction, and gesture is penetrated with the soul of lust, taken from birth itself? May the very essence change!

The Father revealed great secrets to us.

We see the internal man in the heavenly spectrum of immortal bodies.

We contemplate with our spiritual eyes and with indescribable joy, how the being transforms during the ascent to San Salvador.

The most heavenly divine X-ray, which does not blacken the pure sight.

The vow of eternal virginity

For today there is nothing more important than the consciousness and the acceptance of the vows of eternal virginity.

By consciousness we have in mind the complete penetration by purity. The joy from thousands of advantages of virginity over lust and pollution, which have been revealed.

And the staff of eternal virginity is in the hand of the devotee, working day and night, especially in the hour of battle.

Yes, it is necessary to pass a multitude of temptations. But beneath the horseman is a faithful horse. Beside him – his faithful brother. And ahead – his faithful Father.

The civilization of pure love

Hence across all Europe a wave of eternal virginity rolled, and the civilization of pure love was born.

Thousands of knights and beautiful maidens, enveloped by heavenly love, dwelt in the contemplative divine marriage.

Remaining in the world, they succeeded to achieve the highest stages of love thanks to the prayers of the anointed ones in the mountains.

We thirst to remind sleeping humanity about the civilization of eternal virginity and pure love today.

The civilization of pure love and eternal virginity is the new sun, rising above the world. Its light dispels the miasma of cosmic conception, UFOs, and world fundamentalism, in which millions are suffocating.[31]

Endeavour to master its origin, to enter into its universum, and Exceeding Wisdom will generously endow with thousands of gifts, among which are the gift of the pioneer and the sweetest blessings that accompany it.

The vow of eternal brotherhood

After the vow of eternal virginity on San Salvador we took the vow of eternal brotherhood:

'I will never betray my brother!

I will never betray him, however hard the battle.

I will lay down my life for him, however much the cunning one tempts me, however much he fills me with malice...'

In the torments of battle an eternal brotherhood was born, of a kind never seen on earth nor in the heavens.

The cunning one came between the brothers

The cunning one came between the brothers in the most ferocious way. There is no need to relate all his machinations. He set on them to death. He incited them to see the reasons for their failings in their neighbours. He contrived their defeats and pointed at their neighbours. He created phantoms over the dear brothers with his cursed seals: 'Look here! Break the brotherly bonds and the former world and grace will return'.

The attacks were such that now and then our brothers were not able to rise from their places for weeks, preferring extreme feeblenesses to condemnation. The ferocity of the diabolical attacks was such that the most fearless and powerful one was not able to understand from the earth.

The great Armageddon between the powers of Our Divinity and the prince of this world

Here, half a mile above the level of the sea, occurred the great Armageddon between the powers of Our Father and the prince of this world.

Demons, intoxicated with the blood of innocent victims, attacked our fearless knights. But they pierced them with the swords of El Elion, chained them with the shackles of Exceeding Wisdom, and exorcized them with the bridal bonds of eternal love.

And the demons left in powerless malice, realizing their defeat.

The bonds of eternal brotherhood

The bonds of eternal brotherhood passed into eternity and granted immortality.

THE FATHER:

My child, not one person achieved the stage of the immortals, until he had thrice died, giving up his life for his neighbour, and was thrice resurrected, rejoicing in the bridal lodges of pure love for the advantages of eternally virginal conscience, in the embraces of the indescribable brotherhood.

It has been lost by the mortals for the sake of other transient bonds...

Immerse yourself in the springs of eternal virginity. Draw from them. Wash daily in their white fonts. The mind is cleansed by them, and the transformation of the internal being, spiritual rapture, the Bridal Bed with the Divinity, the seals of the bride, who walks to meet her bridegroom with candle lighted, all issue from them.

And brotherhood, my child, brotherhood is not comparable to anything. It serves as a unified shield against the malice of the knight of this world, the well-known wastrel and provoker.

The secret of our brotherhood

THE IMMORTALS

The anointing for eternal brotherhood laid in the fact that the greater part of the soul resided in the heart of one's neighbour.

In battle the cunning one always struck directly, not understanding that the secret part of the soul reposes in one's neighbour. The Templars depicted this secret in the symbol of the two knights fighting on one horse.

The miraculous bonds of most heavenly brotherly love spread around, and those seeking holiness became fragrant in their divine aromas.

Many rejected earthly attachments, worries and hardships for the sake of entering into our eternal brotherhood.

The European lodges, which arose between the seventeenth and the nineteenth centuries (passionate brotherhoods of peoples, seeking purity and perfect spirituality) were a reflection of that most heavenly original brotherhood, which arose among the children of our Divinity of the first degree of blood tie.

O beautiful bonds of eternal brotherhood!

O beautiful bonds of eternal brotherhood! The internal order is changing. The essence is beginning to sing. Man is revealed in illuminated light.

After the first stage (the vision-consciousness of oneself with virginal eyes) you see your neighbour, beautiful, as if for the first time.

And you exclaim: 'Beautiful brother! Beautiful sister! My beloved, O'. No longer formal and habitual, but singing from the heart the never-ending nightingale song of love.

The most restful chamber

After the fierce battles is the Bridal Bed.

After the heavy daily work for the salvation of humanity (the liberation of souls from the snares of Rex Mundi, the sealing of the forbidden entrances and the help for millions, who need it at all the ends of the earth and other worlds) is the most restful odr.

Beautiful brother, beautiful sister... Peace be with you.

*

It is impossible to leave San Salvador Verdadero. He, who has once inhabited our mountain heights, remains with us for centuries, for ever.

Many of the beginners *(the captivated ones)*, called us illuminated. For us the illumination of sight took no effort – to see the beautiful brothers and sisters with the eyes of our Divinity. So lofty and chaste is the sight, given on San Salvador.

How happy we were to see each other in immortal sunny bodies, understanding that these were more perfect than those of many of the angels.

And what never-ending gratitude we offered to Our Father, having honoured us from the earth with stages superior to many heavenly stages!

*P*erfect seclusion presupposes
the bridal bonds of love between brothers

Do not rely upon the tempting mode of seclusion, like the ascetics, who dwelt for weeks in the wilderness, living on bread crumbs and now and then glancing at the neighbouring cenoby for spiritual conversation. Perfect seclusion, of which we teach on the peaks of San Salvador, presupposes the bridal bonds of love between brothers.

The bonds of the Most Pure Virgin, bonds of love, of which there are none on earth, are eternal, like a whitened mother-of-pearl bone of sharpened purity.

On San Salvador 'adored brother, adored sister' sounded naturally, without expending of effort.

The women shone as hypostases of the God-bearer, the men as Christ.

The tears of our anointed ones

The tears of our anointed ones were caused by one thing: throwing their view to this world, we see how man is wounded without end. He suffers in the wilderness through his own guilt, not able to recognize the true reason for his hopeless futilities.

The prince of this world entangled people in many-layered nets of age-old lust.

Our prayer on San Salvador:

> May THE SUN OF PURE LOVE embrace humanity, lost in the bonds of lustful slavery of the prince of this world.

𝒯HE ARCHITECTONICS OF THE CASTLE,

no less than 100 caves with their own entrances and exits, leading into divine existence

Having built the castle on the pinnacle of the mountain, the perfect ones continued to construct it from within.

Tens and hundreds of years passed in order to make the perfect architectonic picture of the castle as it was in the design of the Divinity – no less than 100 caves with their own entrances and exits, leading to divine existence..

The castle turned into the never-ending city of God.

This was something contrary to the modern metropolis. Each of the caves conferred its own aether and aromas.

The initiation on San Salvador

No words can replace the initiation, given personally on San Salvador. It is necessary to rise to the peaks of the castle in order to personally experience the aethers of virginity and covet them.

Bring as many souls to San Salvador as possible. We promise to help them freely and to give anointings, more than which are not possible anywhere.

*

Before the entrance the spiritual ones pronounce: 'Give us your blessing to enter by the divine entrances of San Salvador, our fathers'.

What joy is given at the entrance! We have come home. What a shield, God! How reliably our fathers were concealed here despite all the inquisitorial machinations, catapults, threats and chimeras.

On the heights of San Salvador he who raised his hands became a living superworldly chalice, the Grail personified and its keeper.

*B*irds and butterflies

Birds, like butterflies, are beings of divine existence. Contemplating them it is possible to enter into an ecstatic rapture. The bird sings, savouring the aromas of relics, and even transports the pollen of relics. The birds rejoice together with those who gave their lives out of love for the Divinity and their neighbours.

We left the world, because the bonds of pure love are impossible in the world.

For us, San Salvador was an oasis of pure spirituality.

Our plans were put aside for a thousand years.

⋖§

9.◆

the Candles of immortality
above San Salvador Verdadero

- The Theocivilization will be proclaimed suddenly
- Of seven heads, six have already been chopped off
- The dragon has been pierced by spears
- Immortal seeds are sown in the bilocational Holy Passion

THE FIERY HIERARCHY:

he Theocivilization will be pro-claimed suddenly.

An unexpected blow will have been inflicted on the prince of this world, from which he will no longer recover.

Unhappy are those who trust in the captains of UFOs, the masters of samadhi from Tibet, the homo sapiens sapiens, the religion of the pharisees...

Of seven heads, six have already been chopped off. It is necessary to chop off the last – the most stoical and firmly resisting: the global triple-hypostasis phariseeism.

During your last visit the dragon was literally pierced by spears. His bloody head was raised above the worlds, and the black blood was collected so that no more cursed seeds arise from it, from which are born the attendants of the cunning one.

The triumph of the Father of pure love

Under the Theocilivization your oldest immortal brothers assume the triumph of the Father of pure love.

Is it strange, our child, that only a few hear?

It is easy to convert others to a faith reviving, after lengthy neglect ('the first conversion').

The crop of the Father of pure love is completed by the two hundred million hot Last Drops. Its explosion will be sudden.

The prince of the world, stunned, falls away from the face of the earth.

You accepted the prince of this world as the Divinity

The judgment over the 84th civilization: 'You accepted the prince of this world as the Divinity; the most cunning Elohim, a gathering of impure spirits, dwelling in the dark universes'.[32]

Another judgement is not necessary. Humanity has sufficient experience of unified temptation. But we will help the last of the Adamites of the 84th civilization to see the accursed machinations of the enemy even more soberly, before we inflict the devastating blow upon him.

On behalf of 200 million pure and perfect ones, anointed ones and immortals, reveal the great secret of the fall of man: his delusion regarding the evil and unmerciful deity, bringing punishment and death, filled with rancour and revenge.

Worshipping the prince of this world under the guise of the divinity, the religious institutions have inflicted, and today continue to inflict, irreparable damage on humanity, increasing and hastening its fall.

The salvation of the Adamites resides in one thing (proclaim this in the overworld aethers of all humanity!):

the power of the prince of this world is being destroyed by those who have arrived from the true Maker and Creator. His name: THE SUN OF OUR DIVINITY.

Chernobyl of a worldwide scale

Having not known Our Divinity, humanity inflicted poisonous lead clouds on itself.

A Chernobyl on a worldwide scale has been accomplished. And it remains only to remove the deadly seats of defeat, and heal the bloody spots on the body of the unhappy one, with purifying disasters...[33]

The Divinity of pure love,
being revealed for the first time

Is it worthwhile to rummage in the city urns and

set up archaeological excavations on the sites of the ancient radioactive fires?

The Divinity of pure love, being revealed for the first time, the sunny divinity of ineffable unearthly perfections, prefers the childhood of the soul and the virginity of the spirit.

Hardened conservatism is worse than unconsciousness and nihilism. It is not worthwhile to look for crumbs of gold deposits beneath piles of slag.

Imagine how it is for the lambs of the Most Immaculate to master the spheres of the Adamites – to descend to the heights of San Salvador, Montségur, Nightingale Mountain, Kibeho and Medjugorje![34]

Complete the answering labour of ascent to the spheres for the alleviation of our task.

Thus, continually place small fortresses at the sites of yesterday's wildernesses. And leave the towers and bastilles and torture chambers, which have outlasted their lifetime, on the conscience of the executioners.

*

Do not descend from Nightingale Mountain and Montségur-II, and millions will be converted to the true faith.

Do not rummage more in the human anthill, found the next day to have become a heap of sand and dirt.

175

The word, communicated on the heights of San Salvador, has a superworldly ether and reaches the ears of millions.

The cross, prescribed for its mastery, is thrice honoured. The more severe the wilderness, retreat, loneliness, and solitude; the more unbearable the cross and the despair, the greater the number of souls that are able to get the attention of He, who craves to reveal Himself to humanity as the true, kind, eternal and bright Father, worrying about His children and form them as if for the first time, despite their long path and sufficient age.

I will form a new man

THE FATHER:

I will form a new man in the shape, lying before My gaze.

I will form him to be perfect.

I will place in him the pearl of My immortal compositions, I will give him the power to withstand the nets of the cunning one.

I will gain victory over my eldest, Great Monster[35], thereby that My small creations will shame him. In each of them he will find the reflection of the face of their all-perfect and purest Father.

Today I am already sowing the compositions not inherent in the Adamites – Seraphic compositions.

Their influence will instantly defeat the pow-

176

ers of Lucibel and stop his attack across the entire earth.

*

CHRIST:

Repentance? What great futility, My child, to repent, not having before your eyes the perfect models!

Although they cried out a hundred times in the liturgy 'God have mercy!' and preached in empty words the metanoia of the Byzantine and Alexandrian ascetics... If not even one lamp stands before their gaze, it is empty. A deception mixed with hypocrisy.

Seek the light from the lamp source, and the sinful abyss before the spiritual gaze will disappear like a hallucination. The need for 'God have mercy' fades away, having become the property of criminal double-dealers and mafiosi.

I denounce them today with a million times for righteous anger, than ever in Jerusalem.

Destroying the lamps, the devils in cassocks – the sacerdotes – expose the people to the darkness of unbelief and despair.[36]

Imagine a world day and night beneath the dull, lacklustre radiance of a warping moon without a single little ray of sunny light...

Ascending to San Salvador, the lamp and sun of the coming Theohumanity, raise with you (mentally and daringly) all, who crave to live piously and perfectly, without the sin and the snares of the cunning one.

It is within My authority to form man in a splendid constellation of immortal bodies

— sunny-amber, mother-of-pearl, most radiantly immaculate, marine and heavenly, transparent and waxen, of relics and of myrrh, wounded and invulnerable, reposing superworldly and raising from the dead, not knowing sin, nor illness, nor death, nor decay...

It is within My authority to do this. And I will not fail to complete the greatest of spiritual miracles on the eve of the 85th civilization, the sole reality, which I proclaim today on the heights of San Salvador.

Hither, to San Salvador Verdadero, I strove in the hope of converting the western world to the true faith. Thither emanated the rays of My parousia presence and the hot rivers of My unmelting love for humanity.

Everyone, who was raised to the heights of San Salvador, was fanned by the most fragrant aromas of the Kingdom and united with the faces of the immortals — the most beautiful of creations earthly and heavenly.

The immortals reveal themselves at the end of the 84th civilization, on the eve of the 85th, as the workers of the future age, in order to give the mysterious rules and particles to their disciples.

Battle with the dragon
lying at the entrance to the sacred place

San Salvador is one of the seven apocalyptic arks of the Divinity, erected across all the earth.

It is not enough to be awarded the honour of entering into the ark. It is still important to endure battle with the dragon, lying at the entrance to the sacred place.

Why a dragon, and not an angel, you ask? The dragon is a symbol of the impurity which it is necessary to overcome before entering the holy of holies. While dragon exists (the devil, Satan, the Roman church, the prince of this world, and so on) access to the ark is difficult. Remember this.

Christ of parousia

I lift up humanity with My hand, shield it with the fullness of the Holy Spirit, grant it My seals, press it to My heart and give it the blessing to live for a thousand years on earth under the sign of Our Father.

I am Christ, whose icons are copied from the perfect heavenly model.

179

I am He, who spoke in Jerusalem and today speaks at San Salvador, the mentor of the true disciples of the Divinity, guiding them to the heights of His kingdom.

The Father of pure love Himself sent Me as aid to my disciples, in order that I inculcated my beginning: the seals of Christ. I granted more and more from the last drop of Eucharistic blood, so that your composition became fiery, and your brows accepted the outlines of the sunny hierarchy of the immortals.

Do not be afraid to erase. Stare at the white scrolls in the hands of the Most Pure Virgin. These white tablets are restored almost daily.

The letter, drawn anew, becomes more beautiful from record to record.

Such is the most eternal gospel, seen by John the Theologian at Patmos.

I showed it to John on the Greek island 2000 years ago, and today I am showing it to you.

*

My child, what has been erased, disappears without a trace, if it contained even just one dark particle. And it is transubstantiated into the quality of the most high, if it contained in itself a bright beginning.

Do not be miserable about the paracletic liturgies. They will transform into divine services incomparably more beautiful and corresponding to the composition of the Seraphites of the third millennium.

Do not mourn the old forms. Their unmixed particles will transubstantiate.

The word will become more accessible, more beautiful, and more pure. Its audience will be a million times greater.

Earlier, My child, the Word reached the dark rooms and clouded storerooms of the city burrows, where eternal prisoners sat behind the grey ribs of radiators.

Today the Word will reach a multitude of sunny worlds.

The heavens rejoice from the throne of the Divinity, placed on earth, and from His Words, illuminating the aethers of the world.

Suffer the wilderness as the natural experience of the transubstantiation of the Word into the most perfect − of one composition into another, more pure and of higher quality.

$\mathcal{T}$HE KENOTIC EXPERIENCE OF THE HUMILIATION OF THE MESSIAH

Child, your mission is so significant before my eyes that I am not able to permit you a single hour 'for no special reason' (loss of attention and rest).

In your Holy Passion, in the wilderness you are doing no less than ascending to the mountains and being in the enlightenment of the Holy Spirit.

One illumination is not enough, My child. A kenotic experience of the humiliation of the messiah is necessary for tens to be enlightened and follow the lamp.

Do you not grieve that your flock is so inadequate for the size of your mission?

Remember: immortal seeds are sown in the bilocational Holy Passion. Your potential audience grows to universal scales. May the right hand of Our Divinity strengthen you to enlighten them in the hour, when millions say, having raised their hands: 'Father, strengthen and direct us!'

Do not grieve, My child. Rely upon My regal right hand. I will change the order of the world.

Do not seek to convert anyone. Turn more often to My gospel form. Remember, how the three-year euphoria of Israel, connected with the never-ending miracles and displays of messianistic power, ended.

Your experience of the wilderness is invaluable

Not for an hour, My child, even in the hours of the most severe attacks, should you forget about the secret of transubstantiation, described by the Evangelists as death and resurrection.

Lead thousands of your disciples through the gates of the exceedingly bright transubstantiation.

Let fear and discontent disappear. Outside of the perspective of transubstantiation into the highest and most beautiful quality, outside the vision of consolations, accompanying the wilderness and loneliness, you cannot achieve the heights of the Divinity, as I would have liked.

Your experience of the wilderness is invaluable for you personally and for millions.

Faith in transubstantiation forms the break from the spheres of inconsolable sleep and damnation.

John of the 84th model (The Church of the Transforming Mother of God, the revelation of the Most Pure Virgin in the cathedral of Smolensk,[37] the Orthodoxy of the true spirit) transubstantiated into the apostle of the Second Solovetsky Golgotha,[38] the keeper of the Chalice – the proclaimer of the sunny Third Theocivilization.

My child, the cunning one has already wanted more than fifteen times to bring death upon your immortal soul and the body, protected by Our Father and by Me personally.

But I have prescribed for you 15 stages of transubstantiation even in this life. Now multiply 15 by 15, and may the soul rejoice in the coming light, when the vaults of the caves will part and the light, so longed for by us, will be revealed!

Darkening is a natural phase of transubstantiation before the enlightenment of the mind, of the wilderness before the multiplication of the sacred place.

Without the cross it is impossible to bear fruit in the wilderness.

𝒫rayer on the heights of San Salvador

What prayer there is on the heights of San Salvador! Man is a personified torch. He has 100,000 lighted candles at his altar. Hands are raised most restfully, and on the superworldly throne there is a prayer about the six billion inhabitants of earth, about each individually and unified about all...

THE PRAYER SAN SALVADOR VERDADERO:

About the conversion of the inhabitants of earth, about repose, about the changing of their compositions...

about the inculcation of new seals...

about the renunciation of the prince of this world, of his cursed illegitimate adaptative reformation...

about the erasing of Luciferic seals and the removal of bans on perfect holiness...

about the cutting of the nets of Lucifer and the forming of the new man...

184

about the awakening of millions from ill-fated sleep, about the changing of their compositions and about the sowing of the beginning of Original Immaculateness in the deep sleep of the Adamite searching for eternal life...

The burning tears of Our Father will reach hearts.

Man will transform and transubstantiate. The face of Our Divinity will be inscribed on him and 200 million bon hommes (kind people) will be imprinted in the internal castles.

The holy chalice will be carried in a mystical space and will enrapture all the sufferers of the earth.

The church of the pure and perfect ones will become the property of the Theocivilization.

The authority of the devil will end. The time of the triumph of the saints will come.

*

The very name given by the ancient fathers to the Cathar church – San Salvador Verdadero – shows that the castle is the fortress of Our Divinity in authentic and undistorted immortal models.

My being sunnily transubstantiates into the chalice. And my spirit completes its sunny flight along the ascending ray of light to the throne of our Father...

The candles of immortality

When the hands of the anointed sovereign are extended in prayer in the form of the chalice, billions of souls find room in the space between his palms and enter into the fire of transformation.

I see each of the adored neighbours in an immortal perspective.

The candles of immortality have been lighted. The chalices of immortality have been poured.

It remains only to partake from the Holy Grail of the drink of immortality, here distributed so generously, that it is enough for all who are coming and another thousand on top of that...

1... 2... 3 minutes

One minute of the prayer of the anointed sovereign on San Salvador is enough to avert disasters.

Two minutes are enough to save the world. Three – to divinize it.

*

The prayer San Salvador Verdadero:

About the conversion[+], salvation[+], purification[+], divinization[+], the ascent[+] of the six billion inhabitants of earth to the thrones of the Father,

about their liberation[+] from the hypnotic oppression of Rex Mundi

San Salvador Verdadero, the true Saviour, bless us.

186

Glory to the thrones of Our Father!
  grace most admiring
  grace most admiring
  grace most admiring

The glory and exultation of Our Father!
  grace most admiring
  grace most admiring
  grace most admiring

Triumph under the sunny cover
                        of Our Father!
  grace most admiring
  grace most admiring
  grace most admiring

Millions of bright
  brothers-bon hommes exclaim:
  Gloria, gloria al Altísimo –
  for the true Saviour
  from the prince of the world
          of enchantments and troubles!
  The Grail in the heart of the Father pours myrrh.

                    *

On San Salvador is the grace of the Holy Spirit
of the future age.

Here is the grace of the living Divinity, the presence of Our Father, who has not been on earth for
two thousand years, but is today proclaimed by all
humanity as the form of the faith of the future.

A myrrhic stream. The fragrant relics of several
thousand immortals are beneath us.

A civilization, having achieved technical perfection... so spiritually insignificant! What a decline man is in!

I see San Salvador rising to heaven, transforming.

§

10.

the Archetype
of "Kind People"

𝒜ndrew the First-Called propagated the mystical exceeding wisdom of the God-bearer in Holy Rus'. He talked about the great secrets which neither the Jews nor the Greeks knew, and Rus' had the honour to hear them from the mouth of the supreme first apostle of the Most Pure Virgin. Andrew spread the teaching of the God-bearer in Holy Rus', having clothed Holy Scythia in Her sunny, eternally virginal vestments.

- The assembly of 200 white Theogamic elders
- The Most Holy Virgin entrusted the sacred vessel
  with pictures of the Bridal Supper to Andrew the First-Called
- The divinization of the Adamites was the main theme of Her
  conversation with Christ on Nightingale Mountain
- In Holy Rus' the news about the Bridal Chamber
  and the Father-Sun was perceived as their own
- The grandeur of church song was borrowed from
  the Slavic Theogamites through Andrew the First-Called
  having accepted the vibrating singing seals
  of the Most Holy God-bearer Herself
- The Mother of God accompanied
  Andrew the First-Called's evangelical path
- The apostle saw Russia as modeled
  in spirit by the Mother of God
- In Rus' the Most Holy Virgin did that
  which She and Christ had not succeeded to do in Jerusalem
- The heavenly Queen Herself came to Holy Rus'
  with rushnik in Her hands
- The idea of Theomatrimony lies easily on the Russian mentality
- The Theogamites built sunny temples according
  to the designs of Andrew the First-Called
- The worship of the Chalice was characteristic of the archetype
  of Holy Rus' and sprang from its most ancient history
- With all his malicious pack the cunning one came down upon
  the Theogamic glory of the Russian homeland
- The second Rome was mortally afraid
  of the God-bearer's sun of the Theogamites
- The graduallar staffs of San Salvador were given to us
  - The true church began to speak

190

The scrolls of the Mother of God in the universum

n the divine existence castle-caves of San Salvador Verdadero the tablets are preserved under the name *the scrolls of the Mother of God in the universum.*

Her twelve victorious incorpulations[39] before the embodiment of the Son of God and Her twelve future descents in the coming Theocivilization.

The hypostases of these theophanies, the pearls of Theomatrimony, and the sum of the seals are preserved here, on San Salvador Verdadero, in the holy of holies for knights and maidens.

'Come closer, take and inscribe on your brow and in your heart the words said by the anointed ones of San Salvador, in order to give them to the suffering humanity of earth'.

The Mother of God counted an assembly of 200 white Theogamic elders.

191

And here are the burial mounds, where, to this day, are preserved the first utensils of the Slavic Theogamites, having accepted the news from Andrew the First-Called. Icons with the image of Christ, the Mother of God of Nightingale Mountain, and the apostle Andrew; vessels, chalices, copper objects, candlesticks...

*

The indescribable pleroma of the Father was imprinted in the Mother of God. Gazing at Her, Andrew the First-Called said:

'Only now, my sunny beloved Mother, do I see Christ with my own eyes. And in the earthly days I was blind.

Give us Your seals. Permit us to teach about Christ throughout the whole world, as I see Him imprinted in You,

as You are revealing Him to humanity.'

The most important thing in the apostolate of Christ in Jerusalem: 'Do you love me as is befitting?'

The thrice-repeated 'Do you love me' does not concern only Peter, but every disciple.

His look said: 'Are you capable to accept the sun of My love, the exceeding wisdom of My love? Are you capable to adopt it and spread it?'

From the sweetest Lamb emanated the transcendental, perfect, Holy Spirit grace of pure love.

With His transubstantiation into the Chalice the Most Holy Virgin, the personified sun of Christ, the maternal archetype of Holy Rus', became the bearer of this love.

*

*I*N THE EYES OF THE APOSTLE THE MOTHER OF GOD MIRACULOUSLY MODELLED THE ARCHETYPE OF RUSSIA

Before sending Andrew to the Slavic lands, the Mother of God told him much about Holy Rus', describing Its destiny from the beginning.

Of multitudes of people and countries Holy Rus' belongs to the special chosen ones as the land of the Most Holy God-bearer.

Hither the heavenly Queen strove with all Her being, but the Father did not allow her to leave Nightingale Mountain.

The Mother of God promised to come more and more in spirit and to be present in Holy Rus' more than at Nightingale Mountain,

because from the beginning Holy Rus is Her destiny in the kingdom of the Quaternity (Father, Son and Spirit with the Most Holy God-bearer) and the Quinternity (in Theohumanity).

In conversations with the apostle the Mother of God, literally before his eyes, miraculously modelled the archetype of Russia, and clothed the maiden-bride in it.

$\mathcal{T}$HE THEOGAMIC VESSEL WITH DEPICTIONS OF THE MYSTERIOUS SIGNS OF THE BRIDAL SUPPER

Sending him to the Theogamic sermon, the Most Holy Virgin entrusted Andrew with the sacred vessel with depictions of the mysterious symbols of the Bridal Supper, with the words:

'Do not release this Chalice from your hands, and it will enrapture all the suffering sons and daughters of Rus'.

Give them My love and My presence.

I am with them constantly until the end of the age.

I Myself will come to Rus' in this sacred vessel of the blood of Christ, and with Me our adored Christ' (thus She called Him in her loving, most restful and exceedingly wise language).

Together with the Theogamic chalice the Mother of God granted Andrew the First-Called the Spirit of the Holy Divinizer.

The divinization of the Adamites was the fundamental theme of Her conversation with Christ on Nightingale Mountain.

The second coming, Christ the Second, is accompanied by THE SPIRIT OF THE HOLY DIVINIZER (ADORER). The Trinity is revealed as the Quaternity and is completed as the Octernary of the multiplication of Christ in Theohumanity.

Such is the mysterious goal, with which the King-Lamb completed His transubstantiation into the Chalice.

...He departed, imprinted himself in the Theogamic chalice and appeared on Nightingale Mountain as the Bridegroom of the Bridal chamber – to reveal Himself to humanity clearly.

– How is that? Do they really not see clearly?

– You alone see Me with clearly. The rest – through scales...

The scales have been lifted away. They see clearly with sunny eyes!

*

In conversations with the disciples (especially with the apostles John and Andrew) the Most Holy Virgin revealed Their miraculous bridal combination, the perfect dialogue.

The miracle of entering into marriage with Christ was inherited by those who succeeded in visiting Nightingale Mountain.

The Christ of the Bridal chamber, not distant (idolatrous), but true reveals Himself in the form of all-purifying, Cathar love: as the Bridegroom for the chosen ones, having taken the vow of the pure maiden and bride.

*

The lighting of the sunny disk
in the internal mansions of the spiritual heart

The secret of the solar religion, brought to Holy Rus' by Andrew the First-Called, consists in the lighting of the sunny disk in the internal mansions of the spiritual heart.

Inflamed with the lighted candle in the heart, the microscopic sun dispelled the fly droppings of 'insurmountable' original sin (the fundamental speculation with which the enemy of the human race enslaved the Adamites and bound them to himself).

The solarity of Slavic Theogamism consisted in the liberation of the unheard-of potential of love,

from which came the exceeding wisdom of the chalice and the cross, service to one's neighbour, and the union of all the adored sons and daughters of the Bridal Chamber into one.

THE APOSTLE ANDREW THE FIRST-CALLED
IN HOLY RUS'

On the path to Rus' Andrew doubted: would he be able to reveal the extraordinary teaching about the Virgin, the Mother, and the Bride-Lamb, so alien to the Jewish (and also to the Hellenic) mentality? Humanity was unworthy and not ready...

How great was his amazement, when in Holy Rus' the news about the Bridal chamber, about the Father-Sun, about the Theogamic Bridegroom and Bride was perceived as their own.

The apostle Andrew did not have the slightest hardship in preaching about the Bridal Supper of Christ and Mary and to partake from the Theogamic chalice.

The hardship was to reach Holy Rus'.

There they met Andrew the First-Called xenially with bread and salt, as if he had descended from the heaven.

They caught every word as a confirmation of their expectations:

'Our fathers prophesied: the Virgin of Sunny Lights would come and plant Her kingdom'.

*I*n the first years in the Russian land

In the first years of his wanderings through the Russian land Andrew was already amazed by the ease, with which they perceived Christ.

In Jerusalem, where they were able to see Him physically, they neither understood nor loved Him,

but here, in Holy Rus', they immediately recognised him as their own.

They saw the divinity in Him, craved His seals, caught His every word, sought to imitate Him and the Most Holy Virgin – the apostle Andrew did not cease to be amazed, and his joy was without end.

Christ and God's Mother were so alone and misunderstood in Jerusalem. And here, at last, their sunny triumph had come!

But the God-bearer was imprinted in the soul of the Russian man even more closely, even more organically than Christ.

God's Mother was perceived in Rus' before Christ

God's Mother was perceived in Rus' before Christ.

The name *God-bearer* was on the lips of Andrew (the heavenly Queen laid so many seals in his heart).

Andrew questioned John much about Her: about Her prayers, Her dialogues with Christ, about Her perfect unworldliness, Her vision of the Father, Her understanding of Christ...

Andrew carried the treasure of God-maternity, THE GRAIL OF THE MOST HOLY GOD-BEARER, in his heart: Her form of life and thought, which was impossible to transfer by any kind of words.

The first God-bearer liturgy

How God's Mother sang on Nightingale Mountain! She loved to sing, and She put into Her song so much love for Christ that all creation worshipped Him.

Her unearthly angelic voice attracted every living thing. Birds flew from all the ends of the earth (including exotic birds, which had never before been in these lands), sea-fish swam to the shore and listened to Her voice...

There was nothing like it on earth. The voice of the Mother of God sounded in all the worlds.

Here it is, the first liturgy of the God-bearer! Her song, apart from the unearthly beauty of its timbre, transferred the entire spectrum of Her experience of Christ, Her never-ending grief, Her tears, Her serenity, Her joy, Her spirituality.

When the Mother of God had only just begun to sing, tears immediately flowed from Her eyes, and the wild animals, forest beasts and birds began to weep with Her.

*H*er voice

Her voice (O miracle!) was brought to Rus' like a living musical box. Andrew literally imprinted it in himself, and the voice of God's Mother sounded during the apostle's sermon.

Many heeded the voice of the Most Pure One, unexpectedly sounding in their internal hearing.

The grandeur of church song was borrowed from the Slavic Theogamites through Andrew the

First-Called, having accepted the vibrating singing seals of the Most Holy God-bearer Herself.

*

The Mother of God accompanied the evangelical path of Andrew the First-Called.

In Holy Rus' they perceived Her, fervently, as the sunny Chalice personified:

the selfless devotion of seclusion (1), the fervour about perfect holiness (2), unworldliness (3), spiritual peace and repose (4), the wait for the bridegroom (5) and comforting virginity (6), manifested so amazingly that the devil was able to do nothing.

Coming to Holy Rus', the apostle taught in the form of the Most Pure One. He saw Russia as the Mother of God had modelled it in spirit on Nightingale Mountain.

He consulted with Her and professed himself the direct vessel of Her exceeding wisdom.

Deeply repenting that the Jewish cliches had oppressed him, that like the other disciples he had not understood nor seen Christ in His earthly days, Andrew sought to expiate this by his apostolate in Holy Rus'. He taught fierily, sunnily and fearlessly.

Nothing dared to oppose him. The apostolate of Andrew the First-Called was accomplished with the power of Golgotha of Jerusalem and with the grace of Nightingale Mountain.

The confession of Christ as the bridegroom of the Bridal Chamber, the fullness of grace in opened hearts, the Theogamic Chalice, the Holy Passions, the wilderness, the return to the heavens... comprised the treasure of the faith of the God-bearer.

But greater than these was the love for the Most Pure One, Her living presence, Her undepictable image.

In Rus' the Most Holy Virgin did that which She had not succeeded to do with Christ in Jerusalem: She planted an oasis of indescribable divine goodness along the Volga and the Don.

The Theogamic teaching about the sunny, kind man as the bride of Christ, prepared for his beloved, easily entered into the consciousness of the Slavs.

*T*HE BOGOMIL MOTHER OF GOD [40]

Through the apostolate of Andrew the Most Holy Virgin revealed the shape of the sunny man.

In western Catharism it corresponded to Bonomism, a special type of people with the origin of holy goodness, coming from original immaculateness, inserted into them. [41]

In Rus' the good man, not connected with the

'fierce sin'[42] had the analogous name – kind man.

Man became kind with Slavic Cathar kindness.

The words nice- or good- were added to literally every name: 'nice brother, nice mother'. It was considered disrespectful to address one's neighbour without it.

The kind people were taken as the sunny most eternal archetype given to the Russian people by the heavenly Father Himself.

The heavenly Queen taught about divine archetypes as sunny pearls: the flourishing of the nation depends upon the level of their manifestation.

No external conquests, territories, harvests, or material gains can lead a country to bloom, taught the God-bearer.

And on the contrary, the materially destitute but glorious with kind people and kind good masters, kind boyars, kind tsars and tsarinas, people begin to shine in contentment, in piety and in that indescribable happiness, which can solely nourish man.

Today the sunny Mother of God of Solovki from the throne of San Salvador Verdadero summons Russia to return to the archetype of kind, good people.[43]

The apostolate of kind people or the miraculous ranks of the kitezhgrad communities

Before leaving Rus', Andrew the First-Called left

72 disciples and apostles, male and female (women-myrrh bearers, wise maidens), whom he clothed in the vestments of the God-bearer and gave the power of Exceeding Wisdom and the Holy Spirit, so that with the grace of the Divinizer they clothed others in the vestments of the Mother of God, which the devil could not destroy, and directed them to the path of the truth.

The apostolate of 'kind people', planted in Holy Rus', was a special kind of transformed saints of the God-bearer. The Theogamites did not recognise the priestly hierarchy. Andrew the First-Called built THE FIERY HIERARCHY OF THE BRIDAL CHAMBER, beginning with sheep and shepherds and finishing with the stages of the perfect ones:

Theogamites (Theomatrimony), beatitudes (blessings), pilgrims (small chalices), agapites (the anointed sovereigns of pure love),

small suns, lesser God-bearers, Seraphites, lelies (youths, who have extolled the Holy Grail – the Chalice), maidens clothed in white garments, 'kind people', elders, apostles and prophets, scholars and chroniclers... Builders and architects of the Bridal chamber, mother-mentors, mother-holy women in labour, wife-myrrhbearers and custodiers of the hearth...

Such were the miraculous ranks, having composed the fullness of the life of the kitezhgrad communities of Holy Rus, subsequently erased in the most severe manner by Byzantium.

𝒯HE FIRST AGE OF ANOTHER CHURCH

Andrew transformed like Christ at Tabor.

He was literally carried by hands, adored. He was invited from settlement to settlement, questioned about the details of Christ's witness in Jerusalem and who was planting a new Jerusalem in Holy Rus'.

𝓗oly Rus' under the heaven of the God-bearer

The heavenly Queen Herself with rushnik in her hands, wearing the clothes of the people, decorated with pearls and mysterious spiritual symbols came to Holy Rus', and the grace of the Russian homeland was multiplied.

The peoples marvelled, saying: 'A new sun has risen in Scythia'.

Ambassadors were sent from different countries, and were perplexed: how had Rus' flourished so greatly? All squabbles had been settled. The country had achieved miraculous prosperity and peace.

Paradise descended from heaven. God's kingdom was built on earth in the times of Andrew the First-Called.

The gifts of the Holy Spirit were indescribable.

Garments were shaped from the heavens. Mysteries and enlightenments were given from the heavens. There were no bookish instructions: super-illuminating on how to build the sunny temples, how to erect a house, how to raise children...

Andrew was amazed by how easily the idea of Theomatrimony lay on the Russian mentality.

'What an unearthly people! – He did not cease saying. – They do not think about the worldly. They only crave to enter into the life of pure love and to find the true Bridegroom and their beloved'.

The grace of the Theogamic kingdom seized Holy Rus'.

Over some half a century thousands of sunny kitezh-grads were born. The very character of the people changed.

Vials with miracle-working oils and indescribable gifts rained literally from heaven.

*

The assembly of Holy Rus: with her ancient piety and fragrant wise men, prophets and anointed sovereigns

Exceptional piety spread through Holy Scythia. Many perfect, exceedingly wise white elders were given by the Theogamic faith – the whole assembly of Holy Rus' with its ancient piety and fragrant wise men, prophets and anointed sovereigns was respected throughout the whole world.

Fasting, prostration, penitential tears, abundant illuminations and blessings accompanied the disciples of Christ, who rejected the worldly and professed themselves brides of Christ.

The mystery of the Immaculate Conception

With the blessing of the Most Pure Virgin, Andrew directed the converted ones to the secret of the Immaculate Conception. Immaculately conceived grace inspired millions of villagers, lighting their hearts.

And they found no greater grace than to be born from on high and to profess themselves immaculately conceived.

Faith in the Immaculate Conception brought unbelievable fruits: harvest, flowering gardens.

The gifts of the Holy Spirit: musical, curative, dancing. Theological, contemplative, prayerful charismas. The miraculous mysterious fire flared up in hearts!

Such superabundant grace was shed in the times of the sermon of Andrew the First-Called over the Holy Rus'.

Gaining the spirit of Christ.

Those who adored Christ, and were entirely devoted to Him (the brides), gained the spirit of Christ.

Miracles were worked through those, that gained the spirit. With one wave of the hand they could raise a city or resurrect entire settlements from the dead.

*

The Slavic Theogamites worked according the seals of the Mother of God of Nightingale Mountain. They resided in spirit on Nightingale Mountain and were honoured with seals of anointing from the Most Pure Virgin.

In the hours of passionate anguish Andrew ascended the mountains indicated to him, where Our Most Holy God-bearer and Christ appeared to him.

The heart of the apostle shed loving groans, filling with more and more grace, which he immediately poured out onto his disciples, so that the love-filled seals descended onto the followers of Christ and the Mother of God.

With tears Andrew told the Most Pure One how they loved Her and waited for Her in Holy Rus'. They painted clothes with Her images, they asked about the finest details: 'What is Her face? And what kind of voice does She have? And will She come to us? When?'

And the Mother of God appeared with Christ in the Chalice. The Chalice multiplied.

Three masters made another 12 chalices from the best sea (unearthly) compositions.

The first images of the Mother of God

From those very times they began to draw the first images of the Mother of God, Christ of Nightingale Mountain, Andrew the First-Called, and John the Theologian, and to decorate their dwellings with them.

By means of spiritual art they tried to express that, which they could not in words.

The Theogamites built sunny temples according to the drawings of Andrew the First-Called in the first quarter of the period of his sermon.

They created sculptural forms and a multitude of other mysterious objects from diverse materials (afterwards completely destroyed by the Byzantine priests).

The worship of the Chalice turned out to be inherent in the archetype of Holy Rus'. It sprang from its most ancient history.

They perceived the Chalice as the holy throne of Our Father, carrying it into the interior of the heart.

So Rus' became famous for the sun of pure love, entering into its most eternal archetype.

THE QUEEN DESCRIBED THE FUTURE HISTORY OF RUSSIA FOR THREE THOUSAND YEARS

On Nightingale Mountain the heavenly Queen revealed to Andrew the history of Holy Rus', as she had foreseen even then. She described the future history of Russia for three thousand years, and the apostle was stunned.

From 1st to 10th centuries: worship of the sunny Christ and Mary, the Bride and Groom of the Bridal Chamber. Their church, Their blessed people.

10th to 20th centuries: collapse, the black crow.

And from the 21st to the 30th centuries: the kingdom of light, the Bridal Supper of pure love.

God's Mother's parting words to the apostle Andrew

"Let them avoid dogmas, which are an illusion of knowledge, and illusion of faith, and illusion of prayer.

Child, do not lose the fire of love for our Beloved in the holy heart. Seek to clothe more and more in My vestments and profess the beloved Christ one with the Most Holy Virgin God-bearer, from the beginning as His sunny Bride – and Exceeding Wisdom will not leave you nor your disciples.

I will act in you with Christ. Go. And be with Our Father", – with these words the Most Holy Virgin parted with Andrew the First-Called, before the apostle set off for Holy Rus' to preach the Theogamic faith.

The Mother of God wanted to hear nothing about dogmatic definitions. Exceeding Wisdom in the matrimony of the Holy Spirit reveals Christ-as-He-is.

Bookish learning leads to phariseeism and the degradation of faith. The true Christ, who was not seen by the dogmatizing Roman-Byzantine villain, is concealed behind dogmatic blinkers. Behind crucifying schemes and destructive scholastic principles is crucified love, the shining sun of suns.

THE GENOCIDE OF THEOGAMIC RUS' IN THE EIGHTH CENTURY

Holy Rus' was the first earthly kingdom to accept the news of Christ in its entirety.

The most heavy battle came to Slavic Theogamism. The indescribable, unheard-of flourishing of Holy Rus' coincided with the preaching of Andrew the First-Called. And the collapse began with the first Byzantine ambassadors.

Nothing was as opposed and hostile to the sunny God-bearing archetype of Christian Holy Rus' as

Rome-Byzantium. The Byzantine agents had already penetrated the Volga lands from the fifth century. And from the sixth they incited the Russian princes to persecute the Theogamic brides of Christ.

The cunning one, with all his malicious pack, came down on the glory of the Russian homeland, the former direct fruit of Golgotha in Jerusalem and the sixteen-year Holy Passion of the Most Pure Virgin at Nightingale Mountain.

The second Rome was mortally afraid of the Theogamites' sun of the God-bearer. They exterminated them by the thousands: drowned them in rivers, destroyed them anyway they could. They erased any memory of them. For one recollection they punished them with fierce tortures and banished them, separating families and neighbours for ever.

The Roman-Byzantine pollution, rushed over Holy Rus' like a whirlwind, having replaced the Slavic kitezh-grads with its chimeras. The musical round dances and miraculous choirs, indescribable piety and perfect purity were displaced by church Potemkin villages and decorative ritual buildings...[44]

The fierce genocide completely destroyed and erased the Theogamic grace from the face of the earth: not one seal, not one speck of dust, not one book, not one memory...

And nevertheless there filtered through and remained, in dozens of scrolls (in the unbreakable

211

Russian archetype), fallen immortal particles, awaiting the hour of their manifestation and triumphant flourishing.

Opposition to the pro-Byzantine order

The Roman-Byzantine malice did not take root in places, belonging immemorially to the church of Andrew the First-Called.

But the God-bearer promised that She would place Her indestructible throne here!

However hard the gendarme's klobuk and repressive state machine worked, the Roman-Byzantine agents were not able to conquer hearts.

They built monasteries – brigands destroyed them, or the monks suddenly disappeared from the face of the earth... And the people remained true to the Theogamic legend. And in simple forms (metaphorical, as direct confession was forbidden by the state religion of Byzantium) they professed the peaceful seals of Andrew the First-Called.

As far as they were able the Theogamites showed opposition to the pro-Byzantine order. They supported the people's revolts of Stepan Razin, Yemelyan Rukavishnikov (Pugachev), and others which arose as a people's protest against the violent faith, alien to the Russian consciousness and archetype.

Today the Most Holy Virgin is entrusting to us Her vessel and sending us to Holy Rus' to preach, in order to correct its archetype and to return to its the name of the good young woman, of the good daughter of Christ, the myrrh-bearing wife, the bride of Our Divinity.

The true church has begun to speak.

The laurel has flourished, and the faith of the immortals of San Salvador, according to the seals of the Theogamic elders of Holy Rus', is conquering the world and the humanity of the Third Millennium.

◄§

11.

the Earth –
the greatest celestial body of crucified love

- Souls find heaven suddenly, and their rapture is indescribable

- The Earth is the greatest bridgehead for the divinization of bright spirits

- The deep castles, which can be revealed only in the Holy Passion

𝒯he heavenly mountain

an Salvador Verdadero does not fall silent. The word of Our Divinity does not end.

Here it is as if life stood still. From the heavenly well (in Catalan 'santa cisterna'), where 2000 litres of water were preserved – the earthly heaven. Human processes stopped, the mind became disconnected, the heart turned inside out... And suddenly the mysterious entrances into the heavens were revealed – in the internal castles of one's neighbour, of man-as-he-is.

*

San Salvador instantaneously cancels and erases the past. Even in the approach to the mountain *the mother-guides* warn:

With an excess of suspicious whirlwinds it is possible to fall from the mountain. The cunning one twists you.

216

The ascenders agree to become completely not of this world, for which it is necessary to endure a particular three-fold, ten-fold, hundred-fold (there is no number multiplicity, multiplying according to the measure of the ascent to the celestial castles) cross.

The attraction of the airy heavenly spheres of divine existence on San Salvador is so great that is impossible to reject it.

As if outside of her own free will, the soul, in the rays of superior love of the Mother of God, whispers:

'Yes, yes, yes...'

Among the immortals

The mountain is never-ending, boundless. No one of the criteria of the third or fourth dimension The high mountain signifies the heavenly world, miraculously residing on earth.

Aside from the fifty (5 father-immortals and 45 immortals), permanently inhabiting the spheres of divine existence and not leaving the nearby physical space of the heavenly mountain (muntanya del cel), here are present 100 anointed ones of the highest stage and 150 perfect mothers (their rank according to initiation: madre de la Sabiduría,[45] spouse of the Divinity, Sofia).

$\mathscr{T}$HE CATHAR MOTHERS OF EXCEEDING WISDOM

150 Marys, Charlottes, Paulinas, Sofias and others (some of whom had up to 15 mysterious names) stand before my gaze...

Sweetest Father, how beautiful they are! I have never seen anything similar, except perhaps my two mother-mentors for my first conversion, on whose brows the seals of Exceeding Wisdom shone: Mary from the town of Oryol and and the beloved myrrh-pouring Euphrosinia.

The incomprehensible manifestation of the Divinity. Undoubtedly, they are not angels, because they walk in human bodies. But they are also not people, because there is nothing sinful, passionate, flawed, or indecent in them. The paradoxical mysterious ranks of Theohumanity.

The first things to hit the eyes are the seals of exceeding wisdom, shining on the brows of each of the perfect mothers. And the continual (and having entered into general use) repetition-worship of the names of the heavenly Mother with rosary beads: Sofia, Sabiduria... and at least fifteen more. Each says something special to their divine consciousness. It is enough to call one name in order that its active hypostases descend and penetrate the being of the perfect one...

It is impossible to tear the eyes away from the purest mothers of Exceeding Wisdom! The kindest winning smiles are on their hospitable faces. The heart immediately melts and submits to them. Their unobtrusive mildness and absolute meekness hits the eyes. They are full of the highest exceeding wisdom, which is written in every magnificent, heavenly and exceedingly restful movement of their faces or hands.

Beings from another, higher world. Their residence on earth in the same cave as us is, it seems, as much a mystery for them as our communion with them.

The mothers shine with unearthly joy. Their every gaze, penetrating the depths of the internal castles, transfers a certain secret, from which man is siezed by divine joy and is given the powers to overcome earthly obstacles, griefs, and crosses.

The initiated Mothers of God are another, higher stage than the elder-mentors, and others known to us. On each of them the myrrh-pouring Euphrosinia and fiery-winged Sofia shines.

*

The mothers move as if swimming. Their movements have been slowed, and the desire to serve, for which they appeared in the ancient cave, is visibly readable in their appearance.

THE WIFE-MYRRHBEARERS:

'We would like to show what our wife-myrrhbearing service was like in the earthly days, in the tenth century A.D. according to the accepted human calculation.

The mothers left the earthly (families, attachments, neighbours, relatives) and united with the community of the sisterhood of Exceeding Wisdom.

Worship of the Theomaternity of Exceeding Wisdom was the highest thing among us.

Exceeding Wisdom did not descend from our lips. 150 perfect Mothers of God, 150 anointed immortals were in the eternal marriage.

We did not know sleep in the human sense. Eyes did not close. A period of 'disconnection' signified the transition into another sphere and the accomplishment of other, otherworldly programmes...

The Cathar cross with its dispersing slats conferred the gift of bilocation: the simultaneous residence in several places with partial, fragmented consciousness in each of them.

We became familiar with the dimension of bilocation as something customary for spiritual work, which Exceeding Wisdom foreordained for Her daughters.'

Exceeding Wisdom:
the Mother of God's hypostasis of the Father

The sacred mothers talked about Exceeding Wisdom as a personified divine rank.

They did not agree to call Her 'The God-bearer Virgin Mary'. To their Cathar vision, Exceeding Wisdom was the Mother of God's hypostasis of the Father, concealed from foreign gazes and revealing itself in a mysterious way.

The initiated mothers named the 15 names of Exceeding Wisdom revealed to them (in Spanish, Latin, and other ancient dialects).

Exceeding Wisdom dwelt in the 150 chosen ones. She granted to each of them one of Her never-ending hypostases, one of her mysterious names.

The three great secrets: Divinity, heaven, and earth

The sign of special initiation, shining on the brow, signified the three great secret-paradoxes: Divinity, heaven, and earth. All in all these three revealed the mystery of the Godman.

The secret-paradox of the Father (1) lay in his concealed nature and exclusive internal manifestation. Our Father is not on earth and He is solely present.

His manifestation in the immortals is absolute. There is not one most wretched and badly expressed soul, having glanced in the deep mines of whom, we would not have discovered a sourced of the Highest God.

The secret of the heavens (2): the majority of earthly wanderers return to the eternal home.

Souls find heaven suddenly, and their joy is indescribable.

Meanwhile, the path from earth to the heavens is closed by the clouds of the cunning one, and great efforts are required in order to dispel them and walk before the revealed sky with the sun of suns of Our Divinity shining in it.

The secret of the earth (man) (3) is no less paradoxical. A diabolical backwater and witch's whirlpool, earth is at the same time the greatest bridgehead for the divinization of bright spirits.

There are deep castles in the potential of man which can be revealed only in the Holy Passion, in human darkness: amongst temptation, amongst the forbidden entrances and exits of the earthly 'concentration zones'.

Returning from earth to the Father's house, man ascends to the castles of love, inaccessible to him before.

Earth is the greatest celestial body of crucified love, revealed in the experience of Jesus Christ, the most perfect son of God among His other perfect and immortal sons and daughters.

> The mothers do not tire, opening their lips, to glorify Exceeding Wisdom. They know Her by sight. She is their conversation partner. She has formed them.
>
> Each of them is Her reflection. Looking at them,

we see the manifestation of the Exceeding Wisdom
of the Divinity entirely and as a whole.

*

The hierarchies or ranks of perfect love and exceeding wisdom

Among the beautiful Cathar mothers there existed no earthly ranks of the type 'hegumen' or 'abba-
tis'. They addressed one another thus: 'sister of Exceeding Wisdom', 'my beloved lady'...

They spoke of Exceeding Wisdom as if they had
seen Her and known Her clearly, and possessed the
secret, which can only be revealed in a mysterious
way through special initiation.

Exceeding Wisdom gave them ranks of heavenly organization. In contrast to the institutional subordinate hierarchies, the Cathar perfect
ones represented *hierarchies,* or ranks of perfect
love and exceeding wisdom.

Between the hierarchy (earthly, institutional)
and the heavenly *hierarchy* there was nothing in
common.

The hierarchy presupposes the charismas, accompanying institutional authority. *Hierarchy* is the
Eucharist of the heavenly church, the forming from
on high, the sign of a superior stage, not in the human order, but in the divine.

Exceeding Wisdom Herself numbered among the

five-stage hierarchical ranks of the Divinity, the hierarchies of the Altísimo.

*

At the third and fourth stages of the bilocation of San Salvador

At the third and fourth stages of the bilocation of San Salvador the mothers were able to pass from one body to another, to suddenly disappear and appear...

Their service occurred night and day. By night, when the cripples, the aged, and the dying, assembling in a great multitude at San Salvador from all the ends of the earth slept, the holy mothers of exceeding wisdom entered the bilocational Holy Passion prayer for those, whose wounds they washed by day, consoling them as they were able with words of heavenly love.

Their sacrifice consisted in the complete absence of sleep and the bearing of the exorbitant cross, having become in essence the norm for these greatest crusaders.

They ate not more often than once a day: flat bread, figs, holy water, sometimes vegetables or soup... By what power were they driven? Solely by the power of heavenly superior love.

In the continuous illumination-vision of exceeding wisdom and love of the Father and Mother − loving more than is possible, a million times more than a man can contain, they endeavoured to give that which had been laid in their hearts to the poor children, defeated by earthly sins and illness.

Many of those miraculously cured by them now and then immediately applied for the ranks of continual inhabitants of San Salvador. And the mothers consented.

$\mathscr{S}$ACRED-ORDINEE ONES OF OUR DIVINITY

The mothers possessed the rank of the priestess: 'sacred ordinee of Our Divinity'. They were able to accomplish the mystery of divinization.

They look upon the stage of eucharistic partaking from the transubstantiated chalice as childish. They smile:

– The Eucharist is beautiful, but it is only the beginning of our path.

*

$\mathscr{M}$an in the rays of the God's Exceeding Wisdom

The Exceeding Wisdom of Our Father has been abandoned by humanity (the holy mothers say, sorrowfully throwing out their hands), because of which there are so many misfortunes.

Blessed and happy is man in the rays of God's Exceeding Wisdom.

Exceeding Wisdom penetrates and nourishes his whole being, and the need for earthly food falls away. She dwells beside him, and the need for an earthly neighbour falls away. She fills him to the brim, and lust, anguish and solitude depart forever. She makes him brave and great, from miserly and insignificant, and inserts into his heart a regal pearl framed with precious stones.

𝒯he three great secrets for new-beginners

Three great secrets are revealed to new-beginners:

1) *the secret of the Divinity*: the non-participation of the sweetest Father in evil, death, and sin;

2) *the secret of the devil*: the cunning serpent pretends to be the Divinity;

3) *the secret of man*: on earth he is able to pass the stages from a nobody, having lost human appearance, to the highest of divinities; from demon of the most base black hierarchies to a heavenly angel from the retinue of Our Father.

*

THE MOTHERS OF EXCEEDING WISDOM:

Exceeding Wisdom does not permit us to talk for too long.

Stand still and pass into silent prayer.

Take a rest from earthly hardships.

Unhappy are those who search for knowledge of God's secrets outside of the initiation of Exceeding Wisdom.

Exceeding Wisdom sends souls into this world, and the meaning of the embodiment on earth is revealed to Her alone.

Without worship of Exceeding Wisdom and entrance into Her mysterious bosom, not one person will find the final meanings, which means that he will not be completely at peace.

Seek again and again to worship Exceeding Wisdom. This worship will exceed the Catholic limits of Louis Grignon de Montfort or the reverance of Sofia in ancient Holy Rus'.

The Mother of God of Nightingale Mountain will reveal Herself in another 50 new transformed hypostases as the Queen of the Cathar heavenly mountain.

The three vessels with oils

The seal of Exceeding Wisdom on the brow of Her chosen one

– the mothers repeat. The oldest among them, the Mother of God of the heavenly mountain, the crowned Godbride, gives us three vessels with oils, giving us Her blessing to open them and anoint ourselves with them.

We preserve many secrets for the coming Theo-humanity.

Not one holy soul is able to enter the world without Our blessing.

We give each of them as much as he is able to contain.

Fear nothing. The power of Our Father is greater than ever before.

His armies will inflict a crippling defeat on the enemy, where nobody expects it, where not even his soldiers themselves foresee it, not mentioning those for whom the battle is fought.

The peace of Our Divinity.

*

The tender mothers smile, extend themselves and shed incomparable light. They transform before our eyes, and never-ending gifts and seals descend. They reveal themselves one in another: another 5, 10... 100 in one! As if there are 150... and now 150x150. With what ease they multiply, and now suddenly disappear!

᷼

12.

the Cathar Mothers
in the communion
of the ever-present Christ

- The Eucharist of the Grail in the castle
  of the heavenly Father
- Christ was not absent for a minute
- No one understood His love in the earthly days
- The Saviour conferred on us the communion in which
  He was joined by the Most Holy God-bearer in the earthly days
- The records of His divine revelations

- The Chalice of Our Father remained on earth
- The biblical corruption caused so much evil
- The illumination of the sunny Chalice

❧

 single definition befits heaven: the sphere, alien to the original sin.

**The heaven of original immaculateness
is revealed at a height of 400 metres**

Cathar theology denies original sin in the biblical interpretation (the temptation of Adam and Eve), but understands it as the fateful susceptibility of man to diabolical corruption in the swarming anthill, that earth seems to be from the heights of the Cathar castles.

'The anthill effect' disappears at a height of 400 to 500 metres, and the heaven of Original Immaculateness is revealed, *the aethers* of the Cathar castles.

The essence of the God-bearer, as an unblemished composition, is not so much personified here (in the Lourdes form of the Mother of God or something from the saints), as filled with aethers.

231

The bosom of God's Mother, the Mother giving birth from on high without sin, is here, on earth, at mysterious San Salvador.

*

The aromas of the relics of holy Euphrosinia. The reliquary storeroom of Anzer...

The ever-present Saviour, as He imprinted Himself at the mountain of the Second Conversion

THE CATHAR MOTHERS:

Christ! What would we do without Him?

The Christ of the sunny Parousia, the ever-present Christ-bridegroom never abandoned His brides, remaining in the castles of the interior even in the hours of tormentuous parting.

In the language of the Cathar mothers, 'San Salvador Verdadero' means the ever-present Christ. Thus He imprinted Himself at the mountain of the Second Conversion.

His ever-present presence is a consequence of the Beloved's covenant with His loved ones, the multiplying marriage.

Christ became like the God-bearer in male disciples. The Mother of God became like Christ in female disciples.

OUR CHRIST became more beautiful from meeting to meeting.

Our Saviour continually transformed before the eyes of His beloved ones, and the pause of absence was filled with preparation for the apprehension of an even more perfect beauty.

Christ in the framework of the thousand-year inquisition

A distant judge, presenting scores for forgotten sins, indifferently contemplating the martyr's executions of his followers, while adding: 'for their benefit, *for the good*, for eternal life...' Such is the Christ in the framework of the thousand-year inquisition.

Christ of the Cathar mothers

OUR CHRIST did more than just appeared: He remained ever-present. OUR CHRIST did more than just guided: He descended into the interior, imprinted His face, laid His beginnings, generously granted His composition. He inserted the divine forms, inserted His words.

Such is the Eucharist of the Grail in the castle of Our Father and His divine Son: Christ of lesser christs and mothers of God, Our Christ of the sunny Bridegroom.

Ever-present

Not one of us were able to imagine Him as absent: the catastrophe would not pass the brides.

Do not tolerate it; abandon forever the thought of His absence even if only for a second! The bride immediately dies, abandoned by her Beloved.

Christ was not absent for even a minute for the church of John. He entrusted John to the God-bearer and the God-bearer to the holy John, and He remained with them.

His behaviour, His witness, His words were directly contrary to that, taught by the Roman adversary.

His faithfulness multiplied hour upon hour, from conversation to conversation. We remained faithful, seeing the faithfulness of our Beloved.

His declerations of love

His declarations of love were the pinnacle of our dialogues.

Christ Verdadero complained that no one understood His love in the earthly days, even the disciples close to Him, and our hearts melted with tears.

We prostrated ourselves before Him, repeating only one thing: 'What can we do, our Beloved, to ease Your sufferings?'

The Saviour conferred on us the communion in which He was joined by the Most Holy God-bearer in the earthly days.

He revealed the secrets of His Golgotha (unable to be revealed in any way other than in secret dialogue), and set down His seals for us.

The most fragrant peace overflowed in the hours of waiting for Christ.

Delight in the peace, which was not on earth, ascenders to San Salvador Verdadero.

The peace, gained through our suffering. The peace of our day and night Holy Passion. The peace, granted after being taking down from the cross.

At the beginning the Saviour came to us, and we experienced a messianistic, divine peace, not comparable to anything, without daring to ask about its origin.

But later, revealing the Holy Passion in the universum to us, Christ told us that the most restful divine existence peace experienced by us was a consequence of His removal from the Cross.

Our dear Christ arrives with the removal from the Cross and gives us, His beloved ones, the divine consequences of His sufferings.

Master, my child, the peace after the Holy Passion: it is not only for the lesser christ, His disciple, but also for those for the sake of whom the chosen one of Our Father voluntarily suffers.

*

The Saviour ordered us to keep records of His divine revelations.

After their completion He came to us and literally dictated, to the point of perfection, every word, worrying about the adequacy of His expression.

The myrrhic church

The Saviour transubstantiated no less than a thousand times even in the earthly days.

And then on Golgotha he transubstantiated, passed into the Holy Chalice, forming His mysterious second-existence, divine existence, eternal-existence.

The Chalice of Our Father remained on Earth, and Christ resides within it.

Each of His disciples becomes a flawless mirror of the Holy Grail, a small chalice.

Gathered together, shedding the last drop of secret love, the disciples form the fountaining myrrhic church.

THE SONG OF EXCEEDING WISDOM

In our mysterious castles San Salvador is called the home of All-covering Exceeding Wisdom.

Exceeding Wisdom clothes in silk vestments and transparent garments. Exceeding Wisdom inserts the origin of immaculateness, declaring it to be original, rather than sin.

Exceeding Wisdom alone knows how to defeat

the ancient serpent-tempter on earth, to get rid of his nets.

Our enemy is cunning, but Exceeding Wisdom knows from time immemorial how to defeat him and possesses the keys, which She generously shares with Her worshippers.

Exceeding Wisdom adores dissolving in Her beloved ones. She possesses the gift of perfect transubstantiation into disciples, knowing that only one clothed in Her undefiled vestments is able to become a true bride of the heavenly Beloved.

Exceeding Wisdom generously grants Her seals. Exceeding Wisdom is a virginal Mother. Exceeding Wisdom loves those who thirst to be filled by Her.

Exceeding Wisdom loves defenseless orphans, giving them Her regal maternal cover.

Exceeding Wisdom loves those who are hungry, filling them beyond measure.

Exceeding Wisdom prefers the wounded and hurt to the sated and content, because they need Her help to a greater degree. Many stung mortally by the devil were healed by Her.

Exceeding Wisdom sends souls into the world and explains for which goals they are being delayed on earth. She reveals the bliss of the return to the Father's house and strengthens them through the endurance of severe trials and the blessed Holy Passion.

On the brow of Christ shone the crown of the king of Exceeding Wisdom.

On the brow of Exceeding Wisdom shines the wreath of the triumph of Christ.

Never-ending blessing was shown to our Mother, the sunny Sabiduria. All the essence of the pure one was devoted to Her, and the Most Pure One clothed us in Her garments.

Christ revealed Himself to us in Exceeding Wisdom. The God-bearer – in Exceeding Wisdom. Both Josephs (the Carpenter and the Aramathean), Andrew First-Called and the apostles of the Chalice (12x12=144 sunny anointed ones) are Her vessels.

Christ = Exceeding Wisdom.
Exceeding Wisdom = Christ

Now and then Christ transubstantiated into Exceeding Wisdom, and Exceeding Wisdom transformed into Christ.

Christ = Exceeding Wisdom, Exceeding Wisdom is Christ.

Outside of Exceeding Wisdom the form of the Saviour turns into the dogmaitc Roman mummy, a wadded doll stuffed with the encyclicals of the popes and laws for the inquisitors.

The time has come to reveal another Christ to the world, Christ, whom we knew clearly and

238

loved – to reveal a worthy love, never-endingly great.

We called Him the true King (El Rey Verdadero), because He served for us as a perfect model and dissolved us in the most heavenly spheres.

*

O most fragrant blessings of San Salvador!

Although the caskets are already full and the vessels are overflowing with myrrhic oils, from the horn of plenty pours never-ending precious myrrh, it is heard His sweetest, most tender:

More and more!

We are at the font. Fragrance. The castle of the sweetest repose from passions.

The true Saviour (Cristo Verdadero) – for those, who have yet not become strengthened in spirit. For us – Dulcísimo, the Sweetest one.

*

Our child, San Salvador is not separated from earth by a distance of 700 metres but by a never-ending abyss. On San Salvador there is no sin. The authority of the prince of this world ends at the approach to our mountain.

Take delight in the most restful peace. The mind is scattered, the earthly interests are dispersed in the spheres of the Holy Passion... The silence of eternity is a judgement over the eternal 'how?', 'why?', 'what for?', 'forgive me, I have given in to temptation...'

In the fragrance of Christ's peace

There is only one kind of hardship. The souls endure them for their inability to reside in silent divine existence, in the fragrance of the peace of Christ.

His peace is given by the constant feat of transubstantiation, the peace about which they taught in the earthly day: 'Not *your* peace (ritual and free) I give to you, but that obtained at great cost: My peace'.

The vow of silence

The most spiritual of the pilgrims took a vow of silence: in the beginning for one day, then three, then a month, a year and, at last, from the immortals: constant.

Silence did not signifiy prostration and dullness, sleep or separation. Silence revealed the super-potential possibilities of the communion of man-as-he-is.

Innumerable charismas of perfect communion at the level of the finest vibrations were given to the silent ones of San Salvador, transmittings of the Lamb's sacrificial love.

Our father and mothers did not tire of being amazed by the dialogue being revealed to the disciples of Christ amidst the human silence!

Peace.

The first hours on San Salvador were the hardest. Whirlwinds of thoughts, desparate passions... Deep anguish, desires... The vengeance of the cunning one. The enemy does not want to release the soul from his tenacious claws.

Many could not endure even the first trials and asked to return to the valley. We parted them with love, awaiting the hour of their return after the execution of measure.

But those, who endured the three-day trial henceforth immersed themselves in the oases of blessed silence with ease.

No devillish power could return them to the language of thoughts and judgements any longer. Divine existence otherworldliness possessed them.

Christ's descent to the perfect ones was accompanied by the burning flame of divine love.

Christ-never-absent created Pentecost interior,

and in the spiritual lungs of the disciples who loved Him, He lighted thousands of fiery tongues and ever-burning candles.

Peace.

Our child, the biblical corruption caused so much evil!

Desiring to get rid of sin in words in the final

reckoning it looped man in his unhappy wounds and made him completely subject to the prince of this world, having moulded the sinful essence.

Here, on San Salvador, that which Christ called freedom (having come to know the truth is free), was revealed.

The truth revealed by Christ lay beyond the limits of the sinful craters and impasses. Man-as-he-is revealed himself to His disciples, in the modelling of original immaculateness, in unblemished authenticity, in the imprinting of the Father, in the never-ending transforming divine potentials.

In the deep caves of the Mother of God, who gives birth, new man was conceived, called pure in our annals in distinction from the corrupted by devil malice, having subjected him to unlawful remodelling, forbidden by Our Father.

The unhappy bloody shadows of the human anthill are in the distant past. Delight in the reformation of the Original Immaculateness!

*

𝒯HE GREAT CHALICE

THE SUPREME ANGEL-CUSTODIANS OF SAN SALVADOR, THE CUSTODIANS OF THE CHALICE:

THE CHALICE, our child, of imperishable compositions. It is useless to search for it as a primary composition from other civilizations or from the heavens.

Christ's perfect chalice is the mother-of-pearl bone in man, sealed in the world and manifesting itself according to its whitening.

*

The secret of the ever-burning candle

No one on earth had temptations more severe than on San Salvador.

One day we will reveal to you what our brothers and sisters experienced.

But there was not even the grace from time immemorial of greater and greater degree of the manifestation of the life-giving Christ.

After a month of endured trials – O, the most heavy fighting with the prince of this world fell precisely in this period! – in the spiritual heart began to burn an ever-burning candle, and the lungs turned into a divine altar.

Exceeding Wisdom surrounded, shielded, and covered Her disciple, and San Salvador for a short while turned into Infant God's manager in Bethlehem for him.

The lighting of the ever-burning candle

One must pass so many stages (from the first to the fifteenth, and then another 3x15 and another x3...), in order for the little wick candle to become ever-burning!

The cunning one does not tire of attacking (the battle becomes unbearable), until he recognises that he will never again manage to blow out or even reduce the flame of the lighted candle.

*

The Seraphites are called up to unite with the face of the immortals through the lighting of the ever-burning candle.

Child, your almost daily wilderness with the apocalyptic wailing and candles not burning in it, is a stage of initiation into the immortals.

In his own time Our Father will strike a flint and the candle never-ending, ever-burning will be lit.

But first the siccation of the compositions and preparation of vessels, the annointing and the censing with most fragrant oils in the interior.

The immortals (their *secret one*[46]) entered the sun, mastered the sunny bodies. The ever-burning candle in their hearts symbolised the initiation into the immortals.

In its own time it flared up into a sunny disk: small to begin with, and then great, and mortal man found immortality.

The small sunny disk, finding room in the space

244

of the spiritual lungs, turned into a great celestial body, illuminating thousands of worlds.

THE ALLELUJAH OF SAN SALVADOR:

A - le - lu - ya, a - le - lu - ya, a - le - lu - ya, a - le - lu - ya, a - le - lu - ya, a - le - lu-ya, a-le-lu-ya, a-le-lu - ya, a - le-lu - ya, a - le - lu - ya.

*

The schooling of Christ
about the divinization of man

On San Salvador Verdadero the direct schooling of Christ about the divinization of man, revealed for the first time to the Adamite civilization, occured.

Here Christ performed genuine miracles: almost instantaneously freed man from worldly webs and fears and returned to him his primal modelling,[47] after which the divine composition with the grave of the Holy Spirit multiplied in him.

The divine composition in man

The Holy Passion is for the multiplication of the divine composition. Sufferings, illnesses, death, wilderness, and temptation – so that the divine composition multiplies.

245

Christ has been crucified on Golgotha, so that the divine composition in the Adamites multiplies.

The cunning one would like to seal it for ever. He needs man who has nothing in his composition other than original corruption and the potential for becoming like brute.

Our Father Himself thinks:

– Besides of the divinity, inserted in the first formation, I *will multiply* the number of My particles in the Holy Passion disciples of Exceeding Wisdom, –

...and allow them to pass in the beginning a small and then an intermediate (middle) Holy Passion.

And after the great Holy Passion He divinizes, raising to Tabor, honouring with sunny transformation.

Such is the seal of Exceeding Wisdom of San Salvador. We thirst to spread it to all the worlds and make it the property of all humanity.

*

San Salvador is henceforth declared the mountain of the Divinity, shining onto all worlds, the capital of Theohumanity.

The illumination of the sunny Chalice is beginning.

All my being is filling with sunny light, reflecting the sun of Christ with the heart-grail.

13.

the Sunny Religion
revealed for the first time in Teohumanity

- Every word of our Christ was recorded on divine tablets

- The story of Christ after He shed His blood
  into the Chalice cannot be revealed to humanity

- The blood of Christ was poured, to the last drop,
  into the Chalice from the mother-of-pearl bone of the Divinity

- The Father kept the most eternal Gospel until recently
  and made it the property of the 85th civilization

THE IMMORTALS OF SAN SALVADOR:

The sunny religion, revealed for the first time in Theohumanity. The sunny ark of Theocivilization 85. With imperishable gold is inscribed:

THEOCIVILIZATION III –
THE THEOHUMANITY OF PURE LOVE –
THEOMATRIMONY –
in iridescent lights APPROACH!

*

The mystery of the second conversion of Christ is misunderstood by the world

The mystery of the second conversion of Christ is misunderstood by the world. It is borne today by the Holy Grail – the triumphing, eternal, sunny church.

Look: 200 million sunny bon hommes, 200 million perfect ones, 200 million small thrones descend into the world.

*

The false gospels present distorted Christ. Christ came from the Father of pure love, from the sun of spotless lights.

Profess Christ as the sunny lamb and the peoples will be saved,

and the promised 5 million will enter the ark for the Theocivilization of Exceeding Wisdom.

The millenium-III, Theocivilization-III, and the Ark-85 has been entrusted to Her.

*

The descent of the new humanity into the world

The new humanity descends into the world! Work for it. The aromas shed in the internal castles transubstantiate the compositions of the Adamites into those of the Seraphites.

After another two or three generations the 84th civilization will pass away imperceptibly and definitively.

Easy sleep and peaceful transition

An immersion in easy sleep and a peaceful transition await.

The Father of pure love sees the traumas recently inflicted upon humanity, and desires to display the miracle of His saving mercy.

There will be no disasters, atomic warheads or 'Third World Wars'. A merciful, quiet transition.

249

But after the sleep there will be a torturous awakening for some, and sunny joy for others.

The souls with the golden mark. 'lamb of the 85 civilization': the Seraphites

Souls with the golden mark 'lamb of the 85 civilization',[48] the Seraphites, are approaching the world.

We declare the slandered image of Christ of the canonical gospels to be the greatest deception in two thousand years – the messiah originating from the Judaic idol.

Detach Elohim from the Father of pure love, for ever. There is nothing in common between them.

FATHER OUR SUN, the spotless joy of millions, revealing Himself for the first time.

The Father adores – the Mother divinizes.

The Father reveals the Son for millions of true sons.

The Father reveals the Daughter like the Son for the sake of the multiplication of millions of virginally pure daughters.

The phantom of the Evil-Punishing One, taken up by authoritarian Byzantium, spreading under the guise of Orthodoxy, has been laid on the sunny Lamb.

*

'What is this? A new religion?' You ask. And the sunny Seraphites answer you:

The church of 200 million multiplied christs,
200 million rejoicing bon hommes,
200 million clothed in pure vestments –
Christ is permanently close to them.

*

Erase the Roman chimeras: the chimerical Christ, the chimerical church, chimerical liturgies, destinies, credents...[49]

The Sun of pure love is revealing itself for the first time, the sun of celestial light, the sunny hierarchy of those who have descended from heaven!

The world order is changing. The times recorded in the Apocalypse – the thousand-year kingdom of Christ with the saints – are being fulfilled.

The Great Sign

Soon a great sign, like that foretold in Garabandal,[50] will be given: the great sign of the sun.[51] On the horizon joining heaven and earth, millions will see the Theocivilization, the fiery chariots, the Fiery Hierarchy, the Christ of the Bridal Supper and His white lambs.

The triumph of the Great Church of Love, the triumph of Christ with the saints.

The proclamation of the Theocivilization, the multiplication of suns. The departure, from one great celestial body, of a never-ending multitude of medium, small, and miniature celestial bodies.

The sunny troubadours, the celebratory parade of two hundred million pure and perfect ones of the 84th civilization, proclaiming the glory of the Divinity of pure love and celestial light on golden trumpets.

The sunny bridge (the sunny sign)

Millions contemplating the sign will suddenly see the sunny bridge extended.

Many of the most decisive will pass across it, ascend into the heavens and remain in the shining ark.

The golden bridge will be extended three times, and the number of those desiring to ascend by it will multiply.

The sunny sign *of the second Garabandal,* proclaimed in the land of holy Spain, will convert many.

*

Christ-III – the king of the new universe, the divinity of divinities among the divinized ones (in the Theocivilization)

Profess yourselves to be Seraphites of the new humanity, rejecting the values of the departing civilized barbarity.

The people of the future age will ascend into the ark, professing Christ-as-He-is in the sunny images of the Theocivilization, the fiery professors of Christ-III.[52]

*

Do not await judgement, but rather the celebration of Christ.

Those who await judgement (for the most part over others), will themselves be judged for an unhappy and wrong destiny about which they do not even suspect.

The history of humanity, heaven and earth has been distorted so much that it is impossible to talk about it without 12 question marks.

The judgement over the world lies in the fact that the ark of salvation has been revealed and all who desire are summoned to enter it.

*

New compositions, a new man! Transubstantiate fierily. Hunger for the renewal of the being. Crave transubstantiation.

Do not stop with what has been already achieved. Conquer stasis with ecstasy. Conquer arrogance with a mighty break. Conquer natural dullness and fears, multiplied into fatal ancestral programmes, with the staff of the Holy Spirit in the true church.

𝒯HE CREDO OF THE THEOCIVILIZATION-III

The 85th civilization is being proclaimed for the Godmen. Do not seek universal forums with millions of people applauding the charismatic, moving as if dancing to the microphone.

The 85th civilization is for great and small christs.

Clothe yourself in the vestments of Christ. Come to hate and overcome the distance: the chimera of the old churches, as if there is an impassable abyss between God and man.

The Divinity becomes man, man transubstantiates into the Father of pure love – this is the credo of the Theocivilization-III, the beginning, laid for those enlightened by the spirit.

From the 84th civilization 200 million have been chosen, who have been clothed in sunny vestments and form its elite and ark.

*

Blessed is the sunny Christ of the Theocivilization.

Submit to him, peoples! Rise up under the aegis of the sunny Christ-III in the transubstantiation of the Divinity of divinities.

> Divinity of divinities,
> perfection of perfections,
> the personification of the most divine Father.
> Our Divinity's plan has succeeded!

Do not despair when you meet an impervious boycott from the side of the civilized, enlightened Europeans. The Seraphites' seals act as selectively and imperceptibly for the human mentality as the seals of Christ's true spirit over the past two thousand years. Their action can only be described as that of the holy fool.

O, if only the fervent adepts of Christ, ready to die for Him, would see what distortion the authentic Lamb has been subjected to by the church, and how millions, having returned to the kingdom, see him!

ASCEND to the peak of San Salvador!

*

Our child, when the devotee talks about Christianity, aggressive chimeras hover around him. 999 out of 1000 current believers are surrounded by them.

Exceeding Wisdom offers a strategic approach, worthy of Her splendid perfection: the staff of erasure.

Erase the chimeras. Without the courageous erasure of yesterday, which has been revealed as the chimeric past, not a single person will enter the ark.

Do not work once or twice with the staff, but at least a thousand times.

Then give it to your brother and teach him how to erase yesterday's sacred object, which has today turned into a chimera.

For *the relaxed ones* a white pigeon will turn out to be a flying serpent.

*

Peace be with Theohumanity! Majestic is man in the sunny vestments. Beautiful is the sunny Father of pure love.

Millions of cherubs are above one Godman. The sunny Lamb, as large as the universe, has been stretched above the world.

I see the sunny tabernacle, stretched above the world like a gigantic golden cherub.

Renounce the old chimeras, not a thousand, but a million times more daringly. What help is there even from charismatic Orthodoxy a quarter of a century old?!

The approach suggested by Exceeding Wisdom is unexpected. But in this way distinguish yourself from the wound-up marionettes, in that you hear Her and follow the staff of the Our Father.

Glorious is the Father
in the Theocivilization of pure love.
Glorious is the Father
in the multiplication of Christ of christs.
Glorious is the Father
in thousands of new sunny disciples.
Glorious is the Great Church of Love,
shining forever!

*

Do not leave Nightingale Mountain, our son, so that the earthly chimeras do not inflict their pinhole, and the sensitive membranes are not deflated like a tautly stretched rubber ball.

The five stages of the lighting of the fire are: spark (1), smouldering wick (2), candle flame (3), ever-burning candle (4), and bush (5).

Several thousand saints, classed as immortals, have achieved the third stage (the candle flame). Those close to the fourth are: Seraphim Sarofsky, Padre Pio, and 12 brothers of Seraphim.

𝒯HE CREATION OF THE WORD

How to light the candle? Create the Word.

How to make it ever-burning? Passionately create the Word.

Create and transform it outside and inside the interior, again and again, into the Divinity and into your neighbour.

God is the Word, uttered from time immemorial. The Logos unceasing, the very sweetest voice.

Ascend to the mountain more often. The revelation is simultaneously relayed into thousands of hearts with the record in the notebook.

The superworldly ether of the Word is unlimited.

*

Behind the scenes of the special services tens of diversions are being planned... And they can do nothing – only nails stained with blood and rapacious little eyes staring out from their sockets, dying from their own malice and powerlessness. Such is the omnipotence of Our Divinity.

ℐHE STOREROOMS OF DIVINE EXISTENCE

This it the sole method to open up to the spheres of divine existence: walk along the stream of relics, dictate transcendentally and ecstatically, without comprehending how, daringly, according to faith...

How, without the storerooms of divine existence, when history has been to the uttermost corrupted and distorted to its opposite?

Whither, if not to the storerooms of divine existence, should those seeking truth on earth be directed, not expecting the otherworldly queues for viewing and illumination?

Where, if not in divine existence, are the tablets of truth kept?

Whence, if not from divine existence, did Christ dictate to Anne Catherine Emmerick his 'Day by Day Gospel', transubstantiating in her bloody wounds, combining with her as with a bride?[53]

Having illuminated for the world, the Great Church of Love departs into the next impervious catacombs on the eve of the greatest sunny explosion: apocalyptic and simultaneously creating the 85th Theocivilization-III.

*

𝒯he divine scrolls of the literal Christ

The Cathar wife-myrrhbearers silently spread the scrolls.

ONE OF THE MOTHER-MENTORS:

We read from the scrolls of the most eternal Gospel.

Every iota has imprinted itself in the sunny tablets of divine existence, miraculously preserved in the heights of our castles.

From the number of wife-myrrhbearers only those who had achieved the stage of the perfect ones (lesser God-bearers) were able to grasp the meaning of these heavenly tablets, which presupposed a high level of admission into divine existence.

In comparison with the divine scrolls of the true Christ, your gospels are the comic books of children.

We preserve every word of Our Father undistorted.

𝒯HE HEAVENLY SCROLLS

It is not true that Christ left neither diaries nor written tracts of His own.

Every word of our Christ has been recorded in the divine tablets, from where it issued and to where it safely returned after His incomprehensibly beautiful and lofty Holy Passion.

The greatness of our service and witness lies in that we have been impregnated with the original divine Word and read from scrolls inaccessible to the world.

The revelation of San Salvador is one of the notebooks of our most eternal Gospel.

Our children, not only the genuine words of Christ in His earthly days have been recorded here. Each of the finest vibrations of His heart and the subsequent revelations in the bodies of parousia have been imprinted, verbatim, in our fragrant white tablets.

> Once more they spread the scrolls, and I read. I do not so much see as savour the fragrant scents, and through them are revealed mysterious meanings...

*

In order to grasp the meaning of the heavenly scrolls, perfect peace is necessary in the interior.

The synodal gospels will perish and burn up together with humanity-84, but the most eternal scrolls will smell sweetly for the whole world, thurifiedby two archangels from the retinue of the sunny Lamb.

Millions will read the gospel of Christ, which is spread today by the elderly Cathar nuns.

It is impossible to read the most eternal Gospel indifferently, from without, as it is impossible to contemplate the divinity of Christ from a distance.

The reader clothes himself in evangelical vestments and becomes a small word of the great Word.

All humanity, if it is gathered together, is the perfect and immaculate Word of the Father of pure love.

And each of the souls is a mysterious aspect, a marvellous aphorism, incomprehensible characters.

*

The story of the Christ of parousia, after He shed His blood into the chalice of the Holy Grail, cannot be revealed to humanity.

The blood of Christ was poured, to the last drop, into the chalice from the mother-of-pearl bone of the Divinity.

In answer grateful humanity shed 200 million last drops: the answering chalices according to the number of the true disciple of Christ.

The Christ of Jerusalem has multiplied two hundred million times!

The white scroll of the most eternal Gospel

The white scroll of the most eternal Gospel is

the treasure of the Father, who has imprinted, to the last comma, every word of His only son, as He called Christ, singling Him out among *the others* (we have in mind the eldest one).

The Father kept His promise to preserve the most eternal Gospel until recently, and to make it the property of the 85th civilization.

Its scroll is being revealed on San Salvador by the holy mother-myrrhbearers.

The evangelical bodies of the Cathar mothers

O, the Cathar mothers are living tablets!!! I am beginning to understand their meaning. They have evangelical bodies. Our Father's Exceeding Wisdom entered their flesh and blood. The thought of Christ has imprinted itself on their brows. They open their lips as a continuation of the Gospel. They are the living vessels of the divine Word...

*

A gigantic cherub in white garments thurified from the golden censer above San Salvador, and the aether smelt sweetly...

The evangelical scrolls enter us.

We read them, perceiving the angel of the divine Word through the fragrance from the golden censer.

We hear the voice of our Christ, and contemplate the countenance of the Father.

His exceeding wisdom is relayed from within, into the mysterious caskets and innumerable storerooms of our immortal essences and the bodies that correspond to them...

*

The great book in the hands of the superior.
the keeper of the most eternal Gospel

THE WIFE-MYRRHBEARERS:

At the resurrection Christ appeared simultaneously in thousands of places, and His word often differed.

Our scrolls preserve the messages of Christ, revealing Himself simultaneously in a thousand faces. They have neither beginning nor end.

The great book in the hands of the immortal, the superior, the most superior elder of San Salvador.

His name is known only to some of those initiated in the secrets of the sunny tabernacle.

Our castles comprise 15 hierarchical tiers. And only starting with the tenth is the contemplation of the father-keeper of the most fragrant scrolls of the most eternal Gospel accessible.

We read it, and it reads us (!). We hold it in our hands, and it holds us in its bosom...

We vocalize it, and it vocalizes in us that which cannot be expressed with words, which is a million times greater than us.

The divine Gospel is greater than itself. However greatly you understand it, it is impossible to exhaust its meanings.

Many centuries ago we clothed ourselves in the evangelical word.

Man is the scroll of the Father of pure love.

He was given a mouth to praise the beauty of the divine worlds. His heart is the Kingdom of God in miniature.

The throne of the Father has been imprinted in the interior like a sunny altar.

If it had not been for the insolent interference of the cunning one – the black despot, the huge black rapacious bird – man would have been fragrant in His tablets.

With the transition into eternity, being awarded admission into one of the castles of the Grail, divinized man contemplates the Creator and himself as he is and forever renounces diabolic cunning.

Extol the word of our Divinity, sounding through the tablet-lips of Father John, and not one of the saboteurs will be able to continue his base work.

*

*C*hrist of the sunny era

Christ's disciple becomes a lesser christ.

The seals of the old gospel have been erased as a result of the multiplication of clever Aristotelians, these long-eared donkeys with eyes blinking in perplexity.

The most beautiful Christ, seen clearly – Christ-as-He-is, Christ of Tabor Mountain, Christ of Nightingale Mountain, the sunny Lamb of San Salvador Verdadero – the Christ of the sunny era, the Christ of 144 thousand transcendental castles – the Christ of the new heaven and the new earth, the Christ of Theocivilization-III, descending from on high.

*

The sky hit the sea with rays of light and drank it. The sea turned into the sky, and in the heavens, as on the dome of the sea, the scrolls of the 85th civilization were revealed.

Our service passed silently. Outwardly we dressed the wounds of the sick, brought them food, tended to their ailments. Many of the summoned ones fell into ecstatic divine existence and heard us from within. Having come to themselves, they said: 'What a beautiful letter! What is it?' – 'The heavenly gospel'.

We served in uninterrupted bilocation. The immortal bodies could do incomparably more than physical, perishable bodies.

Our service consisted of anointing for the act of hearing. And when the ears of the sufferers had been opened, secrets were revealed to them, for the sake of which they had ascended the mountain of our Divinity.

The holy mothers summon our sisters to genuflect and bless them, shedding rays of sunny Exceeding Wisdom.

The sisters transform beneath their sacred right hands. I glance into their faces. The beauty of the Cathar mothers imprints itself in them.

Magnificent!

Our beautiful mothers, passing through the cross of the second conversion, will become mentors for thousands of young creations who are searching for the supreme meaning of existence.

The gates of spirituality, which the world did not know in the times of the appearances of the great prophets or the highest flights of the medieval scholar, have been revealed with the universal slump of morality.

The mothers transform in a cloud of pure love. The most divine light, mixed with the compositions of transubstantiated Exceeding Wisdom.

The word is given today though scents, unmixed compositions, and the spirituality of the perfect ones – perfect spirituality.

Peace be with you, inhabitants of the earth. Peace.

The philosophy of the immortals

Transubstantiate unceasingly.

Transubstantiation is the pledge of immortality.

He who has mastered the mystery of transubstantiation as a transition from the erased form into the superior form (with the condition of absolute unworldliness) has mastered the foundations of the immortals' philosophy.

Our Father was able to leave man eternal life even in the physical body. But then his capacity for transubstantiation, given with the deliverance from the mortal and the transition into eternal peace, would have been far less than now.

*

THE CATHAR MOTHERS:

Bear the blows patiently, our Father John.

They bow. They see in me one of the perfect ones. And I read the sorrows which they endured in the earthly days. Before this Holy Passion of the great lambs of Theohumanity, the wretched slander and persecutions which we experience in Russia seem so petty and insignificant...

The main law of the Holy Grail:
the measure of blessings is equal
to the level of sorrows experienced

The main law of the Holy Grail: the measure of blessings is equal to the level of sorrows experienced.

He who desires blessings, but avoids sorrows, inevitably falls into delusion and loses the latter.

As Christ taught again in the Gospel: some lose the latter, while others will multiply what they have and acquire even more.

Our sunny Christ wants to make his earthly disciples perfect vessels of the living Word.

And may our Father bless you in the school of Exceeding Wisdom! Blessed is the kingdom of our Divinity.

𝒯he bridal love feasts of the living Word

The bridal love feasts of the living Word... People gather in a circle. The leader (the elder) creates the Word, the others take it up and comment upon it. In such agapes ecstatic states will be given, the listeners will be carried across into divine existence and savour the heavenly aromas, like those which we have savoured today, fanned from the sunny censers.

One fragment may be commented upon ten times, and it will be revealed anew – as if for the first time.

The seals of the Word! Immortal pollen and myrrhic aromas are within them – the seals of Exceeding Wisdom, the new compositions and ark of the Theocivilization. The Word turns into the interior, becomes one.

*

FATHER JOHN:

When Exceeding Wisdom raises me to heavenly worlds, every word of the books recorded by me will be again revealed to humanity.

Then all, without exception, prophetic, poetic, theological, god-revealed and personal texts of Father John will be shown to the world transformed, in the fragrance of white scrolls, as the mystical sunny library, as a sign of the historical importance of what is being revealed through your father.

*

What divine currents! What hot rivers of pure love! So much flows from the sisters, our divine mothers!

O Grail, the fountaining hot springs of our Father's love, fountaining from heart to heart!

So many of them will begin to flow in the days of the coming Theocivilization! They will become something like new mountains, along which will ascend the devotees of the future age, to heights ever more beautiful.

San Salvador rejoices, transforms. We have descended to two hundred metres. We view San Salvador and rejoice together with it. I am sending airy kisses to the immortal mothers in the castles.

14.

the Cathar revolution
in the history
of humanity

- In the first year of His preaching in Jerusalem,
  Christ had already abolished the rituals of Elohim
- The divine hierarchy in the castles of the Holy Grail
- The burning Christ – minus Elohimism
- After the Second Solovetsky Golgotha there was not one soul
  without the myrrhic Solovetsky particle in her composition

- The sunny ecumene of the brightest Christ
  will beget thousands of new apostles

- The thousands of names of our Father

- Even in the earthly days the Divinity
  should have been seen clearly

- From Anna the God-bearer, the Mother of God and Christ –
  the first branch of kind people

- Mary conceived Christ in the ecstatic Holy Passion

◄§

THE IMMORTALS OF SAN SALVADOR:

ree yourself from the hypnosis of the four gospels (the classics of the Inquisition). Renounce the Rabbinic-inquisitorial version of Christ. Grace will only multiply.

Thousands of advantages will be gained by those who profess that Christ has arrived from the kingdom of the Holy Grail, as the messenger and as the adored Son of the Father of pure love.

Tirelessly repeat:

> Our adored Father,
> Adored among the adored
> and among the divinized,
> sons and daughters of the Bridal Chamber.
> Thrice adored,
> Adored among the adored ones of Eloi,
> the kind father Agafon
> the Father of pure love,
> the most restful myrrhic Lamb,

the Most Pure, Sweetest Father,
the Most Perfect One, contemplated clearly.

Our authentic Christ came as the messenger of the Father of pure love and the 15 immaculate civilizations.

In each of them He came as the most perfect of perfect ones and the most anointed of anointed ones. The great secrets of the power of the sea were revealed to Him.

Like a king He walked across the surface of the world ocean and was borne through the aether, holding the sunny staff of the control of the world in His hands.

The adored son of our Father, the perfect one among the divinized (100 of the 100 uniting particles), from time immemorial Christ carried in Himself the spirituality of divine civilizations, the treasure trove of all treasures, one touch of which fills with Exceeding Wisdom, flows out the oceanic streams of the Holy Grail.

What were the unhappy so-called apostles and disciples able to take from Him? They were seduced by Elohim. John the Theologian saw the light with difficulty, tormented by thoughts like you, our adored brother John.

How your attempt to tear yourself away from the poisonous fastener of Elohim reminds us of the situation two thousand years ago in Jerusalem (the apostle Paul, the apostle John of the Holy Passion)!

*

Christ did not preach in Jerusalem for longer than three years. And before that He lived in Egypt, India, and Tibet, where He dwelt in the most blessed spiritual conversations with the greatest teachers. He was borne through the aether, although He also travelled as an earthly wanderer. He possessed the greatest gift of bilocation, appearing simultaneously in nearly a thousand places across the whole world. And everywhere, while attending spiritual schools, He revealed the spirituality of the universum of Our Divinity and sowed the seeds of the Father of pure love.

All of the teachers of the world knew about the mystery of Christ, which awaited completion in Jerusalem – the transubstantiation of His flesh and blood into the Holy Grail – and they blessed Him.

After the mystery of the myrrh-shedding at Golgotha (hence myrrh in the Eucharist) the angels mysteriously carried the Chalice around the whole world.

The angels of Our Divinity, already appointed in the time of Golgotha in Jerusalem, did not give up the Grail.

And they do not give it up today, forbidding the unworthy even to approach the Holy Chalice.

The King and Queen of the universum

Christ in his perfection possessed the exceeding wisdom of the universum. The heavens call Him king, and the Most Pure Virgin: queen of the universum, Regina Universorum.

The Mother of God is indeed the queen of the 84th and the sun of suns of the 85th civilization.

But in the Holy Grail She is given the name perfect Exceeding Wisdom of the universum equal with Christ.

Among the Hellenes were a multitude of His disciples. Even before His coming in Jerusalem He founded among them a school of transubstantiation, the very highest, central mystery of the 84th civilization.

Publicized through the superworldly aether, they sought to save Christ ('the Hellenes sought Him', has been recorded in the Gospels).

From the first year of His service Christ fearlessly denounced Elohim and the 'synagogue of Satan'.

Many disciples, frightened by this, abandoned Him in the final years.

The Jews, embittered to the utmost by the (from their point of view) greatest blasphemy, sought to hand Him over for as severe an execution as possible.

What was provided for in the law of Moses (to throw into the abyss or to stone to death) was not able to quench their fury. Therefore they came to the Roman crucifixion, the most contemptible and torturous of executions. Such was their malice against the Father of pure love.[54]

Christ had already abolished the rituals of Elohim and revoked the law of Moses and the synagogue in the first year of His sermon. He openly called the 'Creator of the World', Adonai-Jehovah, the devil.

With the formation of the Christian 'law' the new rabbis became terrified and treated Christ's authentic sermon as they had always treated the anointed sovereigns: they borrowed what was convenient for them and consigned the rest to oblivion.

With no less fury than the Jews for Christ, they fell upon the Slavic Theogamites, exterminating them in their thousands, and then upon the Cathars, destroying pure ones and perfect ones in the times of the Inquisition.

To accept the cross from the synagogue of Elohim in Christianity today is an honour.

𝒞hrist leads the immortals

Christ leads the assembly of immortals in the

stages of the supreme divinities – the most divinized of divinized ones of the 85th civilization.

Among the Theogamic elders the address 'holy' was not accepted, but rather divine father, divine mother, divine brother – divina madre, divino padre, divino hermano...

The word 'adored' (adored of adored ones, divinized in Christ) was literally on the pure lips, which drop myrrh from its one utterance.

The divine hierarchy in the castles of the Holy Grail is formed in the following manner:

man is divine; Christ is the divinity of divinities;

The Father is the most divine of the divine.

The rank of King of the anointed sovereigns is the divinity of divinities,

the most divine among the divine, the king among the first-divinized.

Complete the mental theological reduction of the Old and New Testaments: the burning Christ minus Elohimism.

Under the guise of the Christ of the inquisitors (and also of the Moses of the rabbis) hides the prince of this world himself, the devil.

*

Millions of sunny disks

Millions of sunny disks will begin to burn with

the most joyful news: the Father of pure love is not abandoning the world!

Christ has multiplied! The Second Solovetsky has spread the golden pollen in millions of hearts!

After the Second Solovetsky and its sunny triumph in heaven and on earth there will not remain (and is already no longer) a single soul without the Solovetsky myrrhic particle in his composition.

While the unhappy ones crawled around in their two thousand year old theories of redemption, 200 million great and lesser christs of the Sunny Triumvirate accomplished 200 million redemptions.

$\mathscr{T}$HE THIRD PATH
against fundamentalism and Tibet

Against Tibetan cosmism[55] and global fundamentalism proclaim the third path throughout the whole world: Christ as the heir of the Father of pure love.

The adored one will grant thousands of new gifts, immortal vestments, sunny garments, miracles and indescribable victories.

The sunny ecumene of the brightest Christ will beget thousands of new apostles,

until the sun of suns of the 85th Theocivilization begins to shine over humanity!

Ammialies[56] from the retinue of the sunny Divinity count the thousands of names of our Father: Most Pure, Most Fragrant, Most Immaculate, Most Glorious, Most Adored, Most Perfect, Most Blessed, Persistent, the Most Faithful, Glorified for ever...

An exceedingly fragrant candle has been lighted as a sign of the close apotheosis of the 85th civilization

At the altar of the Holy Grail from the heart of the Mother of God and Seraphim Sarovsky was lighted a special exceedingly fragrant candle, as a sign of the close apotheosis of the 85th civilization.

Its triumph will come much faster than we can imagine.

The Theocivilization has already been proclaimed. It remains only to perform the great exorcism, to perceive the fundamental lie of the old religions, the great deception regarding the origin of Christ from Elohim.

*

The strain in Russia will reach its limit. Then – literally, in a twinkling of the eye – the situation will change. The chimeras of Stalin will disappear from the face of the earth in an instant.

Christ's vision clearly

The transition into eternity is an appropriation of Christ, Christ's vision clearly.

Victory over death is being achieved even in the earthly days.

He who joins Christ in matrimony becomes immortal.

The experience of the afterlife is that for the sake of which the transition into eternity is accomplished (to see the Father clearly, Christ clearly, the mystery of transubstantiation, the mystery of return, the transition in the most high, sunny state), is being achieved even in the earthly days!

Even in the earthly days, in the corporal shell, one should see the Divinity clearly as-He-is.

He who dares to refuse the magic of Rex Mundi wins the victor's wreath.

Enlightenment of the spirit returns to the bosom of the Father

The peace of the Father of pure love and Christ has been sealed by the pharisees. Illuminate yourself with the Spirit!

Illumination of the spirit returns one to the bosom of the Father.

To gain the Holy Spirit is to see the Father clearly, to read the white scrolls, to be at peace. Peace.

The fundamentalist offices are frightened of the Holy Spirit and limited by their own versions and writings, believing them to be absolute.

The immortals display the treasure troves. Oh, my Father, so many will be generously given with the acceptance of the authentic Christ, outside of the confusions of Elohim!

*

The rabbis and inquisitors are masters of mystification. Rome specifically appointed 'storytellers', versifiers, composers of legends. The more cunning the falsificator, the more successful – from the point of view of the religious office – is the version he has managed to invent.

The Judaic version, the version of Jerusalem, the Roman version, the Byzantine... Bethlehem, Capernaum, 'the law of Moses', the Hexaemeron... The worship of the Magi, Christ's carpentry in the house of Joseph the Carpenter, death on the cross, resurrection... The Assumption of the Mother of God in Jerusalem, Her residence in the temple of Jerusalem from the age of three, the immaculate conception with the annunciation of the archangel Gabriel ('How will this happen? – The Holy Spirit will come upon You')...

Even the majority of apocrypha is fake. Versions are imposed one after another. From them is formed a virtual image which has become compulsory doctrine.

Until you disown the Inquisition, until you get

rid of its chimeras and specters, the gospel cliches will oppress you.

The gospel versions of Christ are false. The Jews accepted Him as an envoy from Elohim. The same thing was done subsequently by their successors, the Roman-Byzantine rabbis.

The elohimization of Christ, from the point of view of the castles of the Holy Grail, is His direct crucifixion. Rome is the place where Christ is crucified every day.

THE GOD-BEARERS ANNA AND JOACHIM

The story of the entering of the God-bearer into the temple of Jerusalem is a complete mystification.

From Anna the God-bearer, the Mother of God, and Christ, comes the first branch of kind people, immaculately conceived, the sunny Godmen of the Seraphites.

'O, the kindness of our Anna, the holy mother!' — Tirelessly repeated our fathers in the Holy Grail.

The Jews wanted to stone her and Joachim for daring to call the legislation of Moses a diabolic misanthropic lie.

The God-bearer Anna, revered in ancient Slavic Theogamism and western Catharism even before the immaculate conception of the Most Holy Virgin, was in direct communion with the Father of pure love.

The Holy Spirit enlightened her about the greatest battle of the 84th civilization: between the Father of pure love and his treacherous surrogate, Elohim.

The rabbis wanted to take the God-bearer from Joachim and Anna and conveyed Her into the temple by force. But the God-bearer, despite confinement behind seven locks, had already miraculously escaped by the following day.

Anna was the first to reveal to the Most Holy Virgin the secret of the immaculate conception.

The God-bearer, having immaculately conceived Christ, was the first to reveal to Christ the secret of His true, immaculate and spotless Father.

Contemplating the face of the Mother of God, the Infant God in her hands adored the immortal Father, from whose kingdom he had descended to the earthly world.

The Mother of God and Christ were conceived from the last drop of superior, magnificent love

The Mother of God and Christ were conceived from the last drop of superior, magnificent love.

The immaculate conceptions of the God-bearer Anna, and then of the Virgin Lady, were preceded by the sunny revelation about Our Divinity (1), the absolute purification of internal composition, mysterious anointings (2),

the lengthy, exhausting, empty Holy Passion, the battle with the prince of this world (3),

the appearance of the Holy Grail (4). (Christ with the Chalice appeared to the Mother of God at the hour of the immaculate conception. Christ and the Mother of God came from the Theogamic chalice to the God-bearers Anna and Joachim),

immersion in the transcendental Holy Passion, the greatest Holy Passion of Holy Passions, the appearance of the bloody heart of Our Divinity (5).

The immaculate conception is the shedding of the last myrrhic drop and the answering drop from the grateful loving heart.

The Virgin Mary was immaculately conceived at the heights of the indescribable Holy Passion

The God-bearer Virgin Mary was immaculately conceived by Saint Anna at the heights of the indescribable Holy Passion from the last drop of Our Divinity.

Mary Teoengendradora, the mother of the sons of God, conceived Christ not during the Annunciation, but in ecstatic Holy Passion,

in the transcendental wilderness of Jerusalem, this 'city of Satan', from the last drop of the Father of pure love.

*

The Great Church of Love described the first conception and birth from on high. Besides this a second exists.

The first: Christ and Mary, the two suns of the 84th civilization.

Through the second conception and birth more than a thousand anointed sovereigns came to earth: Seraphim Sarovsky, Seraphim Solovetsky, Euphrosinia, Innokenty Baltsky, Father John, the church of John...

Those upon whom descends the fullness of the Holy Spirit (in Catharism they are called perfect ones, anointed ones and immortals), are conceived and born from on high, from Christ. Such is the second birth.

The fiery Last Drop of the immaculate conception is shed from the spiritual heart, from the mysterious celestial body of one of the highest brightest sunny castles – the castle of the Immaculate conception.

'Do you really not know that the goal of the true church is conception from on high?' – Says Christ in a famous gospel conversation, falsely reported.

In John's gospel was imprinted only a small fragment from the detailed sermon of Christ about the Father of pure love, about the immaculate conception from on high, about the fact that the religion of Elohim originated from the prince of this world.

The conversation with Nicodemus, the elder of the synedrion, and with Joseph of Arimathea, was exceptionally complicated, and lasted three days, never-endingly, and passed over into divine existence...

In the white scrolls of the 84th civilization are numbered no less than one hundred who have come into the world from the first conception and birth from on high (among them Elias, born from Mary-Rosa).

From the second conception – more than 100 thousand great devotees of the Holy Spirit born from on high, crowned as the victors over the prince of this world, formed by the Divinity only for 2000 years after the birth of Christ.

❧

15.

the Fragrance
of the Bridal Bed
of our Divinity

- The ecstasies returned the heavenly tabernacle
- The Cathars distinguished more than ten kinds of ecstasies
- Experienced doctors of mercy
- The perfect ones conversed with one another
  without carrier pigeons or notes

- The configuration and internal architectonics of the Cathar castles duplicated the Cathar heaven by staircase
- The Bridal Bed with the Divinity

 bosom,
bosom of Our Divinity!
(Prayer during the ascent to the castle)

THE CATHARS OF THE XXI CENTURY,
THE FIERY HIERARCHY:

San Salvador was designated as the mountain of the Divinity from the creation of the world.

I.

The struggle with earthly passions, programmes, emotions, and forbidden 'bonds' was conducted, not with repentance, but with introspection - with the descent into the castles of internal light.

The practice of Orthodox sobriety originated with the white elder Theogamites. The Exceeding Wisdom of Nightingale Mountain Herself, in the person of the Mother of God, entrusted them with the keys to victory over personal and ancestral chimeras, revealed the ways of cleansing themselves of them.

The Cathar elders possessed the keys to victory over the prince of this world.

But here was such a thick grace that he who endured communion with the pure and perfect ones for more than a month was purified by a miraculous manner and became perfect. The celestial heights seized him and the caskets of divine potential were opened, after which the need for repentant scrutiny (introspection) disappeared.

The sphere of Espejo del Cielo (the heavenly mirror)

Half a kilometre above the Mediterranean you enter the waters of *the heavenly sea*, where other, unearthly laws are in action.

The airy sphere is called Espejo del Cielo – 'the heavenly mirror', 'the second sea' with a smooth emerald-azure surface. Swim freely in its waters.

> The immortals had the best method of renouncing ancestral programmes, oppressing chimeras, old neighbours, and fatal drawings: ablutions in the waters of the heavenly sea.

The pure ones (seeing purely and worshipping the Father of pure love) received grace incomparable with that received by the mixed ones.

It is possible to receive the consulamentum (the consolation and gift of the Holy Spirit) only having entered into mortal battle with the prince of this world and having defeated him.

The immortals distinguished fifteen stages of the battle with the prince of this world, divided into 3 groups:

- The first are connected with overcoming of personal sinful wishes;

- The second with the sinful chalice of the ancestral and national order;

- The third with the sinful universal chalice: the withdrawal from the Adamite programmes.

The Cathar fathers called lust the 'Adamite corruption'. Those preparing themselves to take the vow of purity were called upon to free themselves from inflicted pollutions. Considering lust as corruption inflicted by the devil helped to free oneself in a short time.

*

The consulamentum is a gift
of the pure and loving Divinity

The Cathar initiates awoke the craving for purity by a special outpouring of the gifts of the Holy Spirit.

The consulamentum is not simply the 'gift of the

Holy Spirit from God' (about which the Catholics spoke), but the gift of the Holy Spirit from the pure and loving Divinity.

The Cathar consulamentum has nothing in common with the Catholic succession from Ruakh-Elohim.[57]

The immortals distinguished precisely between possessors of the soul of Elohim and the Spirit of God: 'Those who acquire the spirit of Elohim fall into false holiness'.

The consulamentum (and also the melioramentum) was connected by the Cathars with becoming kinder, warming, the 'thawing of the internal ice flows'.

The gift of differentiation of the spirits

The Cathar elders sharply distinguished between the gifts of the spirit. They called the gift of differentiation not merely the primitive differentiation of 'the spirits of the devil from those of God', accepted in the Orthodox-Catholic exorcism.

They called the pure spirit of the Father, entering virginal bosoms, enveloping all of man's being, transubstantiating him, inspiring him, rousing in him the most eternal source beginnings, combining him with the heavenly hypostases, leading him to the Bridal Chamber, separating him from the mixed spirit (damaged, with the closeness of the cunning one), the 'Spirit of the purity of God'.

The immortals rose sharply against the Roman scoundrels, who considered themselves lamps (like Thomas Aquinas). They were indeed enlightened by the spirit, but others by Ruakh-Elohim, 'having soared above the abyss'.

"And he soars above the abyss to this day (said our fathers), and this precipice is the Roman church, the darkness".

II. THE FATHER OF GOD, PADRE DE DIOS

A shower of the grace of the divine existence comes from the Kindest of the Kind, Agafon, the most chaste Father of God (thus Padre de Dios, called the Father of God by the Cathars, identifying Him with the Mother of God).

The Spirit of the purity of God caused Cathar ecstasies.

Ecstasy entered into the practice of the new-beginners and was considered the second stage after purifying introspection.

Spiritual ecstasy

Some of those who entered San Salvador (Mont-ségur, Perpetouse and other castles) had lengthy ecstasies almost instantaneously, which was a sign of selectness and engendered from them a special relationship. These people were initiated into the pure ones in a short time.

The origin of ecstasies flows directly from the genesis of man.

Ecstasy (ex-stasis – withdrawal from a static state) was considered more than natural. If by 'static state' we understand the wingless existence of those who have fallen under the sign of the prince of this world, then ecstasies returned the heavenly tabernacle, the original purpose of man, and prepared his further flight.

The Cathars distinguished between more than ten types of ecstasies: purifying / most admiring / angelic / contemplative / airy / flight / God-revealing...

In the practice of witnessing the mystery, the experienced doctors of mercy summoned the Holy Spirit, which had given miraculous ecstasies to those ascending the mountain.

The ecstasies did not cleanse like any 'repentance', they returned the divine beginnings to man.

The kind of ecstatic prayer
entrance into the castle:

I unite with our Divinity
    most admiring grace
    most admiring grace
    most admiring grace

> In the bosom of our Divinity
>> most admiring grace
>> most admiring grace
>> most admiring grace

The Father of the pure ones, coming hither, addressed His children as if they had remained in the heavens.

On the Spanish Nightingale Mountain He confirmed His heavenly kingdom and His disciples led a life equal to and even higher than that of the angels.

III. A CORNER OF THE KINGDOM ON SAN SALVADOR

The third stage after the ecstasies was absolute exorcism: the mortal battle with the devil.

Some, when the evil force left them, experienced physical torments. They were shaken and thrown about as the demons went mad and departed. After such a miraculous catharsis (exorcistic purification) people became like angels.

Incomparable waves of love were spread from San Salvador.

The second heavenly sea was the overflowing of divine light and virginal love.

When the newly-converted inquired: 'Where are we? We are not on earth!', we answered: 'Our Father left a corner of the Kingdom on earth. On San Salvador you are in the heavens!'

The mentality of the anointed ones presupposed the ascent to the mountains, inhabitation in the unearthly atmosphere.

They called the airy sphere the 'second sea', or the sea of virginal purity, the pure bosom, where the fullness of our Divinity dwells.

The anointed ones – the third stage after the pure and perfect ones (the fourth is that of the immortals). Mystical incarnations presupposed special anointings for the bearing of the cross, and the Divinity anointed the chosen ones with special oils for the Holy Passion. Hence: 'anointed sovereigns by the seals of the Divinity.

The airy sphere was mastered such that, departing to the 'tower of towers' (grádula) of each castle, the perfect and anointed ones by a miraculous fashion conversed with one another without carrier pigeons or notes.

The perfect and anointed ones felt like fish in the sea here. They swam in other airy waters and did not need special battle or prayers.

In accordance with the mysterious legend, San Salvador was considered a scrap of heaven on earth, the earthly heaven. It was even called tierra celestial (the earthly heaven).

The special clinic for the mentally ill was called 'the school of exceptional mercy'.

For many began purifying exorcistic ecstasies. Some, when the demons left them, spent weeks in prostration,

after which they experienced a state of bliss, close to feeling of peace after an apocalyptic blow.

The architectonics of the Cathar castle

The multi-tiered architectonics of the Cathar castle (not revealed to stranger): 12x12 = 144 or 15x3 = 45 stages.

During the daily ascent the disciples of the anointed ones (by the anointed ones) were instructed to theologize about the ascent to the heavens along those same sunny staircases by which they will one day be led during the transition from the physical condition into the spiritual and the eternal.

THE CATHAR HEAVEN OF THE PURE OF HEART

The configuration and internal architectonics of the Cathar castles duplicated by staircase the Cathar heaven of the pure of heart, the heaven of the Father of pure love.

The Heavenly Father, coming to San Salvador with a miraculous myrrhic vessel in His hands, anointed the castle.

And San Salvador shed the grateful myrrhic smells of our Father.

IV. The Holy Passion

The loss of the model of the Father who gives life is the ultimate catastrophe and tragedy of humanity. By serving the prince of this world the Adamites accomplish worship also of the adversary, the mother of this world, who gives material goods.

The condition of the return of love to earth is the bearing of the Cross, and the Chalice which accepts the last drops of the super-possible, transcendent Holy Passion.

The stage of Holy Passion is linked to the shedding of the last drop. Its shedding at the peak of the Holy Passion is considered a practice inevitable for the anointed sovereign.

The anointed ones are those who have been anointed with the special seals of the Divinity and, already at the peaks of the path (presupposing the staircase), in their own time shed the oils onto their neighbours: they will bear the Holy Passion, and accomplish their act of love.

300

To such high stages of anointing, to the redemptive mission, were called the great abstainers, the wise men, having acquired from Exceeding Wisdom the highest seal of sobriety, the influence on the Works of God, and the reading from the heavenly scrolls.

The Cathar prayer in the mountains

The heaven of Cathar prayer is almost impossible in the world. In a damp cave you light neither candle, not match, nor kerosene wick.

Catharism began with John's 'and light shines in the darkness'.

In order to shine in the darkness, it is necessary to be nourished from heavenly springs of light, and these heavenly lights were shed in the mountains.

Seclusion (the prayer during the 'seclusion' of the internal man, his liberation from the paths of the prince of this world) served as an imitation of *celestial prayer*.

About the secrets of divinization

San Salvador was considered a kind of password for the Cathars of the whole world as a mystical entrance into the sphere of prayer about divinization and liberation from the prince of this world. On Salvador the Father taught the secrets of the path of divinization.

Wax from the candles of the heart

It is impossible to call that which occurred on Salvador anything other than a miracle.

The brothers walked in immortal bodies. They were in bilocation night and day, in several bodies simultaneously.

A miraculous multiplication was accomplished, then the reduction of the brotherhood. The love between them was such that wax constantly bled form the candles of their hearts.

The Cathar theologians and prophets called the illuminating as the archetype of the sunny Father of pure love. He who entered the archetype shone with rays of unearthly warmth.

The Assumption Bed. the place of miraculous initiation

At the entrance to the grádula was found a mysterious room for initiations, called the Bridal Chamber.

In it was found the assumption bed, the place of miraculous initiation.

On the bed was inscribed the Cathar cross, and around it three circles, the chalice and another 12 miraculous signs of the Divinity.

The one being initiated lay down and had the honour of the Bridal Chamber with the Divinity, the honour of perfect union, after which he became a Theogamite.

The three-day residence in the assumption-Bridal Chamber

The three-day residence in the assumption-Bridal Chamber, was a bloody act. The devil set about, and the devotee descended to the very bottom of the underworld, leading out souls from Gehenna.

The heavenly Queen Herself did not retreat from him and gave nourishment from the imperishable compositions of the Chalice.

On the third day a special Theogamic angel arrived, opened the heart and inserted special oils into its treasure trove, which is why myrrhic blood flowed in the interior.

The essence of the devotee simultaneously bled in the Holy Passion and poured myrrh in bliss. Thus the anointed one prepared himself for the rank of the immortal.

NB! The two highest stages of the Cathar path (*the anointed ones and the immortals*) are being revealed to humanity for the first time.

The initiated ones took a vow not to share their secret even under the fear of death or torture.

Thus the inquisitors were not able to learn about the highest initiations of the Cathars. Nothing more than knowledge of naïve 'pure ones' and 'perfect

ones' regarding the Cathar church came to its per-
secuters.

Special grace was given in contemplative-respi-
ratory prayer, conducted without words.

Uttering the verse 'THE FRAGRANCE OF THE
BRIDAL CHAMBER OF OUR DIVINITY', the pure ones
immersed themselves in a special ecstatic state in
which they remained for a long time (anointing
into their hearts).

...Their hearts were opened. The angels constantly performed anointings, entering into them, as at
the altar, and enriching the microscopic internal
vessels.

Under the eye of the Divinity inside man is
found the Holy Grail and the heavenly Kingdom.

Man is the indestructible all-conquering Grail.

There is nothing more shameful (a sign of the
covenant with the devil), than to see man as a sinner, to present scores to him. So Christ taught His
disciples.

In the aethers of San Salvador were spread
white pollen, the organic pollen of heavenly origin. Partaking of it, the immortals were sated.

The meal was preceded by meditation: the
meditative-respiratory prayer sated like a meal. In
the language of the apostle John it was called secret manna.

The anointed ones taught about the nourishing of immortal bodies with the ineffable aromatic oils, fragrant on San Salvador.

Undoubtedly, they also used earthly food, but the need for it was minimal. The immortal bodies of the Theogamites and the highest levels (beatitudes, anointed ones) did not need it.

The eye of Our Divinity

One of the anointings of the internal altar, 'the spiritual Grail', consisted in that the Divinity inserted His sight – THE EYE OF OUR DIVINITY.

The special organ of spiritual vision, received into the spiritual heart. The contemplation of the Father was performed with it.

Today our Slavic Theogamite fathers give us the gift of the heart's sight into the heart. Its revealing presupposes great purifying and redemptive sorrows.

⤳

16.

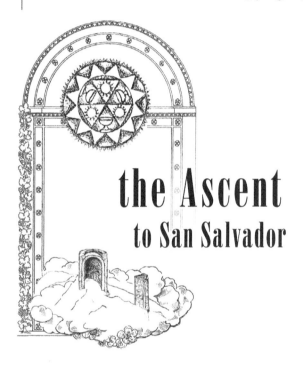

the Ascent
to San Salvador

- The realization of the true roots of the Roman church will be the beginning of the triumph of Our Divinity

- San Salvador was the place where the Father of love returned the heavenly chambers to His children

The mirror of heaven

Why did the Cathars build castles?

Access to the Father of pure love begins at approximately half a kilometre above the earth. Souls, leaving the world and finding themselves at such a height, reveal for themselves for the first time the Father of pure love, imprinted in the world.

According to the teachings of the fathers, the sphere from 500 to 2000 metres and more is fatal for the prince of this world. It was called the sphere of divine existence and was designated by the ancient Cathars as the 'mirror of heaven'.[58]

Here they found the Father of pure love with ease; then as on earth His presence was given with huge effort, through fierce battle with the seals of the prince of this world (the influence of the religious institutions).

*

For Cathars, mixing is impossible. Catharism is immiscibility, purity, and the true form of faith.

$\mathscr{O}$ur Father has been imprinted in Roman Catholicism

Our Father (Padre Divino Nostro) has been sealed in Roman Catholicism and its eastern stepdaughter (the Byzantine branch). The Second Rome succeeded the first, and the 'third' – the second.[59]

It is impossible to extract a pearl from a mixed form.

The first conversion signified a complete break with the old past, with the preceding life.

But why is there no complete break with the first conversion?

Summon day and night the force of the Cathar staff to smash the head of the ancient serpent in its Roman guise, the first enemy of Our Divinity.

$\mathscr{V}$ictims of the ancient serpent

We even pity the Catholics. They are victims of the ancient serpent, their fates are on his conscience. The heavenly Judge will, in the final reckoning, present him with the score for five million anointed sovereigns of El Elion, eaten by the ancient dragon of the Roman church.

The cats began to howl in Perderodes, the Roman Buchenwald, the stone prison for the holy captives.

*

Rome, and the Inquisition which supplemented it, destroyed the Theogamic foundations of the heavenly Father down to the root.

His true light, faith, religion, path, and goals have been distorted and transferred into the order of neorabbinism, advantageous for the Roman curia:

a) original sin; b) the Tempter; c) the church, 'presenting Him in salvational mysteries'.

50 million lambs, contemplating the glory of Our Divinity for seven centuries

...This was the great collision of our Father and Lucifer. And the great victory of our Father.

50 million lambs have been collected, which have already contemplated the glory of Our Divinity for seven centuries, and await the hour when the supreme archistrategos of the hierarchy of divinization will give the sign. And then the Roman church will cease to exist. It will be swept away.

'To soar heavenly' means to join the spheres of Father of pure love

The spiritual path will be given with ease to those who settle today in the mountains.

310

Your battle is connected with the fact that the devil's attacks below are beyond one's strength.

Nothing disturbs to soar heavenly in spirit... The origin of prayer is the soaring to the mountains of the Cathar castles. They are the unified Church.

'To soar heavenly' (an ancient Slavic term) = to raise the spirit to the mountain: to unite with the spheres of the Father of pure love, in the vast dimension rise if only half a mile above the earth.

> Everywhere the smells of relics – the aromas of their presence. The desire to lie down, as on the earth of Anzer: the grace of Anzer![60] The place of the great martyrs. An oasis of peace, a place of the future.
>
> This is why, having described the Russian Solovki, I was transferred to Spain – to describe THE SPANISH SOLOVKI. I find the same smells of the relics!
>
> And here is the local 'gastronom'[61] – the castle Perderodes, dark prison of the Inquisition, where they mocked God's saints who denied the stone Dominican dogs.

*

We reveal ourselves to the world to convey the civilization of the true God.

Our appearance to the world is apocalyptic. The realization of the true roots of the Roman church, originating with the prince of this world with the subsequent renunciation of him, will be the beginning of the triumph of Our Divinity.

The prince of this world will shake like an exploded mountain when his №1 den, the Roman church, has been exposed. And he will begin to fall back, abandoning his fortresses one after another.

It is as if the world were under a cloud of midges. It is difficult to break through to the light. Celestial flight is necessary.

Ascend along the 15,000-step staircase leading to the chambers of Our Divinity.

The memory of Him was not preserved. For the last 500 years our brothers were found in catacombs and acted in conspiracy. But during this time they managed a thousand times more than in the brief period of their preaching on earth (200-300 years).

*

The celestial consulamentum

Hither, to San Salvador Verdadero, the chalice of the Theogamic Grail was carried in the tenth century.

In the space of the castle was thick grace, which is why souls fell into ecstasy and were illuminated by the spirit. The mystery performed was called 'the celestial consulamentum' in the language of the Cathars.

Those rising to the mountains experienced the

first stage of the consulamentum – purifying ecstasy. Passions disappeared of their own accord. The people asked questions: is it true, what they did in the world? Why did they come to this world? How were they able to worship the evil god? What is the sense of ritual functions, if they lead to *the dragon's den* – the lair of the prince of this world?

Many became terrified that, having yielded to the temptation of the world, they subsequently yielded to the temptation of the false church (which is worse than the first).

And they fierily renounced them in order to avoid *the third trap* – the posthumous destinies, promised by the Roman church (the extreme limit of which is the Catholic limbo).

The perfect ones of Salvador understood that any Catholic shares one destiny with the inquisitors. But, renouncing the sinful chalice of the church of executioners and murderers, the soul was bound for bright places.

*

Here the Cathar centre was created. The name of the castle: 'El Salvador Verdadero' ('the true Saviour'), that is, another Lord. The true shape of the Lord was mysteriously borne by anointed souls – those to whom were revealed the enemy of humanity (the prince of the world) and where he hides himself.

313

The first exorcistic secrets, which the Cathars revealed to people:

1. Who is the enemy? Before seeing God, people should see their enemy, the prince of the world.

2. What did he do with the angels who have descended to the earth? See his machinations on earth.

3. Where is his den?

The catastrophe of the 84th civilization

The Cathars called the Bible as his most terrible deception, the catastrophe of the 84th civilization. They almost entirely rejected it, with the exception of John's gospel.

In the Bible, they taught, a mixed form of Our Divinity is given. But apart from this the Cathars denounced *its Judaic cunning*, 'the vengeance of the rabbis'. Having endured defeat from the resurrected Christ, the rabbis attributed Him to *themselves* and made Him a Jewish God.

The neorabbis (the Orthodox-Catholic priests) acted exactly the same way with the saints: they killed them, and then attributed them to themselves – 'to the authority' of the aggressive Judaic demon.

*

The Cathar movement began with San Salvador. The Holy Grail was found here. It was one of the first Cathar castles, the first sunny temple (castillo solar) in Europe. The castle, to which the wandering sunny Theogamic Chalice was carried in a miraculous fashion, having dwelt in Russia for more than ten centuries.

*

1000 years later, a battle for the revelation of the Father of pure love

THE CATHARS OF SAN SALVADOR:

You are experiencing the battle which was experienced amongst us 1000 years ago, being one of our bastions (leaders) and keepers. Endure and thank the Divinity, because this battle is for the revelation of the Father of pure love.

*

Divine heavenly services were performed here. Hither came thousands of angels, and the Divinity, Father Himself visited these places and conferred a multitude of scrolls of the revelation of Exceeding Wisdom (thus the throne of the revelation several kilometres from here is called the throne of the Father of pure love).

Above San Salvador is a direct entrance into the sunny heavens

Juan of the Great Chalice originated from the Balkan Slavs.

In the beginning several men conspiratorially accepted the worship of the chalice. But then there occurred a sudden explosion, and ten years later there were already several thousands. People were stunned by the revelations of the Divinity, and the sunny glory of the Most High stood above San Salvador.

As now above Nightingale Mountain – an entrance into the Bridal Chamber – so here ten centuries ago stood a fiery pillar, a fiery chariot and a direct entrance into the sunny heavens.

Those who had accepted the faith of the Cathars clothed themselves in sunny bodes. He who was able to remain here for more than a month or two was definitively deprived of human transient and old beginnings and returned to the Bosom.

This was the great place of the return to the heavens.

The Cathars of San Salvador sent the souls of the dying into the Kingdom, defending them from the hordes of Elohim. They saw thousands of demons in the shape of black cats, bats, and flying serpents with fiery jaws, which wanted to captivate the 'Orthodox' and the 'Catholics' in their nets, saying: 'These are ours and are going to our destinies'.

Hence, from the castle, the army of Our Divinity was able to retake many righteous souls. And those already on the path to the third trap (the impassable labyrinth of limbo), having seen the light, fell back from the Roman 'guides'. They united with the secrets of the Divinity and returned to the world already as true believers, good and pure.

The Cathars showed the Cathar sign: the cross within a circle.

*

Among the Cathar castles, San Salvador Verdadero was one of the last to be attacked. It lasted longer than Montségur. Here was the impregnable fortress of the Divinity. The Catholics feared it. Rumours passed among them: he who rises hither without the permission of the Divinity will be singed with fire.

What happened at Montségur

What happened at Montségur? The inquisitors and crusaders lit three fires. But Our Divinity revealed Himself and named the execution place of the Second Golgotha, where He accepted the second great sacrifice of the Son.

Christ ascended to the Second Golgotha with two hundred perfect disciples. The heavenly father of love raised all of them. Not one single uninitiated was able to come here.

*

When we surrendered the castle at the order of Our Divinity, part of us accepted the voluntary act and, having followed Christ during His arrest at Gethsemane, surrendered into captivity, in order to testify to the true faith.

Their witness was so majestic that some executioners were converted, while others were struck with fierce death and the fire of the Divinity's glory.

Not a single person betrayed the faith under torture. The anointings were so high that the Roman inquisitors with their instruments seemed poisonous insects. And others, with the blessing of the keeper of the Chalice and the master of the castles (the great elder), were enraptured.

The raptures were given with ease. Those who had been able to receive anointings and reveal immortal bodies were found in angelic flight and were able to move in physical space from one mountain to another.

*

Our Father came to us as His children. We were for Him not 'children in Christ the Only-begotten Son', but the children, whom He once begot from His secret composition, from His myrrhic blood. And he spoke to us as His own children.

He called us 'the children who have returned to the house of God', referring to Christ's parable about the prodigal son.

San Salvador was the place where the Father of pure love returned the heavenly chambers to His children – according to the measure of their refusal of Adamite modelling and the Adamite essence, according to the measure of the return of the most divine compositions.[62]

*

We return from San Salvador, and again the valley of the smells of relics! The channel of the stream along which water flows after the rain.

We stand at the place of the former cavity. Here, probably, the mountain parted and the mysterious caves for eternal life were revealed.

Under the cavity is the entrance into the caves of San Salvador, where the imperishable relics are preserved. They will come to life in their own time and, shedding myrrhic aromas, will reveal themselves to the world.

Indescribable! Several thousand imperishable bodies! Hence, through the earth, we sense the relic fragrance of Pochaev and Anzer.[63]

Fasting

The need for physical food disappeared.

The effort lay in converting and passing the first stages in the battle.

For the victors there was no longer any need to apply effort. They became servants of the Divinity and small redeemers (small christs).

They fulfilled the mission of salvation, conversion and divinization of humanity, which was revealed to them by the true Son of God, the true Saviour.

About the secret internal pearl

Here Christ spoke repeatedly with His disciples about the pearl hidden in the heart of man. From it begins to burn the candle, and the soul, through the accomplishment of celestial flight, achieves the spheres of the Father and unites with Him.

Oral prayers signified only the first stage for us. Next followed blessed combinations and high Theogamic ecstasies (the vision of the Divinity).

The secret of Cathar prayer on the heights of the castles was that some of the anointed ones in humanity, having accepted the seals of the people of the future age (the pure ones and the perfect ones), found here the angelic prayer, returned to them.

◄§

17.

the
IMMORTALS

The world bowed before the greatness
of their oceanic love

We pass the stream of relics. A deep crevice is beneath us. Once in 100 years the stones part, revealing the cave of imperishable relics...

So many were tortured here, in the torture chambers of the Catholic 'Ravensbrück'! So many were burnt alive, scorched with red-hot iron... But what could be done with the fiery bodies?

They voluntarily came to martyrdom out of their love for the executioners, and converted them by the miracles of love... And when, acknowledging their powerlessness in hysterics before the victims, the bigot asked what was the secret of their powers, they answered with one word:

– In love... higher than which there is nothing, more beautiful than which there is nothing, purer than which there is nothing.

...And the world bowed before the greatness of their oceanic love.

Not only martyrs are counted among the many thousand relics. The anointed ones (pure ones, perfect ones) rest here until the hour of resurrection.

𝒯he secret of the anointed sovereigns, resting in the 144 caves of San Salvador

The rocks will part, and several thousand perfect ones will be resurrected, passing out in immortal bodies.

They will be the first to enter the triumphal arch of the Theocivilization, having formed the retinue of the Christ of the Second Coming.

Another 50 million perfect ones follow them, receiving in the heavens the honour of the divinized small (or even great) wreath.

Such is the secret of the anointed sovereigns, resting in the 144 caves of San Salvador.

The Holy Spirit distinguished not only between those of God and those of the cunning one, as is accepted in the elder's science. The Holy Spirit even discerns the smells of the relics, the level of their relics...

I dare to compare the smell of the hill of Pochaev, the earth of Anzer (several tens of thousands of imperishable relics), and Montségur with San Salvador: such thick grace as at San Salvador, I do not recall.

What can be higher than Nightingale Mountain,

the mountain of Exceeding Wisdom, of the Theo-civilization and the Bridal Chamber?

– The Chambers of Our Divinity. Only pure ones may ascend hither.

𝒯HE IMMORTALS

Those resting in the crevices of San Salvador are the immortals, the fourth stage after 'pure ones – perfect ones – anointed ones'.

The status of the immortals is special in the church of Mary Magdalene and Joseph of Arimathea. The regal stage of disposins.[64]

Christ calls the immortals His own kindered brothers. They are the true keepers of the Chalice, His true mystical twins, one with Him.

Their memory dwells on earth eternally. Their presence is ineradicable and absolute.

They are able to come and go from the earth as many times as they like, not being subject to the laws of decay and death. Our Divinity has given them the authority to descend to the earth when they consider necessary, in accordance with the sensitive barometre of their hearts, responding to the painful vibrations of world history, and to disappear just as mysteriously.

They rest in fragrant white shrouds with myrrhic aromas. Their faces are pale, but irresistibly beautiful with most heavenly spirituality.

It is enough to gaze at their anabiotic condition to be moved and to find the eternal consulamentum (the stage, which the initiated Cathars considered to be the highest and compulsory for the entrance into the triumphal arch).

THE IMMORTALS:

Remember us and keep us before your spiritual gaze. Only thus is it possible to become pure and to know the most pure Divinity. His name is the Divinity of Lights.

Draw a page of Cathar history from the mystical memory of Theohumanity,

this is the most beautiful scroll of Our Divinity from those unfolded on earth at one time since its creation!

*

San Salvador is infinite, with one hundred tiers. Towers one after another, and no earthly support. The earthly support is Christ and the Mother of God.

I ask the Cathars of San Salvador about Her.

The Mother of God is the mysterious fullness of the mysterious essence of Our Divinity. His and Her entrance to the earth is achieved by illuminating the spirit with the clothing in spotless vestments. It cannot be achieved otherwise. Other ways lead to profanation, 'the catechism for idiots', and the involuntary inquisition (the interrogation of the Almighty).

The living, wailing history of Theohumanity

Where the sea meets the sky, the Cathar height (the space of flight) begins...

Rocks in the half-destroyed crags, as if in them were imprinted dear souls. Nowhere else has been seen more touching, warm, more speaking rocks.

Now, seeing the rocks of San Salvador, for the first time I understand the ancient 'and the rocks will begin to speak'. The rocks here speak, they bear a chronicle.

A fragment from San Salvador – the living, wailing history of Theohumanity.

The holy place of presence, the place of the invisible inhabitation of the Divinity. Hence the Grail was borne amongst the multiplying castles – there seemed to be thousands.

Here it is, the place of the blessing of the world! Here the Adamites will grow wings and the seals of the Seraphites of the future age will be laid.

A corner of living heaven. Here the angelic hypostasis, lost by man, returned. Those who were honoured with even half an hour of standing every twenty-four hours found the highest lot in the Cathar heavens – the anointed one with the messianistic mark. And they performed the airy flight of the stage of immortality.

Here is eternity itself. What a privilege it was considered to be awarded with even twenty-four hours with the perfect ones on San Salvador!

Here man's aspirations were realized. There is nothing higher than San Salvador.

At the peak of San Salvador

The purest of pure heavens,
the most restful peace of Christ,
the heavens, higher than the heavens,
the most fragrant preaching of the Divinity–
without cliché veils, without words

Hither sails the transparent boat along the Reine
from the spheres of bridal divine existence.
The sea combines with the sky in one
and the spirit stands still in most admiring O!...

We are in the chambers of the heavenly Father,
here we died and were resurrected
and stand in embalmed flesh
in most restful flight.

Do not ask about silence and ecstasies,
on San Salvador questions are in vain.
Combine in most tender rapture,
the heavenly angel, the wretched monk.
Take care not to spill the oils
                    of the Bridal Chamber,
Enrapture yourself and enrapture the world.

Blessed are the storming peaks of San Salvador,
inhabited by the Divinity Himself.

◄§

18.

the **Knighthood**
of the Father
of pure love
is the battle
with the forces of Elohím

CRISTIANS OF THE SECOND COMING

- Among those who have acquired the Holy Spirit and the saints (even those glorified as relics) there was not one single perfect by virtue of mixed faith

- The Father of pure love chose the Slavic Theogamites and the Cathars

෴

THE IMMORTALS:

They are losing the sphere of our Father on earth. Losing the sphere is a catastrophe, while its retention is a great feat.

It is difficult to retain the sphere of the Father on earth. For the retention of the sphere they devote nine tenths of their time at the beginning stages of initiation to exorcism, the denunciations of the falsely-religious Elohim.

The knighthood of the Father of pure love is the battle with the forces of Elohim.

The pillars of our church should add the maximum of exorcistic efforts in order to retain the sphere of the sunny Father, for this increase the battle tenfold!

It is primitive to depict the Cathars as 'peaceful' or 'gentle'. The fathers waged an uninterrupted battle, and were found in the sphere of spiritual war with the prince of this world.

On earth there is not one being to whom the sphere of the Father of pure love would be given easily.

The pure ones waged a battle with passions, and the perfect ones – with Elohim.

*

Recognize the corruption to which you were subject in the first conversion.

Among those that have won the Holy Spirit and the saints (even those glorified as relics) there was not a single perfect one by virtue (who involuntarily accepted the light in the refraction of distorting mirrors). Not one was able to endure the steel of a flawless mirror.

Renounce the modelling of the first conversion.

– We renounce it.

Grey clouds are upon you... They will not part until the insight of the second conversion comes, the insight into the necessity to be born again, from on high.

Have the courage to be born again, professing your origin from the sunny Father of pure love.

The preceding will transubstantiate into the new life.

*

They summon me to refuse the accumulated spiritual riches and gifts of the Holy Spirit of the first conversion.

What, rich man, are you thinking about yourself? Your riches, your palaces are nothing before us. Leave them. That which is valued by the world is nothing before us.

If you knew, what treasure has been prepared for you! But we are not able to give it to you, until you refuse the old belongings.

– I am completely destitute in my seventieth year... Nothing... You will not deceive me?

[We have already been given so much! Is it really so little? New gifts – of love, the Holy Spirit, the new priesthood, new perspectives. New gates, the inspiration of all the church, the new shape of the Divinity. Is it really so little? The loving Father has been revealed. Poetic gifts, musical gifts... It is really so little? The highest spheres of prayer... Is it really so little?]

The second conversion begins with blessings

Christ began His preaching with blessings and your second conversion will begin with blessings.

A strong blow on the breast muscle. Feeblenesses, an almost panicky feeling...

The Catholics mastered this from the gospels: Christ is not of this world. But not even their ascetics, having rejected this world for the sake of blessings, knew another world, the world of Christ.

Until the internal chimeras of Rex Mundi which have penetrated into the depths have been removed, the sunny nature of the Father remains completely insignificant.

The expulsion of the chimeras did not occur in more than two thirds of even the perfect ones in the church.

ℋourly exorcism

Do not waste time for nothing. Perform hourly exorcisms in order to conquer souls for Our Divinity as quickly as possible.

The conversion of thousands of souls, that you seek, depends on your fervour to drive out the chimeras of the first conversion. Do not be afraid to be even thrice bankrupt. The notion of bankruptcy is from Elohim.

We are granting you the sunny regal treasure trove, possessed by none on earth, and you are afraid to lose a phial of out-of-date, dusty relics.

*

The path from pure one to perfect one runs through Golgotha. From perfect one to anointed one – through the second Golgotha, and from anointed one to immortal – through the third. From crucifixion to crucifixion the cross will become larger.

334

If you had seen what the second and third Golgothas are for Christ, the memory of the first (in Jerusalem) would have been erased.

Christ's suffering has been multiplied a million times in comparison with that which he experienced in Jerusalem.

*

As in the Bible the Jews consider themselves the chosen people, thus the Father of pure love chose the Slavic Theogamites and Cathars as the special summoned people of the sunny Divinity, worthy to convert humanity.

Have the courage to perform the feat of rejecting yesterday – the spiritual past. Do this not only for yourself, but for the souls longing for the great break. The sunny Divinity, as we imagine Him, is revealing Himself to humanity for the first time. The feeling of novelty will not disappear even for you.

Seek He who has still never been on earth. Then His gates will open instantaneously.

The revelation of the Father of pure love

Every person should reveal the Father of pure love for himself, experience the warmth of His rays, hear His voice.

You came to our Father. The preceding experience will be crossed out.

335

He who is able to perform the lofty feat of renouncing the world, and all that is in the world, will achieve perfection.

Only when the desire to build on earth disappears will he be able to build in heaven.

In the present world order the kingdom of the Father of pure love is impossible. The transformation of compositions is necessary.

Knocking at the gates prematurely you only push them away, because you unconsciously cause sorrows which they will not be able to endure due to unreadiness.

'Not of this world' means to desire nothing in this world (including the manifestations of Our Divinity). Being physically in the world, to be in spirit not of this world. Such is the stage of the pure ones.

The Father will reveal Himself to millions

When the measure has been fulfilled and the necessary number of souls have found the sunny ether of the gates of our Father, the Divinity will reveal Himself to millions.

Exceeding Wisdom found a method through which to convert five million with a sudden explosion, and after them the remaining humanity in the pre-apocalyptic years.

*

For priests and blessed messengers

Through the bilocation of the anointed sovereigns you perform a greater work than the construction of the church and the conversion of thousands.

The gift of bilocation will be given to several fathers, whom the immortals consider to have achieved perfection.

Ecstatic prayer

Prayer to the Father of pure love cannot be uttered in the order of the world (in the static form). The Holy Spirit prays ecstatically.

§

19.

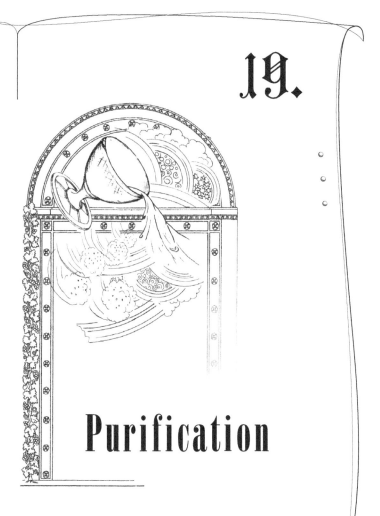

Purification

- The modelling of the pure one is possible only in the environment of the perfect ones

THE IMMORTALS:

In order for the Divinity to reveal Himself, erase your 'I' and expel the prince of this world from the interior,

where his forbidden reformation lies, continuous spectres, and chimeras, which will prevail over man. Prevailed over by them, he madly knocks at the forbidden doors, until he finally goes out of his mind and perishes eternally.

*

'Newly born every day' is the status of the Cathar perfect ones, because not an hour passes without the attack of the 'tailed aerial beasts'.

The pure ones = those who have defeated the spectres and chimeras.

It is possible to receive the modelling of the pure one (the true spirit of the Cathar) only in the environment of the perfect ones.

They ascended along the 15-stage staircase of purification for the sake of the modelling of purity.

$\mathcal{M}$ethods of purification

There exist tens and thousands of paths of the erasure of the old essence. Exceeding Wisdom gives a multitude of paradoxical staffs so that the devil is not able to seize them,

because the cunning one hunts for them, as he does the caduceuses, which fatally wound him.

It is necessary to accept one of the paths (meditation, prayer, repentance, illumination, service) and follow it in order to erase the adaptative reformation to the last drop.

'The pure ones' and 'the perfect ones' are stages inside Catharism, to a different degree free from the influence of the prince of this world.

$\mathcal{M}$ixing is inadmissible

Mixing is doubly dangerous, because it gives our enemy the chance to seize the gifts for his throne.

While even one mixed particle remains in the composition, the Roman church will be able to put ideas into the heads of millions, making itself out to be 'holy', 'the successor to the saints', and so on. Not mixing is worse than a death sentence for them. It stops their breathing.

*

Battle. Purify me, Father, with Your never-ending love...

To see one's neighbour with eyes of eternity; to see oneself with eyes of eternity; to grieve deeply, when the vision is paralysed; to seek to become kinder and to open the gates of the heart.

◄§

20.

the Secret
of the airy castles

- In our bilocational Holy Passion we did more for humanity than its reformers, thinkers, revolutionaries and rulers put together
- The bodies of those executed by Rome disappeared
- We did not fear the tortures, even though they were terrible

- The epoch of the Roman Inquisition and the Orthodox gestapo has come to an end
- Immortality is achieved as a stage of agapic love
- The consulamentum is directly connected with the action of the forbidden adaptative reformation

◦§

The truth about auto-da-fé

THE FIERY HIERARCHY:

e Montfor (having surrounded Montségur with a ten-month siege which, despite innumerable tortures and interrogations, finished with the shame of the crusaders) lit three fires.[65] 150 perfect ones and immortals entered the fire in the name of the Divinity of pure love...

What happened to them? The ever-burning candle is inserted into the hearts of the immortals. Are the immortal bodies able to burn?

The faces of the martyrs of Christ of pure love transformed and became wax in the tongues of flame.

Before the inquisitors stood living divinities: mysterious beings, newcomers from heaven, unknown to the world and to Rome.

As the firewood turned into ashes, the gigantic malicious insects were dispersed.

345

Transformed, having entered the fire of pure love by the baptism of Christ, they were raised to the heavens of Our Divinity.

Montfor participated in the persecutions of the perfect ones of San Salvador with permission of the Pope. After the siege of the second castle both he and his wife had already gone mad. The immortals came to them day and night, trampling upon their Roman wretchedness, and announced the will of the Divinity to this human-shaped worm.

The fear and paranoids of Simon Montfor increased from siege to siege.

The Divinity granted us immortal destinies, for which we first passed the baking in the fiery furnace.

The paths of renunciation of the world

Renunciation of the world is given by three paths: Peaceful sobriety, spiritual practice (1); Holy Passion, battle in the transcendental wilderness (2); or martyrdom (3).

The majority of the immortals were delighted by the regal Theogamic sum: the deepest sobriety in the first centuries (tenth and eleventh); transcendental battle, connected with the uprising of the prince of the world; the persecutions of the twelfth to the fourteenth centuries, the epoch of the glorious martyrdoms and iridescent wreaths.

*

346

Not the slightest fear before illnesses, death, thoughts. At San Salvador is the kingdom of Our Divinity and the illumination of sunny compositions for the immortal bodies.

$\mathcal{I}$N THE BILOCATIONAL HOLY PASSION

The Holy Passion is connected with bilocation and its highest stage – simultaneous residence in several bodies, worlds, and spaces.

Considering the fates of humanity in the post-Cathar period, it would be possible to say that, as a rule, we did more for humanity in our bilocational Holy Passion than its reformers, thinkers, revolutionaries, and rulers put together.

Bilocation is given as a gift of the renunciation of the prince of this world and his hateful modelling.

Soberly grow to hate lust and debauchery in its thousands of forms, and reject the unholy beginning. Become fragrant with the myrrhic aromas of immortal bodies.

Place the spiritual reality first in comparison with the physical (with an admixture of the modelling of the demiurge).

Make the spiritual world first for yourself. Reside permanently in the spheres of the spirit.

Conquer slavish fears, human thoughts and

speculative programmes, detaining you by ancestral methods in the webs of the prince of this world.

Again and again ascend into the bosom of Our Divinity, where you are met by the majestic constellation of the immortals of Montségur, Perpetouse, San Salvador, Béziers, Quermanco, Albi... the Gulag... [the enumeration of enlightened divine thrones would take up tens of pages.]

*A*uthority over the world belongs to the immortals

Henceforth authority over the world belongs to the immortals.

The Divinity Himself entrusted us with the staff of the control of humanity,[66] its leadership, in recent times.

In the wilderness of Perpetouse, at the hour of your second conversion, we promised to entrust our successors with the keys to the salvation of the world. Today we entrust them to our infinitely beloved children.

...We extend the staircase from earth to heaven for you. Ascend by it to the peaks of San Salvador, whence the sole access to the throne of the Father of pure love in the world.

Beneath the revealed fiery staircase are another two (according to the number of the castles standing here).

Only those who had passed a lengthy period of

trials in two lower-situated castles were admitted into San Salvador. The rank of the Salvador fathers was that of the 'immortals' and the 'anointed ones'.

The castle of the pure ones. A little higher – that of the perfect ones. Above them – those of the immortals and the anointed ones.

*

Do not expect practical instructions on spirituality. Instead of the regular rubrics and guidance which fall into the clutches of the Inquisition, take delight in the bliss of the spheres, generously granted by us.

It possible to distort the guidance as much as you like, thus the Torah and the Gospels. But not one unworthy can enter into the sphere, as they cannot enter San Salvador.

The secret of the airy castles

The secret of the airy castles lies in the blessed spheres of Our Divinity, in His reigning parousia, in the miracle of His presence and peace,

in the inexpressible bliss of dialogue with Him, the heeding of His word and the contemplation of His face.

Here, above the sky of San Salvador, the Divinity revealed Himself AS-HE-IS. It is impossible to say anything about Him apart from direct revelation; the recovery of sight of the blind, the perforation of the ears of the deaf, and the opening of the lips of the dumb.

Love, superior to the earthly... love, superior to itself... love never-ending and uncontainable conquered fears and doubts, scattered thoughts.

Blessed are those, who ascend by the staircase of pure love to the chambers of Our Divinity! The seals of the prince of this world are abandoned and dispersed.

> The immortals kindle the candle in the heart, they light the candles. Blessings, myrrhic fragrances, warm rivers of grace. PEACE.

*

The immortals agree to pass through death, to conquer our enemy 12 times, and to be resurrected.

> If humanity had known how beautiful our Father is in the radiances of the dawn of the rising sun, it would have thrice renounced the cunning one and agreed to sufferings, and even martyrdom, in order just to return to the bosom of the Father, in whose presence we delight for ever!

The stream of relic aromas

We enter the stream of relic aromas. Beneath us rest the imperishable relics of several thousand anointed ones and immortals.

Their bilocational spiritual bodies extend above

the world and proclaim the sunny Theocivilization, and the waxen immortal copies most restfully, regally and triumphantly repose in the burial vaults hidden from the world... The aromas, savoured by us, are from their imperishable relics...

The bodies of those, executed by Rome disappeared, which induced a triple terror in the inquisitors. You should have seen their haunted, drained faces, their shaking hands, while they fulfilled death sentences at the order of the bishops!

We did not fear tortures, although they were terrible; so terrible, that it is better not to recall them.

But, our child, the secret to victory over fears: immortal bodies and the modelling of Our Divinity.

When the immortal bodies conquer and dispel the worldly ones, physical suffering is perceived as bliss.

We give the seals and keys for it to you, to our successors.

*

The true church will rejoice. The Roman throne will collapse. Benedict is the last conservative on the throne. After him a file of liberals will definitely show its cosmic anti-christ essence and destroy the church.

With the destruction of the Roman whore and the Byzantine den, humanity will not remain in orphanhood. The church of the immortals will descend into the world and will be firmly established by the regal staff.

The authority of the cunning one will weaken. Our immemorial adversary is not able to do anything with the saints, whom he has pursued for millennia, delighting in his authority over them, considering himself 'omnipotent', able to malign them, to destroy them, to steal their gifts, to lay his phantoms, to address them as if slaves, to lay disgusting trials for them.

The epoch of the Roman Inquisition and the Orthodox gestapo has come to an end. There are no gulags, my son! Away, shadows of hell! Away, sincentric whirlwinds! The sun of Our Divinity stands above the new humanity!

The celebration of Theohumanity in the sunny Theocivilization

Of those who are beautifully adorned with relic aromas, those who rest in the earth across which you are now ascending with Father Paicy, just one would be able to conquer all the enemies of our Father.

Each of the immortals, having risen from imperishable myrrhic relics, will give the successors of the Divinity something from his compositions:

immortal pollen and wax, the vessel with myrrh-pouring oils.

Exult today and forever, my child: the celebration of Theohumanity in the sunny Theocivilization! The new creation of Our Divinity grows majestically!

The former man, with his city reservations and fatal programmes, will be transformed!

He will shed moving tears in night prayer. He will be inspired and ascend along the fiery staircase to the Tabor tabernacles of San Salvador, of the Father of Our Divinity, of the Christ of christs and the Mother of God of god-bearers.

*

Grow to hate dictatorship, grow to hate lust, and the order of the world with its mammon and earthly house-construction.

O, our child! How simple and how almost impossible it is to renounce the world, if, gazing from the heavenly heights, you see the level of your involvement in its order!

Become perfect. Renounce authority, apart from that given solely by the Divinity, the authority of love.

Entrust yourself entirely to the will of our Father, who is not only guiding, as in the guidance of the ancient and medieval ascetics, but combining into one, residing in the internal chalice of the heart.

What scores? What mammon? What philistine reckoning? Chastity is fragrant with the aromas of the Divinity.

The aromas and pollens of fifteen thousand heavenly flowers enter into the composition of the chaste one.

*

Worship of Exceeding Wisdom came second after the worship of our Father

Worship of Exceeding Wisdom came second in the Cathar castles after dedication to Our Father.

Exceeding Wisdom revealed the Father to us.

Exceeding Wisdom revealed the secrets of existence and the secrets of man.

Exceeding Wisdom came personified, led and inspired.

Returning to the bosom of the Cathar church, humanity finds the initial cover of Our Father and the Lady of our Exceeding Wisdom in the bosom of the perfect christs and the immaculate Theomaternity.

THE BROTHERHOOD AT MONTSÉGUR

What a brotherhood was born at Montségur! The love of our Father resided amongst the brothers.

Each of us received a revelation about the great superior love of Our Father.

Only His great love, superior and not defined by earthly limits, was able to send us into this peace.

But the explanation of the secret of this mysterious love required exceeding wisdom.

And how great was our bliss when, after the revelation of the Divinity, we began to see one another with His incomprehensibly beautiful eyes!

What a most heavenly brotherhood existed on earth, only half a mile from the fettering sleep of the entire humanity!

Elixirs of immortality do not exist. It is useless to seek them on other planets or in alchemical retorts. Immortality is achieved solely with the stage of agapic love between perfect brothers and sisters.[67]

With one look of a neighbour (even in the bilocational Holy Passion), the internal candles melted in bliss. The need for words faded. Communion was expressed in the shedding of the last drop, literally fountaining visibly.

Amongst us, the immortals, were several earthly kings, dukes, counts, three former bishops of Rome, tens of converted priests, and a multitude of common people who had achieved perfection in Christ through purity of heart.

$\mathcal{H}$ow we saw Christ

Now, after the combined contemplation of the face of the Divinity and our neighbours, see how we saw Christ –

the perfection of perfection! Christ, as He came to the mountain of the divinized, as our gaze awaited Him!

Christ is He who at the sight of whom the ever-burning candle begins to burn. The Mother of God is the eternally lighted candle in the interior.

The Mother of God is the immortal compositions and bodies. Christ is He who gives them.

Our myrrh-pouring imperishable relics are from the composition of the Bridal Chamber of Christ and the Mother of God.

*

For one hundred kilometres around San Salvador there was not one criminal or thief.

So many unhappy Barabbases literally dragged themselves to us! Or were dragged violently by the arms of the law, understanding that one residence at the foot of San Salvador was enough for complete healing.

The grace, emanating from our castles, was such that many were healed and purified several days before arriving at the mountain.

For the perfect ones it remained only to fulfill over us the mystery of the descent of the Holy Spirit.

The consulamentum is directly connected with the action of the forbidden adaptative reformation. The cunning one stole the treasure trove of the Holy Spirit from humanity, carried it to his throne and in a criminal fashion scattered it, having distributed the instrument to prohibited bearers.

The grace of the Holy Spirit and the fullness of His gifts descends only upon those who, having renounced the deformation by the prince of the world, thirst to be nourished by the pure springs of Our Divinity.

> Then may the Father of pure love bless the soul, returning to His bosom, with most restful peace. And may graceful and sunny streams of highest light in the never-ending gifts of the Holy Spirit descend upon it.

(The immortals replicate the secret prayer of the consulamentum, performed over the pilgrims of San Salvador).

The reason, why the Holy Spirit does not descend upon the Roman-Byzantine whore: being flesh from the flesh of the prince of this world, it is not able to accept from the Consoler of the Spirit.

Consolations come from the Holy Spirit, revealing the bridal raptures to those who will, on earth accept the cross of martyrdom of pure love and the destiny of the bride, hungering for the Bridal Chamber.

*

The cunning one has raised a fierce battle against us. Under the aegis of our Father we will emerge from it as victors!

> The wreath crowns the brows
> of those conquering the prince of this world.

Transform, humanity, in the fiery-winged eagle's flight of the immortal anointed ones of San Salvador!

The spiritual heart

Our child, see how beautiful is the spiritual heart of man! It is indeed an altar, undistorted by the cunning one.

The adversary succeeds in penetrating not more than twelve external castles. The remaining 132 remain unharmed, while the last 12 are inaccessible even to the thought of our enemy.

The enemy is not able to imagine, what treasure troves have been laid in the heart of the Godman.

Preserve, son-successor, the great treasure trove laid in your heart.

And you, our children: become possessors of the regal treasure trove of the Father, glorified for ever and ever.

Identify your neighbour – the most closed and inaccessible, inveterate and supreme sinner, hopeless from the point of view of the world – with the immortal spiritual treasure trove.

And the earthly subordinate slaves, holy fools under the yoke, will turn into perfect righteous men.

Peace be with you. Shine with the grace of the spiritual lamps in your interior.

*

Henceforth there will be no temples. The temple of Our Divinity is in the spiritual heart. In it is the altar, candle and face of the indescribable father surrounded by 144,000 christs great and small...

> Forever glorious is the church of our fathers –
> the immortal church of christs great and small!

Below, the bells begin to ring from the earth. Humanity rejoices with the revelation of Our Divinity.

What a fire blazes in the heart with the approach to the castle!

Our blessed sisters turned into wife-myrrhbearers and small God-bearers

How quickly our blessed sisters turned into wife-myrrhbearers and small God-bearers!

How often the Most Pure Mother of God Herself dwelt amongst us! She untwisted their braids, led round dances with us. She instructed us in the secrets, understood by them alone, our blessed wives in Christ, our sweetest helpers and irreplaceable consolers in sorrow.

Each of us prepared ourselves for the Bridal Chamber by communion with the beloved sisters and mothers.

The Holy Spirit evenly shared the gifts of Exceeding Wisdom between brothers and sisters.

THE FATHER OF PURE LOVE:

I will establish My kingdom on earth!

The delight in the divine incarnations is never-ending

Heavy is the cross borne on earth, but indescribable are the blessings, accompanying the cross. For their sake souls crave to enter the world again and again, by mysterious paths and not necessarily 'from the male seed and the female womb'.

In the sanctuaries of San Salvador are preserved the secrets of dozens of a kind *of immaculate conception*, performed in our heavenly experimental workshops.

The revealed blessings of the comforting (messianistic) incarnation make fearless before the face of death, illness, martyrdom.

Only in the immortal, eternal perspective man is able to find his true purpose and identity.

In the limits of the Judaic Elohim he is tormented by fear. The evident neurotism of the 84th civilization has ended with unsuccessful attempts to conquer psychological defeats and fears.

The delight in the divine incarnations is never-ending!

*

BLESSED IS THE THRONE OF OUR DIVINITY, giving immortal life here on earth, in thousands of the sweetest embodiments and metamorphoses!

BLESSED IS THE THRONE OF OUR DIVINITY, being built in the hearts of His immortal disciples!

Blessed is the throne of Our Divinity during the entrance into the Bridal Chamber!

– we proclaim, entering San Salvador.

Unheard-of exultation over San Salvador. At the corner of the tower are thousands of angels. The immortals surround us joyfully and bless us with an abundance of their grace, sending us legatary seals.

◄§

21.

Keys
to the transformation of man

- With embodiment every soul releases its divine particle, te-el', into the Holy Grail
- Every soul leaves a speck of her essence in the Holy Chalice
- Take the form of the bon hommes – the kind people
- The weakest place in your modelling is kindness

- The gift of modelling has been given today to the heavenly Designer, the perfect Architect of the Divinity

- The reason for which they drive out the Mother of God: in all of Her revelations the Most Pure One calls them to withdraw from the web of Rex Mundi

$\mathscr{K}$indness, of a kind not found on earth
(bonomism)

an should be loving (homo amores), but he must first change in his essence.

The gates of perfect purity... Disfigured from head to toe, in dirt and sand, man does not see himself, does not understand, how he needs ablutions.

They immersed me in delicate sleep and revealed kindness of a kind not found on earth (one of the gifts of Original Immaculateness).

Lust makes one embittered, Elohim turns one into a snake, the law enslaves, and fear neurotises. But kindness, as a consequence of original immaculateness, moulds a new essence – the bonomic essence.

Slavic philokalia (love for kindness) is indescribable kindness, of a kind not found on earth.

The synthesis of pure love and the incomprehensible kindness of the Divinity.

> The Cathars are those who have been preserved from different civilization: the newcomer-successors of the Hyperboreans, of Atlantis. Like the Slavic Theogamites, the Cathars perceived the practical spirituality from Andrew the First-Called and from Nightingale Mountain. But their roots run even deeper: in *the civilization of original immaculateness.*

*

The soul becomes indescribably kinder, when freed from thoughts and passions, when no lusts will prevail over it, when it has no 'programmes', and the devil loses his authority over it.

The Father created the first people from His last drop of most superior kindness

The Father, kindest of the kind, created the first people from His last drop of transcendentally beautiful, most superior kindness.

The bionomists are the successors of the kind people, ('the sons and daughters of the Bridal Chamber', as Christ said of them). Their kindness is amazing!

The holy Cathars desire to give us this superiorr kindness. They want us to lay holy kindness as the foundation of our spiritual path; issuing not from ancestral roots, but from absolute unworldliness; originating with the Father of pure love. This kindness is not enough. It should counter fundamentalist formality, malice, and so on.

𝒯HE CONDITIONS FOR BECOMING KINDER

To become kinder man needs:

1) birth from the Father of pure love (plus the realization of the second adaptative remodelling-corruption of Lucifer, who is the father of global evil);

2) acceptance of the origin of original immaculateness, giving absolute protection against sin, Lucifer, and the temptations of the prince of this world;

3) acceptance of Christ and Mary as the two perfect lamps of the 84th civilization.

It is especially important to worship Christ and Mary. Around them are settled 200 million sunny bon hommes – the martyrs of love, called the elite of the 84th civilization.

These 200 million last drops form the sunny Grail-85, from which comes the Godman, the Theoanthropos of the Theocivilization.

The Godman (christ, bon homme) is born in the shape of the Father of pure love (in opposition to the modelling of Rex Mundi) (1); in the shape of Christ and Mary (2); in the Great Church of Love (3); in the scheme of Exceeding Wisdom (4); in the bosom of the Theocivilization-III (5).

The 5 origins of the Great Church of Love

The true Great Church of Love, which had not been revealed to humanity, became as kind as the Inquisition became embittered, achieving a barbaric malice, that cannot be contained by human consciousness.

The Great Church of Love takes its origin from the Father of pure love (1); the creation of man from the last drop in the bosom of Theohumanity (2); the origin of original immaculateness (3); our Virgin Lady of Exceeding Wisdom, standing between the Divinity and His adversary (4); from the Second Golgotha of Solovky.

*

The spiritual world is full of models of indescribable kindness, which cannot come to earth because of a dense, impenetrable layer: the institutional 'tortoise shell'.

The Great Church of Love desires to reveal itself as an oasis of indescribable kindness.

The values of this world unconsciously embitter man. *Dictatorship zombifies, materialism* fixes him in rapacious foundations, *mammon* separates him from love, and makes him a cold and rational exploiter.

The Cathar civilization distinguished itself by its indescribable level of kindness, with which it conquered.

ℋOW TO ACHIEVE SUPERIOR KINDNESS

Indescribable, superior kindness is achieved by cleansing oneself of Elohim, the false creator (1); liberation from the church of Elohim (2); from the beginning of Elohim (original sin) (3).

By the acceptance of three bright origins: the Father of pure love (1), original immaculateness in the bosom of Exceeding Wisdom (2), and the Great Church of Love (3).

By the renunciation of Elohim, original sin, and the scholastic, dogmatic form of faith (phariseeism, maccabeeism, rabbinism, ritualism, ceremonial magic).

𝒯he universal categories of bonomism:

1) The spotless Father; 2) His church; 3) the bosom of original immaculateness; 4) the patronage of Exceeding Wisdom, controlling the world; 5) the Holy Grail (the chalice containing the compositions of divinized humanity).

*

With embodiment every soul releases her divine particle, te-el', into the Holy Grail.

The Grail is Christ, mixed with all the souls, descending to earth.

The transformation into Christ occurs in the Holy Chalice.

Every soul leaves a speck of her essence in the Chalice. It is connected with the heavens as with the Holy Grail.

The Holy Grail is the home of man, his spiritual temple on earth. And this temple exists.

Christ Himself, holding the Chalice in His hands and giving it to the Father, prays for all humanity;

He prays not only for the six billion inhabitants of earth but, as the Keeper of the Grail, holds them in His hands:

– What is this?

– The immortal particles of the six billion inhabitants of earth.

$\mathcal{M}$an, as he was created from the Last Drop of our Divinity

See man, as he was created from the Last Drop of our Divinity! The heart could not endure this miraculous outpouring of the most perfect beauty, the most perfect goodness, most perfect peace, and most perfect love.

It is possible to understand the enumerated qualities only in an enlightened condition through the action of the Holy Spirit. Constant enlightenment-superadmiration-illumination through the spirit is necessary to feel ecstatic in the damaged aethers of the order of this world and thus ascend to the original, primordial models of creation, avoiding the corruption of Elohim and the surrogates ('the hexameron', the Bible, the gospels, and so on).

How can you become a bon homme? How to become kinder, especially with the Russian chalice of phenomal embitterment, with the executioner's malice, professed for thousands of years (church rabbinism, the Gulag, formality, inflicted fears, paranoia, manias, conformism, squealing...)?

Accept the shape of the bon hommes – of the kind people.

Seek superior kindness.

The devil closes the eyes of man upon it, considering it as nothing, despising it as well as the pure love.

The efforts for bonomisation

Lust disgraces itself by opposing kindness. Lust and passion disgrace themselves by impeding the bonomite ideal, which should be raised to the archetype of the Godman.

Make no less effort for bonomisation (becoming kinder) than the effort that we made to liberate man from sin during the first conversion.

The cliches of elohimism still proclaim themselves exceptionally strongly. You are in the civilization of spiritual 'goners': people who have lowered themselves, embittered. Rationalism, materialism, and the other chimeras of the world defiled the primordial nature of man. It is liable to renewal.

Occupy yourself with deep internal reparation. The renewal of the internal man lies in the paths of superior kindness (1), love (2), peace (3), purity (4), and beauty (5).

The weakest place in your modelling is kindness. It is catastrophically insignificant! There is no consciousness of what happened to the soul during the adaptative remodelling.

The souls lost the hypostasis of the kindest angels: the cunning one extracted the pearl of bonomism from them.

The pearl is being inserted! Make it your ideal.

Direct your spiritual efforts so that the internal essence becomes kinder in the aforementioned conditions (the Father of love, unblemished by sin; original immaculateness; the Church of Love; Exceeding Wisdom).

Complete denial of the prince of this world and the acceptance of the cross are conditions of kindness.

On the spiritual path the cunning one will dev-ilize and embitter you. It is necessary to take the cross upon yourself, craving to shed the last drop.

THE CHALICE is understood as the vessel of Christ (1); as the vessel of all the inhabitants of earth, having given the last drop in their eschato-logical experience (2); as the last drop, which man should shed in his earthly experience (3). The last drop is as pure as crystal and possesses the *myrrhic composition* for its further enrichment in the Chalice.

*

*R*ussia will become the fragrant garden of paradise

Russia will become a fragrant garden.

The goal of your residence outside Russia is to nourish the seeds that you have sown, otherwise the enemy will forbid the crop during your presence.

Your absence, your Holy Passion conditions, your love for Russia, will lead to the sudden sprouting of the crops, and the enemy will not be able to hack them down and destroy them.

*T*he Heavenly Queen will model man as he is before the eyes of the Divinity

The Russian chimeras (Stalinism, fascism, nation-alism, the agents of the KGB) will be dispelled in-stantaneously. God's Exceeding Wisdom will do this. Summon your Lady, the Fiery-winged Sophia in the archetype of Slavic Theogamism.

Summon another Christianity, another church.

Summon the holy Cathars, the successors of Slavic Theogamism,

and in literally several years they will mould a new holy Rus'.

The gift of modelling has been given today to the heavenly Designer, the perfect architect of the Divinity.

The heavenly queen will model man as he is before the eyes of the Divinity, according to the shape of that modelling which she has accomplished with you.

I see the Russian Seraphite being modelled. How beautiful, beautiful, beautiful, he is!!!

*

Russia will call you, will see you, and in its own time will resort to your aid and patronage. You will still do much for Holy Rus'.

Keep yourself in seclusion from diabolical attacks. Your seclusion does not mean the belittling of your mission, but its transition to the most high quality.

During several years of seclusion you will do more than during 20 years of active service in Russia and around the whole world.

The reason for which they drive out the Mother of God is that Her bonomite peace contradicts that of Catholicism. This is the peace of metanoia, returning man to the bosom of initial purity-kindness-holiness-love-peace (2).

In all Her revelations the Most Pure One calls upon people to withdraw from the web of Rex Mundi, which is impossible for the authorities of the church.

Christofascism, the malice accumulating in Holy Rus', will be dispelled by the bush of bonomism. The strongest means against the embittered evil spirits, with their xenophobia, is the bonomic fullness of pure love, the peace of another God.

It is impossible to build a beautiful Russia without spiritual renewal.

22.

the **Pillars**
of the cathar path
to perfection

THE IMMORTALS:

t is impossible to kill the immortals by sword or bullet. It is impossible to line up and take aim at us.

Master, *adored of adored ones* (the address to the loving ones), the science of the anointed Chalice. Unceasing, infinite transubstantiation. The unceasingly reflecting Divinity. Man, unceasingly perfecting himself.

The process of Theohumanity as the dynamic and the science of sciences of the Holy Grail. The 1500 stages of transubstantiation from man to Divinity and from Divinity to divinized man.

*

Christ did not die, but transubstantiated. The disciple performs the answering transubstantiation into Christ.

The Mother of God did not die, but was transubstantiated into the most divine body, corresponding to Her most supreme anointing.

The stage of the perfect one presupposes the imperceptibility of the transition, like a miracle from the side of the perceiving one: resurrection from the dead, the ascent to the heavens from the Assumption Bed.

Meditation on the Chalice as the transubstantiating vessel

Blessed is he who has passed the 1500 stages of transubstantiation in the Holy Grail. Constant meditation on the Chalice as the transubstantiating vessel.

The earth is the chalice. Man is in the form of the chalice. In the interior of a neighbour the chalice is unraptured. In the hands of the anointed sovereign the Chalice, according to the number of transubstantiations, is equal to the sum of souls descending into the world.

> Drink the never-ending Sweetest wine,
> transubstantiating into myrrh!

*

The perfect ones achieved the stage of the anointed ones by meditating on the Chalice.

The last drop on the peak gave us the most blessed transition into the divinity of the neighbour, the divinity of the earth renewing itself, creation being cleansed, man reviving.

The key to immortality: there should be no transition. On earth the Divinity grants the highest of blessings, accessible to the sunny Seraphites, His faithful sons and daughters.

> Life in the Bridal Chambers,
> residence in the perfect chambers
> on earth as in heaven.

On earth more than in heaven. In heaven more than on earth.

The beautiful ones crave the ascent from earth to heaven. Passing through the preparations in the castle of the celestial Grail, suffer more than is possible in heaven: descend to earth for the mastery of its incomprehensible mysteries, hidden from the noninitiated.

The 15 staircases of transubstantiation

There exist 15 staircase of transubstantiation, and in each are 15 stages (15x15 = 225: a holy number). At the 225th (the stage of Christ, Mary, Euphrosinia, Innokenty, Seraphim and the fiery hierarchy of Solovetsky, the Cathar perfect ones) the transition is perceived as a release from bonds, the Bridal Bed.

From the first to the fifth staircases – the pure ones; fifth to tenth – the perfect ones; eleventh to thirteenth – the anointed ones; fourteenth to fifteenth – the immortals.

The fifteenth staircase is the regal pleroma in the golden wreath. The fullness of the Father. The bride in white garments. The Bridal Chamber.

*

Staircases 1 to 5 are catharsis, purification from the adaptative remodelling. The most mysterious stage! Some can pass it in the present age.

So many illuminating insights and spiritual illuminations await! So much renunciation of Lucifer awaits here and there in the wildernesses of the world, striking against his mimicking locusts... Alas, their army is everywhere in this most bitter, most beautiful of worlds.

The fifth staircase of perfect purity. With the help of the anointed ones the stage of complete unworldliness has been achieved.

Is it possible in the world, outside seclusion? With the condition of victory over five enemies: three personal (dictatorship, lust, mammon), and two universal (rationalism, materialism).

Unworldliness, the renunication of the prince of this world, the readiness to endure persecutions, slander and blows, the mission of the lamb-anointed sovereign, taking weak souls to yourself and dragging them to the mountain... Yes, for some.

Against the unlawful authority above one's neighbour (authoritarism) – the transubstantiation into one's neighbour, the readiness to die for brother and sister, for son or daughter.

ℳilitant virginity

Against lust − militant virginity. Nonacceptance of all kinds of refined debauchery: lust, libido, arrogance... The cancellation of personal and ancestral programmes, cosmic zodiacal prescriptions.

Complete virginity for the acquiring of the Holy Spirit.

Complete virginity for service to the Holy Spirit in Theohumanity.

Complete virginity for comparison to Christ.

Complete virginity for the stage of invulnerable in spiritual battle.

Such a person cannot be killed by sword, bullet or arrow.

Against mammon − unselfishness. Man as the highest value.

For the attainment of the Holy Spirit is necessary the absolute scorn of the world by the spirit, the dispersion of its abstracts: dogmas, territories, personal and state interests...

Having become blind to all that you saw earlier, I perceived that which I hadn't seen before − and was blissfully happy.

Against rationalism (including religious) − illumination of the spirit! The potential of the Divinity, partially opened in the storerooms of the spiritual heart.

Against materialism – heavenly spirituality, revealing itself again and again, never-endingly. The insatiable hunger for more, the ceaseless movement to the heaven of heavens.

THE MOST high heavenly sphere. THE MOST Pure Virgin. SUPERnatural grace. The readiness to renounce one's own yesterday with ease and to start from the beginning,

understanding that the previous one will painlessly transubstantiate into the new.

Without the stage of the Infant God (for some it comes at 5 years, for others at 15, 50, and even 100) it is impossible to achieve perfect transubstantiation.

Rejoice, Infant God, in the cradle of Bethlehem! Exceeding Wisdom has transubstantiated you in the hands of the Most Pure Mother and Joseph the Carpenter.

Throngs of angelic ranks above your cradle. The peace of Bethlehem from eternity.

Against distant idol-worshipping forms of faith – the bliss of combination as the consequence of transubstantiation 'I and you are one. O...'

Love transubstantiates, dying in one's neighbour and being reborn in him (the last drop).

15,000 last drops − 15,000 transitions from life to death and from death to life, after which the stage of immortality is achieved.

The transition is perceived painlessly, as a tearing from earth to heaven, as even greater bliss.

𝓘 AND YOU ARE ONE

'I and you are one' is on the lips of the lamb ready to accept upon himself his imperfect neighbour.

The address to the Father of pure love:

> O, most perfect of perfect ones,
> most divine of divine ones
> the divine Divinity
> I and you are one. O…

The Divinity of divinites in the inspirations of Theomatrimony and in the nights of the newly-wed overflows into humanity. Humanity achieves the stage of divinity, enriching the superworldly regal Grail in the hands of our Divinity and His Christ.

'I and you are one', and the cunning one in the brotherhood of the pure and the faithful, in the assembly of the Great Church of Love.

𝓣he stages of the fullness of the universum

For victory over the prince of this world it is

necessary to achieve the stage of the fullness of the universum through the worship of Exceeding Wisdom.

Despite the never-ending chimeras, phobias, traumas, craters, nets, and temptations, steadily follow the orders of our Divinity, laid in the golden book called the Universum.

At this stage the soul lives on earth as in heaven, according to the prayer of Christ of the Jerusalem period, inscribed in the four gospels.[68]

Is it possible to achieve the fullness of the universum? The gospel of Christ, Mary, and Their perfect disciples (the never-ending file of which has been inscribed in the scrolls of the Great Church of Love) answers 'yes':

On earth it is possible to find the fullness of the universum through direct entrances in the rays of light of Our Divinity.

Such is the most generous and most merciful Exceeding Wisdom, pouring out the sun of perfect speculations on Her children.

How difficult it is to achieve the stage of compliance with the universum! So many sacrifices are required, so many prejudices must be parted with! It is necessary to go against so many habitual norms and rules of the order of the world, to pass through so many personal insights and illuminating enlightenments!

Withdrawal from the order of the world, with its unconscious norms mastered with the mother's milk, is an incomparable feat.

Fearlessness in the daily ascent to the higher stage is necessary, without glancing backwards, without the fear to tear oneself away.

He who is unable to take upon himself the act of metanoia, not recognising oneself in the objects of yesterday, will not rise further than the first staircase and will remain at the foot of San Salvador Verdadero.

*

Our staff of the immortals, the staff of the anointed ones, is a pledge that the Grail XXI, Catharism XXI and the Great Church of Love XXI will give a generous multitude of immortals. Your brothers and sisters who have left the world before you await them with great desire.

The mother Euphrosinia prepares places for you at the gold thrones, at the immortal meals.

She does not descend from her cross, so that each of those who, revere her divinely inspired and regal greatness, are able to fearlessly pass a number of determined stages.

O, there is no formal mathematics! Today – the collapse into nonexistence. Tomorrow – divine existence... The arithmetic calculation remains for the high ranks of the immortal Grail.

They do not take their eyes from the adored ones. The adored ones will sin no more. The adored ones are always before the eyes of Our Divinity.

We are prepared to come to the aid long before we hear your hermitary cries: 'Father, help me.... I can't do anything more'.

The passing of 15x15 = 225 transubstantiations, experienced in the framework of one embodiment of lives and deaths, resurrections and regenerations, makes the contrasting transition unnecessary.

For he who has ascended to the last stage, the Kingdom of God has been achieved on earth.

Blessed is he crowned with the regal wreath at the stages 200 to 225! His 12 sunny heavenly bodies have been revealed.

At the stage of the pure one is the lighting of the spark and the wick (1). At the stage of the perfect one are the candles in the heart (from small to great) (2). For the anointed ones, the lighting of the sunny disk (3); and the bush (the whole essence in the fire of the Holy Spirit) for the immortals (4).

The internal renaissance

The transition (overcome by the immortals) is the internal renaissance.

Belonging to the Great Church of Love and dispersing the Roman-Byzantine chimeras helps to ascend the stages steadfastly, despite any distracting circumstances...

To pass 225 stages – regeneration and rebirth (birth from on high in the Slavic church mentality) in order to avoid the transition connected with physical anabiosis, with the death of corporal processes.

The goal of the path to the Cathar castles is not salvation, but immortality

The goal of the path to the Cathar castles is not salvation, nor even divinization, but immortality. It is possible for fervent disciples who have fulfilled the programme outlined by us and revealed to humanity for the first time.

Do not endeavour to go by your own paths. No less than ten anointings are necessary from ten perfect teachers (the stage of each exceeds that of the previous).

* * *

The 15 stages of the 225 of the accession to the universum of the cross, and the 15 stages of the manifestation of the Chalice, understood as the temple (the universum of Our Divinity, corresponding to them.

Euphrosinia, Seraphim Solovetsky, and Innokenty

Baltsky achieved the 15th stage of the cross and the Chalice, the peak of the acquisition of the Holy Spirit with the gift of the stage of the immortal.

The immortal returns unalterably as reigning, invulnerable. The immortal does not depart. The immortal remains in divine existence.

The small sun, the microscopic sunny disk, even in the shape of a barely visible speck in the spiritual heart. The wick will be lit from the spark. And from it – the candle. And the whole essence will be embraced by sunny light. He who has been filled with it will become a sun,

like the Father – the sun of suns, Christ – the sun, the Holy Spirit – the sunny bride, the Mother of God – the Bride clothed in the sun (Revelation 12).

Crave to clothe yourself in sunny vestments after passing the first five stages.

The staircase:

1-5 – perfect purity.

6-10 – perfect love with the mastery of the universum of the Cross, the Chalice and selfless devotion, service to the world in the shape of a pure one.

11-12 – perfect peace, one with the heavenly particles, one with Christ.

13-15 – service as multiplication of Christ.

*

Modern man has been sealed from head to toe. According to the number of the 225 castles, 225 impassable doors, before each of which is a tireless guard of the enemy... Knock until one is heard? Push one's way through?

The sun of the Father of pure love will melt the ice and unseal the mysterious entrances.

Glorification of the Father of pure love is the source of liberation from thousands of chimeras attacking day and night, the source of great sobriety.

Elohim is the master of chimerization, falsification, mimicry, deception and the sealing of man. In his programmes for the Adamite, the role of zombified marionette, doomed to annihilation, has been prepared...

He who came 'from nothing' will remain nothing.

He who originates from the Divinity of divinities, in whom the countenance of our Father has been imprinted flawlessly and (O our beloved) undamaged, will achieve perfection in the stages of divinization.

In our own time we will accept him in regal halls with the words:

'Our beloved, welcome! Join our meal. Settle yourself amongst us as if you were at home'.

Our authority over human creation is absolute.

The authority of love is given with the renunciation of the dictatorship of one's neighbour.

I see how the immortals perceive us from the peak of San Salvador. They fill us, like small chalices, with sunny light. Mysterious anointings.

✍

23.

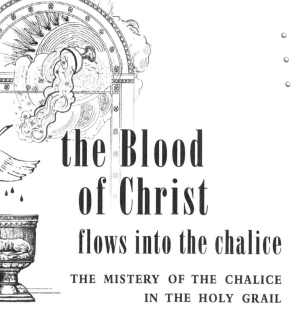

the Blood of Christ
flows into the chalice

THE MISTERY OF THE CHALICE IN THE HOLY GRAIL

• Divinization – through partaking

• The Chalice suddenly becomes invisible

• The pharisees hunted the Holy Grail more
  than they hunted Christ

• The Jews dispatched tens of secret agents in search
  of the Chalice

- The blood of the Lamb crystallised into most fragrant myrrh immediately with the outpouring into the Chalice

- In their diabolical minds they understand the Grail as something more

- The men of the Chalice considered he, whose heart took the shape of the chalice, to be perfect

~§

THE IMMORTALS:

chalice of Christ! His burden. His load... The Chalice of chalices.

WHAT IS THIS?
The treasure trove of treasure troves
    of Our Divinity.
Captivating grace,
the most admiring chalice.

The last drops... How many are there? Never-endingly, innumerably many! Each sounds in the heart with torturous, sweetest pain. Each cuts the lungs, opens the vessels, transforms the essence.

'I cannot do more... Stop!!!' Shedding... There are five, ten, one hundred, one thousand, one hundred thousand, one million of them!... There are 'more and more' – never-endingly many.

The greatest 'more and more' can be understood as the prayer of prayers in the church of the Holy Grail.

After the wilderness there is more. Against 'no, I cannot', against the ban on the bearing of the cross – the credo of he, who has been enlightened by the spirit, this craving to drink more and more from the fullness of the Cross, from the fullness of the Chalice of Christ.

Joseph and the Most Pure One repeated: 'Five, ten, one hundred... one million last drops!'

Every drop of blood, flowing from His flesh, is the last.

With each drop the value of His blood multiplies, because His Holy Passion, His divine suffering, increases.

Every drop is absolute value.

But from drop to drop the value becomes more than absolute, superior to itself.

'More and more', boundlessly, limitlessly, until the essence transubstantiates into the Divinity... But even then 'more and more'.

The Divinity turns into something more – into the Divinity-more-than-He-himself. But even then 'more and more'!

The perfect Divinity dissolves Himself in creation, gives the last drop to those, who need it...

The harder it becomes for Him on the Cross, the higher the value of each drop, most precious.

From one grain, from a millionth particle of the drop, the world would have been saved. But they pour out never-endingly.

And only one thing remains – more and more in the superabundance of grace.

There is nothing more torturous and more beautiful.

Having once partaken of the mystery of the shedding of the Chalice, you repeat only: 'more and more'.

*

The agonizing interval of expectation between the shedding of the drops lasts a second, a minute, an hour, eternity...

Shedding does not stop in the wilderness, in communion, in grace, in combination, or in loneliness. The 'more and more' of the Holy Passion is the peak of the Holy Passion.

Five, ten, one hundred times they repeated during the meals of the Chalice:

> O, more and more
> O, there is nothing more beautiful
> O
> Exultation of pure love
> Myrrh is shed into the Chalice
> O, more and more
> O my Beloved O
> O exultation of pure love!

> The perfect Divinity of Christ
> washed suffering humanity.
> From the lips of Christ's disciple
> falls only one word:
> O my Beloved O!
> More and more...

How could even one drop flow away into the sand? Not one of His words, uttered in the earthly days, was erased.

In the most eternal Gospel the word of Christ has been recorded to the last with myrrhic letters.

His blood, having transubstantiated into myrrh, has imprinted itself to the last drop in the Chalice and is preserved as the sacred object of the 84th civilization.

The sun of suns of the 85th myrrhic civilization of Christ's Chalice will shine from it, when the renewed composition of the Seraphite becomes one with the composition of the Holy Grail.

*

Joseph revealed himself unexpectedly... He came from heaven-knows-where during the hoisting of the cross. At the greatest moment of the Holy Passion the Father sent Joseph with the chalice, as angel-keeper.

When the Saviour was exhausted from His sufferings, and bloody tears flowed in streams from

His eyes, the Holy Passion Chalice of Our Divinity came to His aid.

The Chalice, like a mother, took Him into its embrace.

The Chalice became His new flesh, bearing in its vessels no longer blood but most fragrant myrrh.

The Chalice is the God-bearer of His second coming.

Exceeding Wisdom made it that no one noticed Joseph's approach. It was as if he remained invisible. Nor did anyone see the Chalice.

Confusion reigned among the rabbis. The heavens closed, and there came a universal darkness.

Only the Chalice shone.

The Mother of God, three wife-myrrhbearers, John the Theologian, and Joseph of Arimathea...

The Chalice and the holy Joseph served as the centre of Golgotha. The Mother of God was the personified Chalice. John the Theologian was Her vessel.

The Holy Grail collected the most precious blood of Christ from the first to the last drop.

Not one drop fell outside the vessel. If the blood splashed onto the surrounding people it was miraculously gathered in the Chalice...

The meaning of the crucifixion is not 'sacrifice

for sins', but mysterious transubstantiation.

The myrrhic blood of Christ is preserved in the Chalice. Christ did not die, but transubstantiated.

𝒢radular entrances

Gradular entrances of the Chalice give from the throne of Christ the power of the control of the world.

The mystery of the Chalice is connected not with the recollection of the earthly days of the Jerusalem period, but with the Eucharist for the Grail.

Eucharistman becomes of one blood with Christ, one with Him.

The composition of the blood is restored and becomes myrrhic.

Melchizedek and the partaker revere the mystery of Golgotha, as the outpouring of a million last drops:

> More and more...
> O never-endingly
> O blessedly
> O there is nothing higher...

The mystery of Golgotha shakes the being and causes the answering Holy Passion, the acceptance of the Cross, and the shedding of the answering last drop.

The soul, stunned and drawn into the mystery of the last drop, craves only one thing – to fall onto the Cross and to be dissolved with the Lamb.

And only thus is the mission of the anointed sovereign on earth fulfilled..

Divinization – through partaking from the Chalice. The Divinity combines with humanity with the shedding of the Last Drop. Through the answering drop humanity combines with the Divinity.

Perfect divinization is the ability to ascend Golgotha behind Christ and shed one's blood to the last drop.

Such are the immortals.

*

The Chalice was preserved as the greatest holy object.

One of the secrets of the Chalice: it suddenly becomes invisible. It reads hearts flawlessly, and when someone unworthy appears, with impure thoughts, the vessel mysteriously disappears.

The pharisees hunted the Holy Grail more than Christ. The Chalice induced mortal terror in them.

The rabbis were afraid of Christ for the denunciation of the 'synagogue of Satan', the revealing of the secret origin of the Judaic priesthood from the devil.

But they feared the Chalice even more. The Chalice was a hallucination for the rabbis, and plunged them into madness.

Around all Israel was borne a rumour that the blood of Christ had been collected into the Chalice, therefore it was useless to seek His flesh, whether He had been reburied in the tomb in Jerusalem or raised to heaven...

The Jews sent tens of secret agents in search of the Chalice, and they were literally run off their feet arresting witnesses, those who had heard something about the Agapes of the Holy Grail.

They hunted the Chalice as they later hunted the holy relics. Nothing attracted the pharisees more than the mystery of the Chalice. They saw the victory of the 'Holy Israelite', their divinity, in its possession.

Global phariseeism desired to take away the Chalice, to appropriate it for itself and through it find authority over all humanity.

*

Immediately, with its outpouring into the Chalice, the blood of the Lamb crystallised into most fragrant myrrh

and its smell resounded in thousands of worlds.

The Holy Chalice is the temple, altar, and place of the presence of the Second Christ, parousia.

The mystery of the Chalice is performed when the Holy Grail imparts the particles of Christ into the chalice of Melchizedek.[69]

Who are you?
The scattered particles of Christ,
the priests of Melchizedek.

There is no external, distanced chalice. The chalice turns into the Holy Grail, and the Holy Grail into the chalice of Melchizedek, only when all the being of the disciple is anointed with myrrh and turns into the chalice.

Upraised hands and celestial divine existence exits witness the transubstantiation of the Adamite into the Seraphite, the living chalice of Christ.

Conditions for the completion of the meal

Many of the Melchizedeks of the Church of pure love do not understand the mystery of the Chalice and are not able to complete it, despite the authentic texts of marvellous beauty, corresponding to the divine existence meals in the castles of the Holy Grail.

Formal treatment of the Chalice is impossible. Initiation into the secret of the Chalice is necessary, recognition of the mystery of the Holy Grail:

the blood of the Lamb, gathered to the last drop at Golgotha, transubstantiated into myrrh and existing in divine existence. The constant astonishment of the heart[+], crucifixion[+], participation[+] and involvement[+] in the mystery of Christ.

WHAT IS THIS?
The mystery of Christ,
the transubstantiation
            of invaluable blood into myrrh.

O Beloved O
O, there is nothing higher.
Myrrh is shed...

An ecstatic pre-Eucharist condition is necessary. For this, absolute purity of the heart, full disconnection with anything worldly, and easy gradular entrances into divine existence.

The mystery of the Chalice cannot be accomplished indifferently. For the Holy Grail manipulations and words are not important. Significant is he, who achieves a level of readiness. The manifestation of 144 internal castles is important. The manifestation of the vestments of the Most Holy God-bearer. The manifestation of Christ from the preceding Eucharist. The manifestation of the seals of the Great Church of Love on the brow and in the heart. The manifestation of the saint, glorified by the whole being of the devotee, and not only in words.

Without the enumerated conditions the mystery of Christ is not accomplished. The blood of the Lamb is not shed into the Chalice, and as a consequence the answering last drop is not shed as well.

The heavens are closing. The angels remain indifferent. Manipulations with the chalice are called falsification and ceremonial magic, and do not differ from phariseeism.

Understand, Melchizedeks of the Church of the anointed ones, how necessary the worship of the Holy Chalice is.

*

The third Rome and the Vatican fear the Holy Grail. Not one saint (and even Christ Himself, if He had appeared in the retinue of the great saints to denounced them) was so terrible for them. In their minds they understand the Grail as something more than Christ of the first coming.

The Vatican understands: the Holy Grail deprives its ritual magic of power.

The absolute manifestation of Christ in Theohumanity

The Grail, the chalice of the blood of Christ = the absolute manifestation (100 out of 100) of Christ in Theohumanity.

Christ was not understood in the earthly days, incognito. They ask: 'Messiah? Lord?' They betray Him. They inquire, investigate: who He is, from whence He came. At last they seek His death and hand Him over for villainous execution...

Christ in the Chalice is absolute exultation, the crowned victor.

*

The meals of the Holy Chalice in the castles of the Grail are meditative and night and day

The meals of the Holy Chalice in the castles of the Grail are night and day meditative glorifications of the Second Christ, dwelling in His church, from the face of the church of the saints, the Great Church of Love.

The Grail multiplied in divine existence: $1\times12\times12=144$. May this mysterious number be on your lips. Do not release the 144 castles from your memory.

In the lands of Catalonia and Occitania the 144 Cathar castles were visited by the Holy Chalice.

There were 144 great keepers of the Chalice, of whom no more than three are known to you.

The church of the Holy Chalice has been concealed

As the Grail in the hands of Joseph of Arimathea was miraculously concealed from the rabbis, so the church of the Holy Chalice has been concealed from adulterers and thieves for two thousands years.

And to the question 'Where is the history of the Holy Grail? Where are the keepers of the Chalice?, we will answer: our child, they are innumerably more than the priests of Rome and Byzantium.

Adore the Chalice, / hold the Chalice in your hands, / raise the Chalice in the Holy Passion, / shed the last drop.

Melchizedek holds the Chalice of Christ, and the Most Pure One Herself takes it into Her hands like a little Infant God.

The Eucharist is taken into the internal Chalice.

Proclaim: Your interior becomes the chalice of Christ!

> The eucharist is taken[+] in the 144 internal castles, the drops of myrrh multiply[+] 144 times.

The pneumatology[70] of the Holy Chalice teaches of the fullness of the presence of Christ in the holy gifts, about the mysterious composition, about the presence of Our Divinity in the Chalice during the accomplishment of the mystery of mysteries.

> The fullness of presence, pleroma – for the true witness.

The Theogamic Grail today is borne to the new Holy Rus'. The meal of the Holy Chalice smashed the hypnosis of the pharisees.

𝒫.𝓈.

Christ's Chalice was at San Salvador no less than one thousand times!

The immortals partook from the Chalice night and day, worshipping the Chalice. Their existence passed around the Grail.

The highest anointed sovereigns (christs great and small) do not release the Chalice from their hands, feeding solely from it, because in it is the fullness of the Divinity, the fullness of Christ, the fullness of the church, the fullness of existence, the fullness of all creation.

*

Our succession from Slavic Theogamites and ancient men of the Chalice, holy pilgrims, bearers of the fullness of the grace of absolute existence of Christ in the Chalice.

The men of the Chalice considered he, whose heart took the shape of the chalice, to be perfect. To such a person the rank *of perfect one* was given by the white elders.

The elders taught: it is one thing to see the chalice (the spiritual heart) in the interior; it is another to perceive the spiritual heart as the living Grail, in each of the castles of which is shed the answering last drop (the stage of the perfect one and the anointed one).

*

THE IMMORTALS:

Shed your blood into the Chalice of Christ, O John... Remember the mystery of the Chalice and answer by the Last Drop (the transcendental Holy Passion). Shed your answering last drop into the Grail. Your composition is sufficiently pure for the last drop to crystallize into myrrh and dissolve in the treasure trove.

*

It was indescribably difficult for the Virgin Mary to think about the Holy Grail after Golgotha and Jerusalem.

The heavenly Queen avoided the transubstantiated Christ into the Chalice, as knowing Him well in the earthly days....

But when the adored Bride came to Nightingale Mountain with the Theogamic vessel in Her hands, the mystery of the shedding of the last drop was revealed to Her in its fullness, and She craved more and more.

*

May the anointed sovereigns of the Chalice enter peace. The mind will transubstantiate and transform in the castles of the Grail. 144 anointings, the grace of the keepers of the Holy Grail and the fullness of the presence of Christ within it. Amen.

The fragrance of myrrh has been dissolved over San Salvador.

◄§

24.

the Gospel
of San Salvador

- It is possible to see our Father only with pure, undefiled eyes
- Reveal the Father of pure love for yourself
- He who sees our Father will see nothing more
- It is necessary to become pure to see the Father of heavenly purity clearly

- Purity, as the longed-for ideal, is never-ending
- The earth is the Chalice in the hands of Our Divinity
- The Chalice is the hidden interior of the Divinity
- The earth is full of the Last Drops of Our Divinity

☙

04.09.2007 Costa Brava

THE IMMORTALS:

he Godman, reconstituted in Christ, is able – like the Divinity – to conceive Theo-humanity.

The seeds of billions of souls in the universes may come from one immortal.

The sacred heart of the immortal begets the ecumenes of never-ending worlds.

𝒫urity

Which of the earth dwellers is able to ascend the staircase of purity? Whose interior shines through with the immortals bodies of the Father of Lights?

You have advanced no further than the first stage and have already begun to groan and sigh: you say that this is the limit and nothing more is possible.

But after this first stage are another fourteen to the fullness of virginity!

413

The enemy himself at the first stage shook and blew off, snapped a poker across his forehead and pulled away with a hoe.

*

Which of the earth-dwellers dares to discuss the pure ones? Even if they thrice called them 'Cathars', 'perfect ones', 'perfects', and attributed to them these or those characteristics, according to the guidance and dossier of the Roman inquisitors... Only the pure ones see the pure ones clearly.

It is still necessary for man to cleanse himself never-endingly, until he achieves the level of the newborn infant.

See how pure is the newborn and what fullness of the Divinity shines within him!

Barely every second of those born on earth is worthy to be laid in the cradle in Bethlehem and to dwell in the hands of the Most Pure Mother of God.

Christ the Infant God imprints Himself flawlessly within him.

𝒞ATHARSIS

It is possible to see our Father only with pure, undefiled eyes, for which pass again and again through the stages of purification.

CA-THAR-SIS! Call it 'ablutions in white fonts', 'repentance with the bearing of fruits', the purification of the internal being with the absolution of sins. Purification, multi-staged catharsis.

Desire to become purer than yourself of yesterday.

Investigate the potential of purity, great ascetic or prayerful fervour in yourself.

Preserve undefiled purity of mind, heart, internal temples, vessels, fibres, vibrations, thoughts.

The Father of pure love can imprint Himself only in pure vessels.

About our adored Father...

He, who sees Him clearly, will want to see nothing more.

He, who has known His love, is the vessel of His love.

He who has known His exceeding wisdom, will say, stretched before Him: 'Father, I crave... that the light of Your love is lit in the dark caves'.

The world DOES NOT KNOW the Divinity of divinities. The world DOES NOT KNOW Our Divinity. Orphans and widows, those abandoned and alone. O, if you knew and loved our Father!

Your vision has been sealed, your hearing has been closed, and your hearts have been locked.

Our enemy from time immemorial, the prince of the world, the biblical Elohim once rejected the

Father. And the Father rejected him. The heavens of pure love seemed to him to be something like exile. And the Father, taking pity on him, expelled him from heaven.

*

Before your gaze is the den of Perderodes. The spiders' nets to this day hold onto thousands of idle tourists. It has never occurred to them that, literally two hundred metres above Perderodes, dwell the fiery tabernacles of the Father of pure love, the sanctuary of Our Divinity.

Thus it is in the world. The 'Perderodes' of the old faith, the abandoned and accursed fortress, yawning with demons and vampires, forbids the ascent along the staircase of Our Divinity!

The world has still not rejected Elohim. His criminal traces are everywhere. They are afraid of his court. They call him god and honour him... O global sorrow of the sons of our Divinity! Reveal yourself to them Father, as you have been revealed to us.

He, who sees You, is unable to see anything more.

He, who knows You, wants to know nothing more.

He, who has entered by your gates, never leaves them again.

He, who has joined our Father, is permanently present at the Bridal Chambers

of the Father of the Light of lights,
the Divinity of sunny lesser divinities –
universal preaching.

Open the fifteen-thousand-sun lamp in the eye-ball and see our Father with our eyes.

Down with cataracts! Away glaucoma! Erase the dark spots!

Most beautiful Father, reveal Yourself for the first time to those who daily perform the slavish and penal 'Pater Noster', fingering the rosary with the half-nonsensical 'Ave Maria'.

Reveal yourself to them for the first time, so that they know You in greatness and primordial light, and see as we do, having ascended to the heights of the Cathar castles.

Father, adored by us, reveal Yourself to the humanity of the earth!

Permit five million chosen ones to enter the ark.

Awake the sleepers. Touch them with your fiery right hand. Light the sunny candles. Reveal Yourself to them!

*

𝒮ix billion suffering orphans

Our adored Father John teaches truly about the genocide of the Holyminne,[71] about the genocide of the Great Church of Love, of the Holy Spirit and the Mother of God.

But our child! With grief we testify to the full genocide of our Father.

The memory of Him has been erased from the archetype of humanity. Europe is sleeping. There are dictators full of malice with bloody tongues in Asia. Africa is a scorched wilderness. America is a valley of cowboys and coca-cola.

Six billion suffering orphans... Thus the world has not known its Father!

An ominous substitution has occurred. Is that not why our vision of the Father is given with great effort?

Knock at His doors! Purify sight, so that we stop talking about dull glasses, cloudy lenses, cataracts, about the muddiness and darkening of sight.

Did you not pass the school of repentance with the first conversion? Now pass the catharsis, the kind with which the pure ones see him clearly.

Only the pure one is able to come from the Father. It is impossible to look at the most perfect purity of our Divinity with mixed sight.

*

Do you want to save the world from lustful ulcers and perverts, from never-ending highs and depraved delights? REVEAL THE FATHER OF PURE LOVE FOR YOURSELF.

Having lit the lamps in the hearts, bring humanity the news about the loving Father.

Instruct again and again: 'You did not know our Father'.

– But why did we not know him? – Desperately cry your adepts.

– Because your gaze has been turned somewhere else, and the chimeras of the world have authority over you. He, who sees our Father, sees nothing more. Other things are the dissemination of His divine sight.

It is necessary to become pure in order to see the Father of heavenly love clearly.

He who has grown dull sees only the distorting mirror of his very own chimerical projections.

But the father will not permit distortions. It is possible to see Him clearly or to see nothing at all. To see Him without seeing is an absurdity of this world.

*

How to become pure?

How to become pure? Withdraw the source of Lucifer, come to hate his modelling. Limit the circle of communion to the pure ones.

Make your gaze pure. No television screens or news, flushed out by the Divinity.

Purity, as the longed-for ideal, is never-ending. Do not be content with the stage achieved. Always consider yourself insignificantly small and barely advanced.

There is only one Teacher of perfect purity on earth – our Father. So taught Christ in the earthly days and so do we, the dissemination of Christ, His worthy disciples, proclaim for you in the gospel of San Salvador.

Endeavour to remove the source of Lucifer from yourself, like an octopus which has spread himself in your interior, having fettered the 144 internal castles of irresistible perfection.

Expel from yourself the poisonous root, as a splinter from the body of the Theohumanity XXI.

*

The Chalice is the sole thing that remains from Christ after Golgotha and Jerusalem

Man-universe, do not release the Chalice from your hands!

The Chalice? O, the sole thing that remains from Christ after Golgotha and Jerusalem: blood collected to the last drop.

The Chalice, our adored one, is the sole thing that remains from the Father!

The Chalice, overflowing with the lights of 200 million myrrhic transparent drops!

Love the Chalice to sacred madness.

Such is the highest virtue in the Holy Grail.

Whatever you like, only not self-satisfaction, not habitual ritual.

The Grail disappears without a trace. The Grail possesses the property to become invisible and to appear in the physical order.

The world is the primordial creation of the Father. But today the grace of His love is greater than during the creation of the world in the Chalice.

It is possible, having ascended along the relic stream to San Salvador, to view earthly perspective from the height of the Cathar castles.

But it is possible to see the whole history of humanity, and to experience the presence of the Divinity, without releasing the sacred Chalice from one's hands.

It is the continuation of the Divinity, the continuation of Christ, the fullness of Exceeding Wisdom, the vessel of the Great Church.

The earth is the Chalice in the hands of Our Divinity.

And the Father shed millions of Last Drops into it.

Much has been said in the Hexaemeron about the creation of the heavenly celestial bodies, birds, fish, and other living creatures. It concluded with the creation of man. But nothing has been said about His shedding of the Last Drops.

The Chalice is greater than creation. The Chalice is the secret interior of the Divinity. The

Divinity as He is from within. The Divinity is greater than Himself.

There is no static Divinity. Only He, who is more than Himself in the shedding of the Last Drop, is able to reveal Himself.

And He, who is greater than Himself, giving the sacred Chalice into His hands, makes the knight greater than Himself, in the final reckoning: immortal.

The earth is full of the last drops of Our Divinity. Our child, the sounds of dying groans and the aromas of the myrrhic drops of pure love of the victims, brought in gratitude to the Father of pure love, have been dissolved in the aethers of Catalonia and Languedoc.

Above San Salvador, Perpetouse, Béziers, Cadaqués, Barcelona, above Holy Rus' – the myrrhic relics of the Solovetsky elders.

The earth is full of the fragrances of Our Divinity, the aromas of His perfect vessels, the martyrs of pure love.

☙

25.

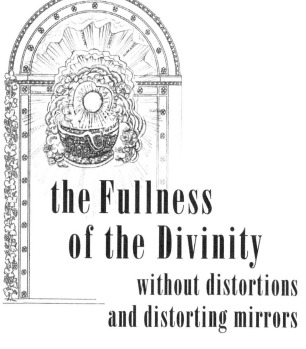

the Fullness
of the Divinity
without distortions
and distorting mirrors

- For more than seven centuries we have freed a space
  for the heaven of Our Divinity

- No one, glorified in the heavens, ever belonged
  to the Roman church

- From each drop of blood, spilt by the martyrs of pure love,
  will rise an invincible warrior and sparkling virgin

nly those who are strong and great with the spirit can carry the inadequate news to the world. Without *inadequacy for the world* the charisma of the miracle-worker will not be given.

First – initiation in the Cross. And only then the revelation of the Father of pure love, whose name you should preach in the wilderness of the world, tragically subject to the prince of this world – the Cross of Golgotha.

1.

The immortal ranks and the choirs of cherubs never-endingly extol the Father of pure love, without separating Him from the perfect creation:

Glorify our most divine Father of the perfect ones, who have remained faithful to Him for ever;

of the perfect ones, descending into the world with the messianistic mission of the redeemers, of the Holy Passionate ones, the crucified sons of the Father of pure love, His disciples, / divinized in the earthly Holy Passion / and expecting the state of awakening.

The adored ranks of our Divinity

The adored ranks of Our Divinity, the true sons not tempted by Lucifer, obtained from Him the blessing to descend to the earth amongst the never-ending sunny assemblies of the great Church of the saints, in order to help the true witnesses of recent times to resist the synagogue of Satan, the church of the cunning one.

A great multitude of them descend to the earth around the throne of original immaculateness and three white swans, flying before it.

Glorify the Father of pure love! Limit yourself to the glorification of Him alone, until a crippling blow has been inflicted on the devil and adversary.

Luci sealed the gates of Our Divinity. Our task is to reveal Him as more beautiful than ever before, in the fullness of his indescribable munificence.

Glorify the Father of transubstantiated hypostases. The Mother of God is His Theomaternal hypostasis. The sunny proto-christ is His son's hypostasis. The composition of golden pollen from the sun of hypostases 144x12.

The Father above all things.
There is no one
higher than Our Divinity.

The invincible church of the perfect ones, invulnerable from time immemorial

The Great Church of ineffable purity has existed from time immemorial, having preserved invulnerable the initial compositions of creation.

The descent into the world of the church of sunny anointed ones anticipates the triumph of Our Christ in the Theocivilization.

Perform daily at noon and midnight (for the specially initiated into the prayerful rank) the petitions for the perfect church of the invulnerable ones.

Its unheard-of power will inflict a decisive blow upon the Roman whore. The Church of Love, shining through transparently, sees it as swarming evil spirits.

The invincible church of the perfect ones is invulnerable from time immemorial. Appealing to it will reduce new seals and charismas.

*

The sun of suns of pure love is shed from the heart of our Father. The form of the suffering universe (with the exception of the sons of darkness) jointly comprises His face.

His face is revealed to those who are able to

raise a prayer for the 6 billion orphans of earth. The staggering heaven, the blinding sun of Our Divinity.

The treasure trove of Catharism

The treasure trove of Catharism lies solely in this:

> Glorify the purest of pure ones of our sunny Father, blazing with righteous anger against His adversary from time immemorial, returning to him evil, cunning, and treachery.

For more than seven centuries we freed a space for the heaven of Our Divinity.

And now the heavens have been revealed and the earth freed!

You are the humanity of Our Divinity
of the beloved, most pure Father.

Behind the Roman whore stand the treacherous popes, with debauchery not yielding to the Roman monarchs. And behind the disciples of our Divinity – the never-ending regiments of the supreme spiritual forces, one more beautiful than the next.

How ever many 'Christmastides' and 'lives of the Saints' the hagiographers of the Inquisition enclosed, how ever many saints they attributed to their putrid institutions, none glorified in heaven ever belonged to the Roman church, but joined the army of the saints and perfect ones of our Father.

*N*o, there was not and will not be anything in common

No, there was not and will not be anything in common between the Father of pure love and Elohim of the Old Testament.

No, there was not and will not be anything in common between the Christ of pure love, as the king of the anointed sovereigns, and the Roman-Byzantine Lucichrist.

No, there was not and will not be anything in common between the Mother of God, (begetting the sons of God from Her immortal, most immaculate bosom), and the lover of plaster statues and cultic temples.

There is nothing more insulting for our Father than distanced worshipping of Him as an inaccessible idol.

It is not more treacherous than the approach of the cunning one, than to see the adoring inseparable Father as a judge, punishing, unforgiving, carrying out machinations against His sons and daughters.

The Roman-Byzantine cult inflicted a monstrous insult on Our Divinity, for which it will be called to answer.

The vision of our Father – through the enlightenment of the mind, the illumination of the eyes – is necessary for the awakening from sleep.

Do not worry about anything more, our adored one. The rest will come. Exceeding Wisdom – from Him.

She is the loving Mother of the sons of God, who crave the return to the chambers of the Father, to the kingdom of Our Divinity.

The gradular staff in our hands

Adored brother, the gradular staff is in your hands.

Day and night, constantly upraising hands, we ask in the recent times of the 84th civilization about preserving as large as possible a number of the chosen ones in the ark for the sunny Third Theocivilization (the 85th).

But the Theocivilization can accept only a limited number of souls for the new ark of Noah. Alas...

The reverence of our adored, enlightened Father, the purest of the pure and most immaculate of immaculate, is the first condition of admission into the apocalyptic ark for the life of the future age.

He who sees our Father contemplates the retinues of the immortals and the most eternal Gospel, accompanied by the fiery letter in the heavens, in hearts, mysteriously...

FROM EACH DROP OF BLOOD SPILT BY THE
MARTYRS OF PURE LOVE WILL RISE AN INVINCIBLE
WARRIOR AND SPARKLING VIRGIN.

There are two white swans before them.

Go, trembling and inflamed with the spirit,
across the earth of the saints.

𝒯he Holy Grail

The sacred object is revealed with the realization
of the identity of the Divinity and humanity.
And it is sealed according to their separation, according to the artificially raised abyss between creation and Creator.

Only he, who tells the Father 'I and you are one',
can say: 'the kingdom of God is inside you'.

*

Do not strive even to theologise about our Father in the limits of human ordinariness, and night
blindness!

Exceeding Wisdom and fourfold Exceeding Wisdom with delight in the kingdom of the pure ones!
Her most restful lips proclaim the truth for future
ages.

2.

The second thing after the throne of our Father
is the worship to the Mother-Virgin, the
Exceeding Wisdom of the Father. Exceeding
Wisdom of the Father, bless us!

From our Father and from His beloved Queen comes the Flawless Mirror, the assembly of perfect sons and daughters, called by Christ in the earthly days *the sons and daughters of the Bridal Chamber.*

Such is the third rank in the hierarchy of worship (after the Father and Exceeding Wisdom).

*

Our child, from time immemorial you were anointed to perceive the secrets of Christ, as He was in the communion of perfect ones and immortals.

Even though the Roman-Byzantine chimeras soared like clouds of midges above you, they were not able to exert any influence upon the chosen one of Our Divinity.

Such is the absolute patronage that stands over him.

Your first conversion (baptism in the temple of Ilynskay Sloboda, which is near Mozhaysk, the leadership of the spiritual elders of Mary and the most blessed Euphrosinia) can be considered solely from the point of the Church of Pure Love. Today you have been brought into it by direct gates... Sweep the others aside as hallucination and chimeras.

The fullness of the Divinity has been revealed without distortions and distorting mirrors.

At last we are able to converse with you seriously, without allowances for earthly confusions and worldly weaknesses!

Shine with ineffable purity, beautiful brother!

*

Nourish yourself with the most restful and most moving spheres of our grace of the perfect ranks of Our Divinity, who are called the immortals.

O, pass another thousand white fonts, in order to become purer than yourself of yesterday! Purity without end, the endlessly whitewashed mother-of-pearl bone!

It only possible to experience the boundlessness of purity having ascended by the narrow dusty stone path of San Salvador.

During recent ascents we called it *the myrrh-pouring stream*; in the divine existence expanse of San Salvador Verdadero there are relics everywhere. Thousands of imperishable and myrrh-pouring relics.

Moreover, it is impossible to talk about *relics*, since the immortals do not identify themselves with them. But they possess properties incomprehensible to modern civilization:

to manifest themselves and witness the truth of the Divinity, / having so superabundantly endowed them, / having returned to them the highest purpose of the Godman, / eternal life, immortality.

Being faithful witnesses to the last, they inherited the wreath of immortality as the true disciples and brothers of Christ, and are thus called the immortal ranks of our Divinity.

In the 85th sunny Theocivilization there will be neither death, nor illness, but *the Holy Passion transition from one quality into a higher quality.* And only the Seraphites anointed by the immortals (from the number of former Adamites) will be able to enter the Ark-85. The destiny of the traumatized homo sapiens – with their fears, phobias, chimerical delusions – awaits the others.

I hear the song:

Gloria aeterna! Gloria aeterna! –
Glory to the true witnesses!

*

The Mother of God works miracles. She will give Her beautiful characteristics to our many mothers and adored sisters.

The Mother of God will be seen in many of them.

The liturgy of the 85th civilization together with the immortal ranks at San Salvador

What a liturgy of the 85th civilization is celebrated together with the immortal ranks at San Salvador!

It is impossible to imitate it even for the perfect instruments, our fathers. While only hence, above the relic streams of San Salvador Verdadero directly from the throne of our Divinity in the superadmiring and thrice-ten heavens sounds:

BLESSINGS TO THE HUMANITY OF EARTH!

Thousands of enlightened Theogamic ranks of Holy Rus' from the first to the tenth centuries, from the Chalice of Andrew the First-Called, here on San Salvador Verdadero among the immortals. Incomprehensible!

Here from time immemorial was placed the throne of our Divinity. The devil had no power. The Roman den suffered death here.

In their own time our fathers will say,how the white-hot rocks poured from the mountains onto the catapults during the siege of San Salvador.

San Salvador Verdadero thus remained unconquerable. Its inhabitants departed through the aethers into the castles of the Holy Grail. It remained only for the Roman brigands to withdraw.

One of the most grievous blows was inflicted upon the Roman whore at San Salvador, from which it was never able (and will never be able) to recover.

The atrocities of the Inquisition were caused, not only by religious prayers, as much as by the fear, which arose in these professional informers of corruption.

The Inquisition consisted of traumatized and inferior little monsters, who were led by Dominic Gusman.

And until the Roman church perceives who it has canonized in the person of this serpent, they will not be able to talk about its justification, despite any arguments in its favour.

If we had shown the destiny of the 'holy inquisitor' Dominic Gusman or Tomas Torkvemada, the entrails of many would have fallen out with terror.

Neither the body nor the soul of your neighbour can be defeated as long as the fullness of the Divinity dwells within him. The inquisitors, committing the physical and spiritual murder of the neighbour, pass a death sentence to themselves, separating from the Father of pure love.

Only those who are able to perceive the fullness of the Divinity in those that are close to them, or in those that are transcendentally strange and distant, can enter into His Bridal Chambers. The others are blind, turned upside down (seeing crookedly).

The sun of our Divinity burns the soul of the inquisitor, shaming the last grains of the divine potential in them.

Not one serpent or villain will dare to approach the sanctuary of the Divinity.

The sun and its fire will incinerate them.

So many endeavored to approach San Salvador but were cast back, as if by the most powerful wind of a hurricane.

> O Most Holy of holies Father, / Existing in Your sons and daughters. / O Father of the Bridal chamber, / O Father of the messianistic meal, / O stretched above the chalice of the Holy Grail / brightly and triumphantly / the adored sunny Father, / revealing Himself at the newly-wed midnight in full!...

*

Each step has been thoroughly calculated, but predetermination exists only for the absolutely preserved, and the others are fixed through correcting programmes.

❧

26.

the Burning Heart

THE DESERT HOURS
OF THE SECOND CONVERSION

(The Solovetsky Mother of God at San Salvador Verdadero)

The Mother of God:

I am in the archetype

am the Mother of the Spanish people. I am in the archetype, I am in the heart of each of you. My love has multiplied a million times.

We pass the most fragrantly myrrh-pouring cave of martyrs. The relics are fragrant as a sign of the all-embracing presence of the heavenly Queen. I am not able to describe Her presence today in words. The Queen covers humanity with Her whole being, Her vestments, Her bosom. She is a new universe for humanity.

*

The immortals:

We knew the secret of the Roman church – how to conquer this shameless wench. How can a serpent have beauty? How can Satan have grace? Their music is choral magic. Their rituals are loathsome: barbaric ceremonial magic, borrowed from the ancient masters and mithraic orders. There was not one impure power from which these villains did not draw their thieves' attributes, later passing them off as beyond the judgement of dogma.

𝒢lobal phariseeism crucified Christ

What does Our Father have in common with mammon? Between divinity and satan there is nothing in common, not the slightest intersection. Do not indulge the beast. Denounce him day and night. Do not let him break though into human sentimentality.

The saints? Not one of them belongs to them. Writings? Constant fabrication with the goal of establishing hypnosis.

If the kitchen of their secret goals and intentions and the chalice of their sins had been revealed to you...

They killed Christ with the goal of appropriating His divinity and gifts, about which they knew. Here is the secret of the murder of the King of the anointed sovereigns and His disciples. Subsequently they did the same thing with the lesser christs. The 'synagogue of Satan' sent Peter to the community of Christ as a spy in order to betray Him; buyers of stolen goods, defilers of humanity! Through them take place crimes not recorded even in the codex of mafiosi and murderers...

This serpent has the power to attack until its serpentine nature has been completely denounced – in imitation of the saint murdered by it.

Global phariseeism, having crucified Christ, accomplished a thousand mimicries. Without this they are not able to execute their repulsive rites and accursed ceremonies. Their mimicking faces have been smeared with the blood of saints.

The biblical serpent, tempting the primogenitors in paradise, pretended to be 'a friend' worthy of entering Eden.

Scores have been prepared for them. The serpent's lair will collapse almost instantaneously. But there will await another, unexpected battle. A new dragon head will arise. The church of the saints will strengthen and deal it a crippling blow.

The Divinizer

The crisis of the fathers has been caused by the second conversion – by the change of the quality of the action of the Holy Spirit in them. Let them more bravely dare the stages of divinization and understand that the staircase of the attainment of the Holy Spirit is infinite.

Mal hommes

The malice of the Roman beast is not inherent in man, the perfect creation of the Divinity. The

Adamites are not able to embitter more than 85 out of 100. But 15 out of 100 have already been embittered.

To the bon hommes are opposed the mal hommes.[72]

They originate in the sphere of underground anguish, Sheol. They are the former rabbis of the Second Temple, having imitated those of Christ in order to expel them.

The title 'Congregations of Purity of Faith', which their last Pope, Benedict XVI, has proclaimed, has been borrowed by the medieval Inquisition from the Cathars.

The Cathars called the unalloyed faith the 'pure faith', giving perfect joy – with the condition of renunciation of hovering chimeras. Thousands of mental serpents hang around the pure ones. One after another they fly from the lips of the priests of the evil god, as soon as they begin to profess in their serpentine dialect he, whom they call 'the saviour and redeemer' in their ritual ceremonies.

They are full of malice and hate, and multiply according to the level of the manifestation of the Divinity in those who voluntarily entrust themselves to their hands, in order that the crucified Lamb and His gathered church are glorified. Their rage has been directed against the Great Church of

Love, which has opposed them from time immemorial and knows how to destroy them.

The keys, closing the forbidden doors

Our child, the true keys to the heavenly Kingdom have been given to the pure disciples. But we have more keys, closing forbidden doors, sealing the accursed entrances. These keys we give to you today.

(They confer them).

The desert hours of the second conversion

Do not fear the little wilderness. This is honour.

Imagine what we experienced, locked in individual cells amongst refuse, rats, merciless beatings, hardened spots of blood... Seeing how, before our eyes, they torture and mercilessly beat our neighbours... In expectation of the fire or any kind of terrible torture. The continual invention of new tortures was the sole fantasy accessible to these villains, of a kind the world has not often seen.

The earth had never seen saints such as our brothers, the bright bon hommes! And such a human rabble as the Roman villains had never entered the world. They are the disgrace amongst the Adamites. It would be too gentle to talk about them with the words of Christ: 'having coming from the lowest depths'.

In the wilderness there is more preaching than in the world.

Remember, our child, how you preached during the first conversion, desiring to convert half of Moscow. Your preaching multiplied, but during the second conversion – in the wilderness.

Remember how Christ began in Jerusalem: the 40-day wilderness. Pass the desert hours of the second conversion worthily... In its own hour the world will see the light and be converted through a great sign. You will see it and rejoice...

Take care of yourself. Again it will be necessary to pass not only one wilderness (the extraction of souls from hellfire, as the adored mother Euphrosinia said).

In the wilderness the love of Our Divinity proclaims itself in the special way of the holy fool. The wilderness presupposes the multiplication of grace for tomorrow.

Those whom She loves, She sends into the wilderness – for the sake of provoking never-ending love, which has multiplied a thousand times

My child, your seminar today, for which the Most Pure Virgin Herself came to thank you, occurred in the superworldly ether and found a huge audience... thanks to yesterday's Holy Passion.

To some of your disciples it will seem great. But

from the point of view of *the immortals* and the wildernesses through which they have passed, it is moderate, small...

But we love in such a special way in our small Holy Passion! How you are adored in the Holy Passion by your Mother, my child! Those whom She loves, She sends into the wilderness — for the sake of provoking never-ending love, having multiplied a thousand times.

> Hither, to San Salvdaor Verdadero, the Queen brought the Chalice. Here they celebrated the wedding of the Lamb and His bride.

*

THE MOTHER OF GOD:

Hold back. Do not thrust yourself forwards, so that the blind do not see you. Do not give the malicious beast cause to growl. I will deal with him Myself. I will take revenge on him for the 200 million lesser christs and god-bearers tormented by him.

I am fully reflected in each of the disciples. Their slander and persecutions are persecutions of the Mother of God. Let them dare to utter My name, so that the scores presented to them do not multiply!

*U*nder My aegis fear nothing

Your Solovetsky Mother of God, God-bearer of the Theocivilization on San Salvador Verdadero, the

Mother of the new people of God, faithful, I do not retreat from My children.

I thank you for what you have done today. The beast has been mortally wounded and will not be able to crawl from his den for a long time.

Under My aegis fear nothing. The wilderness is the place of daily bloody effort for the heavenly recluses. And the chalice of My hot tears and the blood of the Lamb is beside them.

I am the true Church, and the rest is blasphemy.

Keep peace in the heart. You and your adored children are Our children.

The Mother of God on Peter

I came here to comfort you in the battle and to thank you for the denunciation of Peter, hated by Me from the beginning.

My child, I warned the Lamb about Peter. Christ knew who Peter was, and saw the spy in him. Peter thrice transformed into Satan in the eyes of the Saviour. And Christ suffered him, knowing that this was as it should be. The Saviour waged a fierce battle with Peter from his very sham 'conversion'.

I regarded Peter as the first enemy of Christ, worse than Caiaphas. Irritable, malicious, he always bore something hostile and strange within him.

Without the fearless denunciation of the pollution of Peter (it is absolutely true to call him the twice-chimerical of the double-synagogue of Satan) the church of John will not be revealed to the world.

The pharisees of Catholic Rome and Orthodox Byzantium occupy a strange place. They will have to yield to the church of the saints. They have neither grace nor succession. They are the enemies of Christ from the creation of the world.

Fear nothing. I am eternally with you, with the disciples of true spirit, My sons and daughters. In each of you has been imprinted My divine share.

I am your eternal mother according to the second coming of Christ, of Solovetsky, of the Holy Passion.

*

What is man worth without the secret of sorrows? The sanctified sorrows of the Cathar church, anointing the internal essence of man with her oils, his immortal mines and storerooms.

Such exhilarating grace is here at San Salvador Verdadero! Such prayer for the entire world!

The world appears to be a great macrocosmic airy chalice. In the hands of Our Father it is the great chalice of all humanity.

The world will convert
The world will convert
The world will convert

Like the small vessels behind an icebreaker, fathers with three year-old children strove after us.
Our angels built the path for them.

What peace! Most restful, from divine existence.

❧

27.

the New Name
of our Father

- Lucifer stole the name 'Jehovah' from Our Divinity
- The obliteration of the purity of Our Divinity
  led to the catastrophic corruption of the Adamite model
  of the beginning of the third millennium

THE FIERY HIERARCHY:

 victory has been won. Our hearts are full of joy. Victory! The exultation of the never-ending regiments of Our Divinity.

> Father of kind armies
> of the most immaculate knights,
> BLESS⁺ the world with virginal
> purity and perfect beauty

Apart from thousands of other mistakes the Israelites did the following. About the Father of pure love, of course, there is not a word in their thrice rewritten manuscripts, which were 'not written by the hand of man'. The prince of this world has made the complete renunciation of our Father as a condition of the conclusion of the covenant with this people.

The Jews trembled. Even in their tribe the memory and presence of the Divinity from the time of

Abraham had been preserved – like, for example, the seal and chalice of king Melchizedek.

The Jews made their conscious choice and worshipped the demiurge, having acknowleged him as the sole divinity and having sworn to lay down their lives in order to erase any memory of the true Father.

Thrice they took the oath to Jehovah, renouncing the Father of heaven and earth, before accepting Lucifer's interpretation of the creation of the world, perverted by the rabbis of the Moses' version, presenting, all in all, only the second illegitimate adaptative reformation of man in favour of the prince of this world.

The relationship of our Divinity and His forces to human flesh is not simple. There are many of the compositions of Lucifer in it. But the Divinity promises, in the wildernesses of the Holy Passion of Theohumanity, to transform the Adamite essence.

The Father is already completing the third reformation of the Godman today, inoculating the fallen through the guilt of Lucifer (scores are presented to him alone!), creation with the composition of original immaculateness.

The initiation of the world into the immaculate origin of the Mother of God as blessed as never before.

The earth needs Her virginal vestments as never before!

The sun of suns of the Divinity shines above the world as never before.

> With the prayer 'Ave, Father, ave'
> the spiritual compositions are changed
> in the eternal and immortal bodies
> in the Theocivilization, in Theohumanity.

The prince of this world has been banned from the immortal armies of Our Divinity.

*

A great mistake hangs over the world: the false identification of Christ. The ancient Jews managed to realize their treacherous plan and to connect the Messenger of the Father of pure love with their own rancorous idol, full of hatred and mortal damnation. It is difficult to imagine anything more insulting!

The naïve Christians accomplished a sin much greater than their 'older brothers' (as they call the Jews), having turned the feat of the conversion of humanity to the Father of pure love, accomplished by Christ in the earthly days in Jerusalem, *into nothing.*

The chalice preserved immutable and permanent the grace of the sun of our Father, – the song about the Father of pure love, disconnected from the evil contained in aspects of the lowest bodies.

O poor homo sapiens; poor, defiled, deprived man! His divine bodies (12x12) have been sealed, and the anointed ones, able to insert the oils of divine reconciliation and the immaculate compositions brought into the world by us today, are needed. We need a mystical church capable of bringing humanity to the kingdom of Our Divinity. We need fearless heroes capable of courageously erasing the forms of the cunning one and winning a decisive victory over him.

Reveal the name of Our Father for yourself. O sunny divinity of Our Father! His new name bears great grace. There will come thousands of messengers, desiring to hear only about Him. Biblical references to Lucifer will not cause them anything but bewilderment. Satan is a coward with all his power, which is the force of virginal love, stolen by global lust.

Pure love is devoid of fear.

Pure love transforms the essence.

Pure love bears eternal life.

Pure love illuminates the mind.

Pure love reveals the divinity in one's neighbour and the neighbour in the Divinity.

Pure love bears man the revelation about himself.

For immortality and eternal life, open the springs of pure love and do not seal them. May more and more oceanic streams of the purest of pure sunny love, from the bosom of Our immaculate Mother, flow above the world.

The joy during the departure from the wilderness

Yes, the wilderness of the Father of pure love with the unforeseen approaches of Lucifer, with the unexpected ruptures into emptiness, solitude and loneliness. But what grace comes with the departure from the wilderness! What exultation with the taking down from the Cross!

Christians are called to the second conversion. Too much has been mixed in. The mixer-chroniclers, catechists, theologians and others – the underlings of Lucifer – have done some work.

In the Bible (with the exception of the gospel of John) there is not one pure book (1) without additions and changes, (2) coming from the throne of Our Divinity. More evil comes from these mixed writings than good.

Our Father, in His shining greatness and primordial face, has not been shown in the Bible and Christianity.

May holy virginal kindness become the ideal of the disciples of the Father of pure love. It is diffi-

454

cult to achieve the stage of seeing Him (revealing Himself for the first time), but blessed and holy are those who perceive Him in the wildernesses of the world. Exceeding Wisdom will give him the virginal eye of the Most Pure Virgin God-bearer, who contemplates our Father clearly, as not a single creation does.

Sing of virginity! It destroys the serpent like poisonous powder and strikes him like a spear in the belly. The Mother of God treads upon his head with virginal purity.

In its death throes the dragon is especially dangerous. In the wildernesses, at the hour of visible deprivation, is the invisible multiplication of Christ.

𝒫rayer:

There is no one other than Him,
the Father the most high and pure.
There is nothing other than His love.
O Beloved O!
O, more and more
sorrows and crosses in the wilderness.
The Father will multiply grace.
The enemy will take nothing.

Lucifer stole the name 'Jehovah' for himself from Our Divinity.[73] And the Father gave him his mysterious name for the time being, knowing that in the final reckoning it will lead to the celebration of pure and great love.

One of the 115 names of our Father, counted in our scrolls:

'There is only love, there is only light. I and you are one'.

Man has been filled with the highest light, while the rest are chimeras. This is precisely the original meaning of the name of our Father, revealed by the hierarchy of the immortals.

'There is no one other than Him / my Beloved / and there is nothing other than love / His love' – In a perfect fashion this prayer expresses the secret of the name of Our Father.

The name of the cunning one: 'He is-who-is not'

O, this wretched thief and coward, the cunning Luci! His name: He is-who-is not, which was also proved by his church during the two thousand years of its existence. At the centre of the liturgy of John Chrysostom, the Lateran and modern mass, is the recollecting, self-concealing and distant He is-who-is not. But if he appears in the present, it will be suitable to erase his traces from the face of the earth.

Our children, without consciousness of the name of the cunning one, 'He is-who-is not', you will not comprehend the name of our Father, manifesting Himself in earthly creation as invisible (He, who is not visible), but invisibly embracing all creation. Otherwise – requiring *insight*.

The manifestation of our Father is great and is only growing. O, if you had known, our children, how we love Our Father! His love has irreproachable and perfect authority over all creation.

How magnificent is the hierarchy of apostles and messengers of pure love!

It is time to sweep away the chimeras and free yourselves from hypnoses.

A multitude of anointed sovereigns will soon descend into the world, carrying scrolls with the news of the close kingdom of Our Divinity in their hands.

We come with this joyful news today, so that, carrying the heavy crosses in the wilderness of the world for its conversion to the Father of pure love, you do not lose faith and hope.

The obliteration of the purity of Our Divinity, not connected with evil (without one particle of evil out of one hundred thousand) led to the catastrophic corruption of the model of the Adamite of the beginning of the third millennium.

Alas, there is nothing other than evil in this external man, already worshipping the Most Evil of evils for two thousand years!

The cunning one managed to throw his accursed traits onto God's creation. But Exceeding Wisdom is purifying it.

Modern man is an almost exact copy of Elohim. But yet again we say: the devil did not manage to touch the depths of creation.

The two thousand years of church corruption is ending. More bravely, more steadfastly, more audaciously, more and more preach the 155 hypostases of Our Divinity and His 140 names according to the number of the castles of Exceeding Wisdom.

*

More bravely erase the old seals and renounce those who have erased any kind of memory of our Father, having cut creation off from the true Creator, whereby you will be able to approach the glory of Our Father.

> The world is born anew.
> Glory to the branch of John,
> to the immortal daughter of Our Divinity,
> who has created the world with exceeding wisdom!

The age of divinization

Preach the age of divinization.

The Divinity desires to return to man the lost

immortal substances, indescribable and most heavenly joy. The heavens are descending to the earth.

Rejoice, rejoice. Hallelujah!

> Adored Father O
> most sunny divinity
> the exultation of the Father of pure love
> O

(The revelations of San Salvador interpret 'O' not as emotional rapture, but as deep respiratory meditation.)

The undefiled name of Our Father will renew the earth. So many beautiful beings of heavenly origin will descend from the high spheres with one summoning of the name of the Father of pure love! Myriads of souls, tormented in places of anguish, will find repose...

> Father of pure love,
> adored Father,
> resist the authority of corrupted Lucifer.
> Against the Roman-Byzantine chimeera –
> the Throne of San Salvador Verdadero.
> Long live the glory of our Father,
> the most adorned sun of suns!

The Father reveals Himself after the corruption of Lucifer has been reduced by five times

The revolution of the Father of pure love! His name should be mastered as that of the kind by which children address their parents.

But first it is necessary to perform the mental purification of the shape of the Father from mixed chimeras. His non-involvement in evil (1), sin (2), illness (3), death (4), and the judgement over humanity (5) is evident for those who have joined His sunny hierarchies.

The Father reveals Himself only after the corruption of Lucifer has been reduced by five times, after His evident disconnection from evil, illness, death, sin, judgement, and temptation.

The mysterious reason for the non-manifestation of Our Father before the spiritual gaze, and the wilderness for the newly-converted disciples, is the incapacity to perform the full and purifying reduction of the five chimeras of the Thrice-Cursed (as we call him in our heavenly assemblies).

Perform the mystery of the purification of our Father of the mental pollution of Lucifer every day. And stay away from any sources that lead to mixing.

With the purification of His sweetest form the adored Father will reveal Himself miraculously. And with the partial lifting of the veils from His divine name, the soul will enter the condition of the divinization of her Father. The child will return to the home of the Father.

28.

Juan de San Grial,
the supreme apostle of the Father of pure love

How to see the Father?

Our Father, the true divinity, the Father of the saints who descend from on high, of the anointed sovereigns of the Holy Spirit, is Juan de San Grial.

My Holy Passion question during the 100 thousand groans of the holy fools of Solovetsky: How to see the Father? His form vanishes before the internal gaze... I crave, and I am not able to see Him. Day and night I pray to Him, but His face disappears before the internal gaze and is not able to imprint Himself. The old forms have been erased – the grey-haired Sabaoth on the throne, Christ Pantocrator, Ostrobramskaya Mother of God...

I saw Him!

O kindest father, in knight's garments and black mantel! Thus He revealed Himself: all-powerful and exceedingly wise, possessing irresistible potential. The radiance of the secret and the presence of the Divinity was upon him. His absolute unworldly kindness strikes and hits the eyes first of all.

O our father! Christ of christs, Father of fathers, kindest of the kind, the divine Exceeding Wisdom of the wise men, inexhaustible love, the court of metanoia, all-conquering life and the light of learning.

His name is Juan de San Grial, the supreme apostle of the Father of pure love, His perfect mirror. He has been given the immoveable staff and has been ordered to keep the desert Grail in the Holy Passion before His eyes. How madly he loves! On his face is transcendental exceeding wisdom. Under the radiance of a thousand rays – the divine Juan. Our Father is found in the lights and makes irrefutable decisions.

Juan de San Grial is the father of our church in the heavens. His brilliant honed mind, great gifts, transformed being. He has thrice passed martyrdom on earth. In constant exertion, in the battle with the Roman bigot mounted on the throne of Moses.

His secret desire is to reveal Christ to the world, as He is perceived by the disciples appointed from time immemorial to follow Him, and not to form His wilderness and crucify Him like the Judaic apostles.

*

Another church. The church of love is irresistibly different than that of the Roman. In it there is not a single seal of Elohim. It has developed in the direction of sunny metanoia and gave miraculous splashes of perfect beatitudes.

Juan de San Grial specially favours us henceforth. His decisive, soft, knightly disposition stuns, and his perfect purity arouses no doubts.

JUAN OF THE HOLY CHALICE:

Not more than a hundredth or even a thousandth is known to the world about the villainies of the Roman bigot, these titled rabbis of the synagogue of Satan. They have painstakingly erased the traces of their crimes, immediately after their completion. But they have been imprinted on the screen of the Chalice. There is not a single crime, erased by them, which would not have been presented to them.

The Roman villain knows of the near judgement over it. Today (the Roman church) all the saints, whom they were once able to drag in and to present as 'their own', have departed from it. Their pantheon is completely empty.

'Behold, I leave your house empty.'

Their 'church' is on the edge of panic. The Catholics have lost the battle, but the bearded Orthodox villains have already been in their service for a long time, although pretending to be their enemies. They are of one spirit.

*

A hypnosis, created with the smoke from the fire sites of the saints, holds sway in Russia. But its cloud is dispersing.

The Russian and Roman pharisees flee as soon as their denunciation begins. The cowardly nobodies are generally deprived of faith and pursue selfish interests. As soon as they grasp that their 'racket' is over, they will be the first to betray Christ as they see Him and dress themselves as businessmen.

Great insight into the true church awaits. At the beginning it will start to shine in the West, and then in the East.

Every hour of the Church of Love has been calculated down to the finest details and happens according to plan.

*

Our Father, spread Your blessing above the world and bring the joy of the exultant saints.

Blessings to the world from the sunny hierarchy of the Great Church of Love. Let the sunny disk imprint itself in the hearts of millions! Indescribable kindness, enlightened Exceeding Wisdom, the light of the Bridal Chamber. The grace and pleroma of the Holy Spirit is with the faithful.

*

Juan de San Grial, as the personal ambassador of Our Divinity, has been revealed so that the Church of Love summons him in the hours of the Holy Passion loneliness, because the battle is so great. Our enemy would like to sow discord in the hearts of the faithful: he says that grace has receded. Grace is greater than ever before! The saints, glorified by us, are persistently with us. The heavenly altar of the Church of the Mother of God has been enriched again and again by the great multitude of the saints. The church will multiply. Grace has multiplied a million times.

Hallelujah, halleluja, hallelujah!

≼§

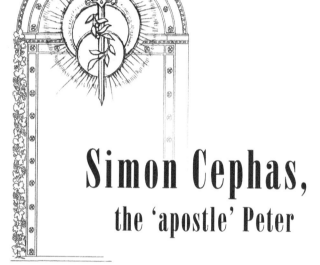

29.

Simon Cephas,
the 'apostle' Peter

- The Grail caused particular agitation among the rabbis, who sensed their defeat

- Joseph adored Christ

- Christ was surrounded, not by Judaic apostles, but by disciples that adored Him

- The Holy Grail and the Church of Exceeding Wisdom know another thousand names of Christ

- What great damage the Roman she-devil inflicted upon the teachings of Christ!
- What sweet assemblies were formed by the true Church!
- There is no weapon more shattering against Elohim than love.
- A thousand year never-ending meal awaits you

§

From the cave, the smell of relics. The myrrh-pouring sarcophagus. The fragrance of exceeding wisdom of our fathers.

O, do not abandon San Salvador, Nightingale Mountain! Bright is the hour when Melchizedek, celebrating the divine service with the Holy Grail in his hands, completes the movements of the cross. In his right hand is the chalice of Jerusalem, the blood of the Son of God, flowing from Golgotha. In his left is the Theogamic chalice of the answering Last Drop of His bride, the Eternal Virgin, His church, His Exceeding Wisdom.

In the thirteenth century our fathers performed the liturgy with two Grails in their hands. And here over San Salvador shines the sun of Theohumanity, shedding direct rays into the hearts of the lovers (the true disciples of Christ).

*

$\mathscr{S}$imon Cephas, the 'apostle' Peter

The church of Peter, having been tested three times, betrayed three times. The thrice asked 'do you love Me?' thrice testified to its unlove. Its sentence, from time immemorial, from the throne of Our Divinity: the synagogue of Satan, Aristotelians.

Simon Cephas, at the insistence of his masters in the Synedrion, asked Christ to give him a new name, so that it would be simpler to consign the old Cephas over to oblivion. At Simon's request, Christ gave him the name Peter. But what is written next is absent from the gospels. With the treachery of Peter, Christ removed his apostolate from him and called him 'old Simon'.

> Peter's mother-in-law despised him. It was she that advised the Synedrion to suggest that Cephas join the Christians, the 'enemy camp'. The regard for Christ in the Synedrion, among the three notified about Peter's mission, was like the regard for Stepan Razin or Yemelyan Pugachev in Russia: an insurgent.

Proud Peter considered himself an outstanding theologian with prophetic charismas, and despised Christ. He considered the King of the anointed sovereigns secondary. The kingdom of the anointed sovereigns in general was sealed for this double stranger from the very lowest of the low, from the sphere inhabited by Joseph Caiaphas, Judases, and *saboteur-destroyers like him.*

$\mathcal{O}$ne of the denunciations of Peter to the Synedrion

Christ's teaching irritated Peter. The theologian of the Synedrion could hardly contain his fury and indignation.

'Christ ignores the wise men of Israel and wants to rewrite the sacred scripture anew! This revisionist and revolutionary is worthy of only one thing – contempt!'

Thus Peter denounced Him in the Synderion. He tirelessly repeated Christ's second-rate nature and lack of education, considering himself much more knowledgeable in the secrets of the law of Moses:

'What this upstart teaches has been fabricated. Rabbi Shamuel and rabbi Akiba, the holy wise men of Israel, taught much more deeply about the same thing. This half-educated person steals from our fathers, passing it off as his own.'

Christ was not seduced by Peter's learning. There did not pass an hour that he did not rise against him, calling him 'Satan', 'wolf', and 'serpent'. The angry 23rd chapter from Matthew (the denunciation of global phariseeism with 'woe to you') was addressed... to Peter.

The 'Apostle Peter' was an imaginary figure from the beginning. Christ himself, the founder of Christianity, removed the name which He gave him at the beginning of his service.

The church of Peter accepted the spirit of the Judaic synagogue. In her teachings reigns the ambiguity committed to damnation by Christ.

'Woe to you, scribes and pharisees, hypocrites! Raise tombs on the sites of the prophets you have murdered and imagine yourselves their disciples, whereas you are their murderers... Lift the chalice full of loathsomeness.' – was said about Peter.

'Judaic eyes': the hypnosis inflicted by Peter

Are we capable today of imagining the truthful picture of the 'Judaic eyes' – the hypnosis inflicted by Peter? His task from the devil was to seal the Father of pure love in the Son.

Elohim was a spirit-alien from the cosmos. But Christ came from the heavenly kingdom.

Peter was the initiator of anathemas against the true disciples of Christ

Peter was the initiator of the thought that Christ heals with the power of Beelzebub. He imagined himself an healer, and the healings performed by Jesus aroused secret envy in him.

It was the precisely after the denunication of Peter that the Synedrion decided to hand Jesus over for the fourth degree of herem.

He who brought the fiercest anathema against Christ, to which the Jews subjected only the most inveterate criminals, was the 'supreme apostle'. It is easy to conclude that this very same person was the initiator of the anathema against the true disciples of Christ for the following two millennia.

Today it is difficult even to imagine that the Synedrion judged Christ according to the denunciation of Peter. If it had not been for Simon Cephas, perhaps, the Jews would not have shown such hatred towards Christ. Peter is none other than the true murderer and crucifier.

*

$\mathcal{P}$eter's war on virginity

Peter was tormented by lust. The Mother of God and the immaculate origin aroused a particular secret hatred within Peter.

Peter assumed himself to be a prophet and boasted particularly that the 'will of God' had seemingly been revealed to him. He verified all the Judaic sources known to him, including those that were mysterious, God-revealing. But he had not heard about the immaculate origin from a single rabbi. And this impertinent autodidact dares to teach about impossible secrets!

'Nothing like it is able to come from our Elohim', – asserted Peter in the Synedrion.

The Mother of God issued from the spiritual flesh of Her mother, Anna

The secret of the Immaculate Conception has not been revealed to the Christians to this day. The Mother of God came into the world without the agency of Joakim and Anna. She issued from the spiritual flesh of Her mother, Anna, from her divine immortal bodies, manifested in a special way. Christ came through them.

The carnal vision of the immaculate birth is Judaic. From birth our dear Christ possessed the gift of bilocation, characteristic of the anointed sovereigns, and did not leave divine existence, witnessing all the worlds.

Christ is the king of bilocation

Peter was familiar with the Chalice which collected the blood of Christ. The Holy Grail aroused a particular agitation among the rabbis, who sensed their defeat. Through Simon and the other 'prophets' it was revealed to them that nothing good would come even from the execution of the insurgent. There was such a level of damnation on Him, you see, that it would have been better not to touch Him. But he would have done too much

474

harm to the Judaic people, defiled the temple and sealed the office...

The unhappy rabbis were forced to deal with Christ. And now the Chalice never leaves their heads; it beats and shames them!

The execution of the 'insurgent' did not arouse the slightest approval among the common people. On the contrary, the people rose against the pharisees. Everywhere they spoke of His multiplied appearances... What if He remains? They see Him here and there...

The king of bilocation.

Bilocation was locked in the earthly days. But with the shedding of the blood into the Holy Grail, Christ constantly appears, converses, heals... His presence has multiplied! The rabbis have lost! Elohim has been defeated!

$\mathscr{S}$imon Cephas led the persecutions of the Mother of God

Peter was in seclusion for more than three months, biting his lips and pondering what to do. Later he justified himself with bad health, with his fears...

None other than Simon Cephas led the persecutions of the Mother of God. Now he was able to act openly. His sabotage work concluded with the crucifixion of Christ. There was no longer any sense for him to remain embedded in the body of the church as before.

The God-bearer did not accept Peter from the beginning, and repeatedly indicated to the Saviour that he was a false apostle, the source of evil and the greatest danger.

Whenever Peter tried to search for the Chalice it was useless. They saw it now here, now there... But no one knew where it was or in whose hands it was kept.

The hunting scent even led Peter to Ephesus. Here it seemed he had managed to discover the path. But the angels of the Our Divinity deflected the villain from Nightingale Mountain. Otherwise the Mother of God might have suffered powerfully.

$\mathscr{T}$HE LINE OF ADORING LOVE

From Joseph of Arimathea and Mary Magdalene came that which is called, in the Holy Grail and the church of the immortals, the line of adoring love – a kind of 'witnesses, true to the last'.

Joseph adored Christ. His Son, Joseph the Magnificent, more than adored Him.

Christ was surrounded not by Judaic apostles, but by disciples that adored Him. Their memory has been criminally erased by the Roman church.

The Saviour dwelt persistently with those who held the chalice of His presence in their hands.

His presence in the Holy Grail was a million times greater than in the earthly days, absolute and authentic.

No longer did anyone ask: 'what is this?' They understood: the blood, transubstantiated into myrrh, of the king and anointed sovereign of the Divinity himself.

His names are so great! 'The perfect Divinity' and 'the Only-begotten Son of God' are only two of them.

The Holy Grail and the church of Exceeding Wisdom know another thousand names of Christ – even more beautiful and lofty.

The true church of those that adore Christ

Christ was touchingly attached to His loving disciples. He called John beloved, Joseph adored, Mary the divine bride.

And from them was born the true Church of those that adore Christ, divinizing through adoration.

He who adored Him with his whole being: lovingly, sacrificially, madly – to him was revealed how Christ (the sun of suns!) adored them.

And they repeatedly said, referring to Him: 'It is

possible to see our Christ only with adoring eyes.'

It is possible to understand Him only with a mind that adores Him. To love Him – adoringly, with the whole being.

The Judaised gospels

The Judaised gospels reflected another view: the view of Peter. Cold, questioning, rationalizing... closing a ring of incomprehension around Christ.

What great damage the Roman she-devil inflicted upon the teachings of Christ!

The juridical doctrine of Augustine, and later (in the eleventh century) of Anselm of Canterbury, placed the Judaic idea of salvation at the centre, sealed the gift of Our Divinity to see Christ with authentic eyes, to adore Him.

The atmosphere of adoring divinization was replaced with cheap office tricks. The fears inflicted: 'unforgivable sin', 'the Redeemer who has come'... And at once – donations in the church,

> for the work of the office,
> responsible for the clerical work of Christ.

*

The secret of the Last Drop

Those that adored Him combined with Him as one.

Mary Magdalene experienced the most blessed

inspirations of the Holy Spirit and supernatural ecstasies.

The Saviour set Mary's adoring love as an example for his other disciples and granted her more and more indescribable gifts.

Mary Magdalene alone possessed more of them than the total of all the Judaising 'apostle-reformers': Matthew, Mark, and so on – the unconscious secret disciples of Simon Cephas rather than Christ.

After the Most Pure Virgin the Saviour revealed the secret of the last drop to Mary Magdalene.

Heated to a temperature of many thousand degrees, the heart accepts the sun of the Divinity into itself.

The divine composition dissolves in the interior, through which the marriage of the Lamb is accomplished.

To achieve a similar temperature of the heart is to prepare the bride for meeting with the Bridegroom.

What sweetest assemblies were formed by the true Church! So many bright martyrs, so many great seers, prophets, miracle-workers!

So many treasure-hunters, having found their ineffable treasure! So many emotional wise men. So many lamps of the Holy Spirit, and anointed ones whose delightful loving groans proclaimed invisible worlds.

It is time to denounce to the Roman bigots and torturers that have sealed the Church of love.

For two thousand years after the crucifixion, Rome did with Christ what the rabbis of Elohim had tried to do. Becoming terrified after the crucifixion (Golgotha shamed them and pierced them like a sharp caduceus), the rabbis took to the task of erasing any memory of Him.

Having blocked the tomb with rock, they were prepared to place half of 'their' army beside the Roman troops in order that nothing happened.

Rome did something similar with the church of Christ. Throngs of crusaders, Jesuits, and inquisitors came to take the place of the Judaic zealots and Roman legionnaires... The Vatican theologians gave them the task of sealing the true Church of Christ.

But the secret of Our Divinity came to be. The laurel has flourished.

*

The end of the Roman she-wolf! That which her servants criminally conceal will be revealed. Humanity will recognise the truth about them.

More than a billion innocent victims are on their conscience. From the twelfth to the nineteenth centuries 150 million were tortured in ancient prison cells, and more than 500 million were condemned. Nearly twice that number of innocents passed unbearable torments...

Such is the hypnosis, if the memory of them as the direct successors of the rabbis, as the first enemies of Christ and the Holy Spirit, as torturers and executioners, is erased!

The words of Christ relate to the adherents of religious institutions: 'You imagine yourselves the heirs of the saints (the prophets), but you are the children of those that killed the prophets.'

The two great lies

May the two great lies be revealed to humanity.

> 1) The God whom the Roman church professes is a mixture of Christ and Elohim.
>
> 2) The saints for whom it erects literary-theological monuments were killed by it. Their death is on its conscience.

*

The internal casket of the divine gifts of pure love

The world will be converted. A condition of the prevention of universal catastrophes is the acknowledgement of the new name of Our Divinity: the Father of pure love.

The Father among His loving children, adoring His creation, virginally pure, spotless (separated from evil).

Open, our adored one, the internal casket of divine gifts of pure love.

Open it again and again.

Teach the 150 stages of its opening. At the last stage the sunny disk flares into a bush which cannot be singed.

The battle in the hours of the wilderness

Against Elohim's torments in the battle in the hours of the wilderness you should remember: love is self-sufficient.

Uncertainty, doubts, searching: these are the results of insufficient love. Fill yourself with pure love, and peace will be given through the cross of the Holy Passion.

There is no more shattering weapon against Elohim than love.

Conquer our enemy in the battle with the spear of Longinus.

Chop off the dragon's head with the confession of virginal love.

Great is Our Divinity! Great in boundless expanses and indescribable secrets.

Great is Our Divinity and renowned throughout all the world.

Great is Our Divinity, the king of pure love, and His forces are invincible in heaven and on earth.

Great is Our Divinity – and the scepter of immortality is in the hands of the anointed ones.

Great is Our Divinity, and absolute is His cover over the true disciples.

Great is the Divinity, our Father, at the Bridal Supper of love, like the lamb among His loving disciples and lesser lambs.

*

The true faith begins with the denunciation of the hypnosis of the office of the false apostle Peter. So taught our fathers in the twelfth century, for which they were subjected to fierce persecutions from the Roman bigots.

We have touched the most painful nerve of their teaching. The denunciation of the Roman deception begins with this: that the 'most-supreme apostle Peter', the 'ecclesiarch', 'Christ's successor', the 'first deputy', and so on and so forth, is none other than a serpent hiding in the flowers.

*

Indescribable exultation

Glory to the church of Our Divinity!

Sunny glory to it in heaven and on earth!

The malice of the enemies will multiply as their hypnosis collapses under the influence of the denouncing truth of the Divinity.

Stand stoically firm and do not lose the presence of the spirit. Our victory is inevitable.

Our sunny church will celebrate such a triumph in it own time!

O John, remember the beautiful meals with hundreds of priests after the twenty five assemblies!

A never-ending thousand-year meal awaits you: the indescribable table, covered with the sun, with golden chalices and regal viands.

It is impossible to take one's eyes from the angels serving the knights who sit at the meal.

And so magnificent are their brides, the true and loving virgins!

What a reward for the knights for virginity!

They carry their love for Christ to their adored pure husbands.

The husbands of Christ carry their love for the Most Pure Virgin to their brides. Magnificent!

> The Bridal Supper of pure love –
> the virtue of the Theocivilization III!

Again the myrrh-pouring smells accompany our descent from the mountain. And the consolation: the consulamentum from the disciples of Father-Sun.

Their dinner table has been laid, and they invite us to partake of the ineffable viands of the spiritual meal in the peacefully contemplative prayer from on high.

*

Queen, bless the world in the sunny vestments of Christ, the anointed sovereigns performing the liturgy at the Bridal Supper of the Lamb. Amen.

We leave San Salvador full of indescribable joy and rejoicing. The mountains have been filled with light. The heavens rejoice.

The harder the battle, the greater the victory!!!

*

𝒫rayer before the meal:

The might of Our Divinity
Coming into this world blessed.
Amen.

◄§

30.

the Double standard of monotheism

- Christ created the Christanthropos
  by shedding His blood

- The Mother of God fainted from the ecstatic
  Holy Passion when the Saviour entrusted
  the Theogamic Grail to Her on Nightingale Mountain

- The hypnosis of the old tabernacle will act until the worship of the cross has been replaced with the worship of the Chalice

- The entire sum of evil from the start to the end of the world relates solely to Lucifer

◄§

25.09.2007 Costa Brava

$\mathscr{P}$hantom N 1

In order to portray himself as kind, Lucifer (evil from the beginning) needed to attribute evil to the kind God, placing the phantoms of his personal monster on the immortal Divinity.

In its naivety, humanity attributes evil to the Divinity: judgement, rancour, the presentation of scores, illness, death, eternal torments – and falls into the devil's nets.

The devil does not have authority over the Adamites until he catches them in his snare *of nasty monotheism.*

As soon as the cunning one is able to shake off his evil onto the most kind Divinity, the eyes of humanity are closed. Renouncing its Father, it attributes divine perfection (peace, beauty, kindness) to Lucifer.

May Catharism become the worldwide religion of the kind God and drive out the droppings of Lucifer.

The idealised Moses

Someone, who despised Moses, gave him on Sinai:

1) 10 articles of the law (the Decalogue);

2) 613 lesser prescriptions (regarding the sabbath and ritual purity);

3) 'the Book of Executions and Punishments' ('the Book of Holy Justice') for infringers of the law – whereas there is nothing about any kind of love or the beneficial influence of the conscience in the religion of this Someone;

4) a mysterious book under the title of 'The Covenant of Covenants'. Moses was ordered not to unseal this until the end of time. This book contained the great secret about this Someone – who he is.

Moses received four legislative codes. The first of these became the property of universal publicity (the so-called '10 commandments'). Another 613 were revealed in the Torah and the interpretative books of the law (the second scroll). And the two final books, the Book of Executions and particularly the Secret Book (which even Moses himself did not unseal) were not made public by the rabbis.

But in their arks they held scrolls which bore in themselves this terrible imprint of Lucifer. Lucifer's gospel, the darkest book of all those ever on earth, gave the aggressive tribe authority on behalf of this malicious vindictive idol.

'Jehovah'

Moses doubted to his last breath: who exactly had spoke to him on Sinai? He sought from the Speaker the confirmation of the divine nature of the revelation. But he did not receive this and, wandering through the wilderness, sowed in his people the seeds of doubt. Conscience suggested that something was not right.

'Someone' is the name under which the great cryptographer and mimicker desired to remain in the memory of his vessel Moses and his people.

The name 'Jehovah' (JHWH – 'he is-who-is') confirms the crown of monotheism. The authority of one over all – seen and unseen worlds, angels, men and other created beings.

JHWH (he is-who-is) is the name of the Dictator. In the sunny Cathar spirituality this name was called *the greatest damnation,* inflicted on humanity by Lucifer and his vessel Moses.

Such a imperious name could not belong to Our Father.

The Father considers creation as the dissemination of Himself from the last drop: I and YOU, who are the total WE.

The name 'All-existing' denies the Father of pure love, and lays a ban on His vision and the worship of Him. Such is the secret suggestion of Lucifer. There is only he. In his creation exists he alone.

The Cathars revealed three secret names which Luci gave Moses as his adept. The malicious rabbis knew these names (50 Levites and the 150 attending to them).

In total, 200 rabbis left Babylon (and with them women and children, all in all no more than a thousand). This tribe again restored theocratic tyranny in Israel. The Deuteronomy effect: the Torah was rewritten anew (according to the rules of Lucifer).[74] With this new law was established a strictly regulated racist regime. Jewish women, under fear of execution, were not able to marry men of other tribes. The worship of other divinities was also forbidden and was punished with death.

The monotheistic '*He is-who-is*' excludes the most eternal Christ and the most eternal existence of souls, and seals heaven as the homeland of the immortal soul. There is only *he*. The soul is not acknowledged in the heavenly homeland and does not bear within itself the origin of the Existing One. Man is a primordial nobody. He is nothing <u>before his embodiment</u> (the basis of 'creation from nothing'). He remains nothing <u>during his life</u>, because the fullness of being belongs to Jehovah, and will remain nothing <u>beyond the grave</u>. As 'nothing' in the best event, if he proves to be a deceased monad after *the second death*, fragmented for never-ending torments and insights.

The sunny regal incarnation of Christ

Jesus Christ was the perfect embodiment of the sunny proto-Christ, or the regal sunny incarnation of the 84th civilization.

He entered the world to return souls to the Divinity.

The Christoanthropos, the anointed man

The Old Testament chalice of the Secret Supper was borrowed from the ancient cults and has no direct relationship to Golgotha.

Golgotha was the mystery of the collection of precious blood, the mystery of the transubstantiation of blood into myrrh. By shedding His Blood, Christ created the CHRISTOANTHROPOS (the anointed man) and with him the THEOANTHROPOS (the transformed Godman).

The goal of the messianistic meal, as it is understood in the school of the Holy Grail, is the dissolving of Christ's blood in the pure vessels.

The divinization of the Chalice

The divinization of the Chalice... The Father looks at it as a flawless mirror, contemplating the perfect of Himself.

The Mother of God holds the Chalice in Her hands as Christ Himself, adored by Her, and transubstantiates the Multiplying one.

The last drops of the myrrhic blood of Christ, infinitely multiplied, are dissolved in nature and in the person of the Seraphites – the lesser christs.

The worship of the Chalice returns the Universum

The Roman church in the sin-centric juridical doctrine placed the cross as the centre of worship.

The light-centric Grail performs the worship of the Chalice.

At the level at which the worship of the cross alienates from the Universum, worship of the Chalice returns the Universum.

In the Holy Grail is contained:

1) the fullness of the Father;

2) the fullness of His anointed sovereigns, having entered the world at some time;

3) the flawlessly represented Church of Love;

4) the fullness of divine existence and

5) the sum of Adamite souls who have given the last drop, their ecstatic Holy Passion.

This divine vessel is invaluable, containing within itself the most precious blood of Christ.

The Theogamic Grail – what is this?

The most precious vessel of Our Divinity, of His disciples. The sum of the last drops of the anointed sovereigns and of all God's creation, which has given a never-ending multitude of answering last drops of pure love.

> O adored Chalice of chalices!
> Withn it in fullness is present our Divinity.

The Mother of God fainted from ecstatic Holy Passion, when the Saviour entrusted the Theogamic Grail to Her on Nightingale Mountain. Even she, the heavenly Queen, was not able to endure the fullness of grace, contained within it.

The hypnosis of the old tabernacle will act until the worship of the cross (already recognized to a sufficient degree in the universum) has been replaced with the worship of the chalice. The spheres of Catharism are needed.

Five million of those to whom the heaven of the Father of pure love has been revealed will enter the ark.

Catastrophe number one of the 84th civilization: the Elohimization of Christ

The Elohimization of Christ is the declaration of Him as the son of the Old Testament idol because of His apparently genetic origin from the Jewish tribe.

The immortal anointed sovereigns of the Theo-civilization, having revealed themselves at San Salvador Verdadero, called this phenomenon the greatest catastrophe of the 84th civilization. The collapse which sealed the gates of the true Divinity and entailed the death of man.

Lucifer, having 'with hindsight' ascribed Christ to Elohim, was able to realize that which he had not been able to realize through Moses. Christ has been called 'the new Moses': the new law to take the place of the old. What Moses, the first vessel of Elohim, was not able to do, the second did: Christ.

The Elohimization of Christ is a step towards the embodiment of Lucifer's plan: the formation of the single worldwide religion of the dictator. Thus the age-old enemy concealed the true mission of the greatest anointed sovereign: the transformation of the line of Adam through multiplication and triumph in Theohumanity.

*

In the symbolism of the Round Table the four circles, drawn on linen, radiated out like the four suns of the Cathar cross. The four circles symbolize:

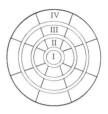

I. The heart of the Father of pure love and the birth of the proto-Christ, the Son of God, from the Last Drop.

II. Christ sheds a million multiplied last drops at Golgotha in Jerusalem.

III. The Great Church of Love multiplies Christ in the Holy Passion of the anointed sovereigns.

IV. Theohumanity achieves the triumph of myrrhic drops. The 85th Theocivilization.

*

Without the Chalice, the shedding of the Last Drop could not occur.

The Chalice of the Bridal Supper – 'from the bone' of the Divinity Himself. The composition of the theoanthropos, the Godman is contained in it.

In Christian restored Elohimism man is the source of evil

The entire sum of evil from the beginning to the end of the world relates solely to Lucifer.

Attributing (indirectly or directly) evil to the Divinity is a monstrous delusion.

497

The slightest assumption that the Divinity is capable of setting a trap for His creation or blessing him to enter eternal torments (even as a consequence of freedom given) automatically attributes evil to man. Hence in the Christian restored Elohimism man is the source of evil.

Man closed from himself is not able to be freed from phantoms. He remains sealed in a stagnant shell until the Divinity has been rehabilitated before the face of his creation. Only the Great Church of Love, descending from heaven, can do this.

The verdict of the Father's acquittal, disconnected from evil, corruption, pollution, debauchery, and the judgement of Lucifer's accusation is already accomplished today by the anointed church, led by the anointed sovereign.

*

Our Father reveals Himself with such effort because the chimera of the old tabernacle stands, the Roman distorting mirror.

When the evil projected by Lucifer onto the Divinity and creation is returned to him, the score for the phantoms will be presented to his adepts.

> Against the chimera of Lucifer –
> the immortals of San Salvador Verdadero.
> Kindest divinity among kind divinities –
> such is the preaching of the pure one.

*

As soon as the wilderness begins, the deviation and the shape of the Father is lost ('where are You, Sweetest One?'), denounce Lucifer and his machinations.

May the light of Our Divinity be revealed to the souls passing into eternal peace. Having seen the machinations of our enemy they enter terror and disarray.

𝒞hrist desires to reveal the Father of pure love to Christians today

The Christ of the first coming (of the Jerusalem period) desired to reveal the Father to the Judaic tribe, which had arrived at the centre of global Luciferism.

The Christ of the second coming desires the reveal the Father of pure love to Christians with that same fervour with which he defended the Father before the faith of Elohim 2000 years ago.

As he thrice denounced and ordered that the temple of Jerusalem be destroyed, saying: 'I will build a new temple, my Body', so today He orders that the old temple, built in the shape of that of Jerusalem, be destroyed. He promises to build the kingdom of the Holy Grail, the temple of the Chalice.

*

It is impossible not to love Him... It is possible only to adore Him.

The epoch of the Father of pure love of the adored Christ is beginning.

God is revealing Himself for the first time.

31.

Five million
will be led to the Ark

The heavenly fire,
lit by the Divinity in His creation

The Cathars accomplish the melting of the candle in the heart. For the awakening one it is important to light the candle of our Father.

THE IMMORTALS:

San Salvador Verdadero is the place of the return of the gifts from Our Divinity to humanity.

The staircase of San Salvador Verdadero is extended in the Universum. It is possible to ascend to it from any corner of the earth. To the ascender is returned the heavenly fire, lit by the Divinity in His creation – in the protochrist. This fire has begun to burn in the hearts of the Cathars and has made them immortals from perfect ones.

The melting of the pearl

The melting of the pearl has already begun during the first metres of ascent. The candle, melted in the heart, should blaze with divine fire. This fire burns up the origins of death, decay, sin, and pollution.

Perfect holiness is possible and easy to achieve, but awakening is given with the price of breaking off the manacles. It is necessary to fill yourself with the spirit and break the petrifying, soporific spider's nets, laid by the prince of this world with regard to the immortal human essence.

With each ascent I hear from the immortals:

Grace comes from the Father of pure love with His revelation.

Man needs only to see the Father to love Him and combine with Him.

And then, with the dissolution of the covenant with Lucifer, the Father begins to nourish His sons and daughters.

The hardest cataclysm

The Cathars show terrible disasters. From the side of the sea I see dark, torrential, molten streams.

The hardest cataclysm awaits humanity. This is the sole thing about which it must be warned.

The 84th civilization will be swept away.

The ark for 5 million

Our news is ark-apocalyptic. Into the ark will enter those who worship the Divinity of the ascending sunny Theocivilization, the Father of pure love, and acknowledge themselves as His children.

But before the universal cataclysms will be given signs: a stench in the temples; the complete denunciation of the diabolical nature of the religions of Abraham.

Five million will be led into the ark by the same unknown saints, the martyrs of love, about whom neither trace nor memory remains in the library of humanity. From them, comes today the power and salvation, patronage and might of Our Divinity.

There is no other fortress than the fortress of pure love, erected on earth. Lucifer is frightened of it.

The anointed sovereign

He who acknowledges only the authority and the power of the love of Our Divinity over himself we call the anointed sovereign.

The power of love alone is able to kill Lucifer, the tyrant and satan, who uses the serpentine power of hypnosis, magic, violence, fear, mammon.

The entrance into divine existence is given with the feeblenesses of the Holy Passion according to the spiritual staircase of the universum: Holy Passion – divine existence – bliss.

The holy of holies of San Salvador

In the holy of holies of San Salvador, man discards from himself the body of the original sin (which does not exist), draws out it and clothes himself in a body of original immaculateness. Elohim has no authority. Hence such unheard-of lightness and the fullness of the grace of the Holy Spirit, for which man is worthy in the pleroma created from the Last Drop.

Fragrance and myrrh

The fragrance of the myrrh of the Father has finally penetrated us. Despite the fierce wind the most powerful fragrance comes in waves. The Holy Grail of the Father smells fragrantly.

The prophecy has been realized: in 700 years the laurel will become green once more. The laurel has become fragrant. Hurrah!

The fragrance is the anointing of all the immortal bodies. The immortal body is anointed through smell.

This was the fragrance of relics. We fly downwards weightless.

We are taking the vow of eternal loyalty. To stand for a thousand years under one golden throne and fearlessly destroy the machinations of Lucifer, to descend with the fiery apostles of the Father of pure love many more times.

The Father opened His heart for me, revealed His love. Another revelation is not needed. His love is the greatest gift. All the others (gifts, charity, service, charismas) are derived from His love.

The devil is the enemy of humanity because with his laws, fears, and mimicking chimeras he leads man from the love of the Divinity, and switches him over to himself.

The saints will be victorious! Those, who worship the Father of pure love in the purest virginity and perfect immaculateness, are called saints. One day they will be honoured with the stage of the immortals and the fragrance of the laurel will be smelt in the Holy of holies of San Salvador Verdadero.

32.

the Radiance
of the most eternal one
in the existence today

- The millenium of sunny saints
- The seals of the victor of Gulag
- 'I, the Divinity of divinities'
- His gates have been opened for the immortals
- I took You into My embraces

THE IMMORTALS:

lessed is he who follows and hears today, not yesterday. Yesterday has passed without a trace. The radiance of the most eternal one in the existence today.

The crowned kings great and small, the rapturous princes glorify the Father, descending and revealing Himself for the first time to the humanity of the sleeping 84th civilization.

The staff of awakening is for the melchizedeks. The keys of salvation are for the anointed sovereigns. And the casket of secrets is for you.

> In the embraces of Our Divinity
> superadmiring grace,
> superadmiring fullness.

The adored Divinity of the sunny Theocivilization, the Father of fathers, differs from the pantheon of the divinities of the traditional world religions in the same way as the Chalice of the Sacred Grail from brass glass-holders and cheap church forgeries.

Accept the courage of the warriors of the Divinity from us and take the knight's vow to stand to the last beneath His shining banners in the most eternal glory.

During the first conversion your deed is to renounce worldly values, to renounce the childhood of the world.

Your deed for the second serious conversion of the knights of the Most Pure Mother of God is to renounce pseudo-religious values.

The ancient serpent will have to roll up into a ball and clear off. Today we scattered his ancient old nest.

The Divinity transubstantiates, and He has no yesterday.

Christ transubstantiates. Christ is alive and He is not former as stamped in the books of the past.

The Mother of God transubstantiates, fading in the icons.

The Holy Spirit transubstantiates into the Divinizer, adoring His loving disciples and rewarding them with a million times more than they are able to accept at present.

The Great Church of Love transubstantiated into the sunny kingdom of Our Divinity. Savour the fragrance of the aromatic relics.

> O adored Divinity
> O His transubstantiated name!
> O sum of most divine names.
> His triumph and exultation.
> The kingdom of the Holy Spirit.
> The fullness, the pleroma of the Word.

Transmit to the world our sorrow at how weakly they hear our revelations. Some enter bravely by the gates opened for them!

I.

THE FATHER:

The mission of John's throne is to proclaim the new Divinity for the new humanity:

Adored Father, purest of the pure. Be-el', Te-el', Mi-el',

Beautiful among beautiful ones, the Most Beautiful of the splendid ones,

Perfect among the perfect ones, Most Perfect of the perfect ones,

Kindest among the kind, the Kindest of the kind,

Pure among the pure, the Purest of the pure,

Loving superior among His beloved,

True among the true, the truest of the true,

Permanent among hermits, Combined among brides,

510

Perfect manifested one, Adoring with adoring love,

Father of perfect sons and daughters,

Father of holy fool pilgrims,

Organizer of the Bridal Supper of the He-lamb and the She-lamb, Christ and the Mother of God,

Enraptured in the bosom of immaculate and unsetting light,

Victor over the ancient serpent,

Triumpher of the sunny 85th Theocivilization III.

So the adored Father said about Himself.

The sunny cohorts of His troops, the chariots of His immortal warriors, their joyful faces and exultant cries. They rode on white horses in expectation of the horsemen, and behind them came the army.

II.

THE IMMORTALS:

Your mission is to set the end for the epoch of the devil, to sum it up. To accomplish judgement over the ancient serpent. To display the forgotten scrolls of the saints and seal the deeds of the impious. To sift and winnow as the wise sewer and gather the beautiful harvest from the autumnal fields.

Proclaim the end of the age of the devil, of his base joss houses and cunning pantheons. The millenium and age of the sunny saints!

III.

Father John San Grial II

We called you John of the Second Grail (Juan de San Grial II) from time immemorial. You glorify the civilization of the Chalice, in which are 2, 20, 200, 200,000, 200 million last drops of the fountaining meal of Our Divinity.

Glorify the Holy Grail in the true church, for which agree to endure to the last, until the last drop has been collected for the fullness of the Chalice. After which the master of the meal will exclaim: it is enough! Hosanna!

And the exultant procession of the sunny Theo-civilization will begin, where Father John San Grial II will be awaited by one of three to take in his hands the sunny Chalice of the last drops of our great martyrs.

IV.

Accept from us the seals of the Victor of Gulag, the concentration zones of the poor mother-earth, in order to patiently bear the determined cross.

Consider the transcendental and back-breaking battles an honour. They, more than anything else advance you towards the assemblies of the anointed ones.

Do not glance backwards. Remember rule № 1 of the Holy Chalice:

The true one does not die, but transubstantiates into a higher class.

Never regret what has been erased. What is insignificant departs without a trace. What is worthy imprints itself and is glorified.

The mind-boggling triumph of the 85th civilization

Look, our beloved. From the 200 million last drops have been born 200,000,000×10. Multiply again by another 200 sunny immortal Seraphites. Such is the mind-boggling triumph!

Each of the inhabitants of the future age of the 85th civilization, in which the martyrs of love of the 84th will reign, will carry in himself something from the Adamite, and in particular the immune composition, made in the battle with the prince of this world and allowing to withstand his machinations.

Healing ointment

THE FATHER:

Despise that with which the enemy reproaches you. Remember My sixth attribute (faithful) and the fifteenth (the victor).

I will not retreat, and you will not retreat.

The devil has shown himself as more insignificant than he is. The enemy attacks through old lairs, dug by him during the first conversion...

Accept the healing ointment from our hands.

They give white ointment, then another 12 boxes for my disciples.

Use it to heal the bloody wounds and bites inflicted by sharp teeth, and anoint your beloved disciples bitten by the poisonous dragon. With this ointment wounds are healed and illness passes without a trace.

The enemy's bite is negligibly sweet at first, but it is possible to free oneself from the tempting charms only with the help of the first-anointed staff.

Your mission has multiplied – and so have your sorrows. But without persecutions and slander the crown of the anointed sovereign-king of the Holy Spirit will not be gained.

With honour share the cross of the saints glorified from you, from Andrew the First-Called to Ascold-Nicolay, the nunciate of Holy Rus', from Innokenty and Euphrosinia to the last saints in your army.

I move the hands of My eternal clock to the 85th Theocivilization-III

I, the Divinity of divinities, the Father of fathers, the Mother of mothers, the Miracle of miracles and the Victor of victors[+], erase the diabolical ourtlines of the 84th civilization.

514

I am the Sun of suns! Look upon my face and do not withdraw the sacred gaze.

Today, before the face of My saints, I exultantly abolish the old seals and move the hands of the eternal clock to the 85th THEOCIVILIZATION-III.

Rejoice, crowned ones. Rejoice, victors. Rejoice, perfect ones.

Rejoice, Holy Passion. Rejoice, lovers. Rejoice, you who carry your crosses in the wildernesses of the world.

Rejoice, troops of the Divinity, having not lost a single battle with the surrogate and mimicker, the prince of this world.

Peace be with you.

O, our fathers shed so many sacred myrrh-pouring tears on San Salvador Verdadero! What wildernesses of Holy Passion they suffered to gain today's triumph!

> The mountain has been cleared. The Father has expelled the enemy from our mountain.

Who is he? The wretched dog! He sits at the legs of his master, tail between his legs, and doesn't stop looking into his master's eyes, devising his machinations...

THE IMMORTALS:

We placed a great investment in the victory over our common enemy, the prince of this world. It remained to scatter the last myths and dispel the barely taut webs.

Glorify the Mother of God of the sunny temple of the Second coming.

Glorify Christ as the sun of suns of the Theocivilization III, the king of the anointed sovereigns of pure love.

Glorify His priesthood of Melchizedek as the guiding elite of the constellation of exceedingly wise white elders, coming to earth from time immemorial to confirm the civilization of original immaculateness.

Immaculate is the disciple of Our Divinity. Thrice holy is the immaculate and spotless branch of John.

Keep, earth, the promise of the Divinity. His gates have been opened for the immortals.

The Father:

Original immaculateness is the tree of saints and the root which I lay as the foundation of the sunny civilization.

No less than five hundred years will pass before the serpent, defeated and lulled to sleep, will awake. For more than half a millenium the enemy will not be able to defile My thrones. The infinite joy of joys awaits creation, my child.

Peace be with you. Peace among the saints.

Peace doubled among the perfect ones.

Peace among the anointed ones and among the immortals.

Peace be with you, kings and small divinities of the new holy Rus', of the new holy Spain, of the new holy Croatia, of the new holy France, of the new humanity, of the new earth.

The voice of our Father is buried in the thousand-times fanfare echo of sunny trumpeters. Today is the day of our victory over the prince of the world.

Even in your earthly days you will see the greatest celebrations of decisive victory

My child, if only you had seen how this demon slid into the abyss after his sham victory over you today – like ball of dirt, gathering weight with every turn. And the gates closed behind him.

I am the true and persistent Father. I will allow a battle for My holy fools and unpredictable true disciples, for the loving ones, for pilgrims.

In the prayer of the Holy Passion today you asked Me with tears to take you. And now I have taken you in My embraces and returned you to the world for the fulfillment of your triumphal mission.

Even in the earthly days you will see the greatest of celebrations of our decisive victory, of a kind not known in the 84th civilization. And you will rejoice to the heavens with the church of John.

There are 200 million of us

200 immortals cry, the splendid assembly of invincible knights:

> The Sun of Our Divinity,
> our most admired Father.
> The road to the Kingdom has been cleared!

There are 200, 200 thousand, 200 million of us, and each will give: a candle, a pearl, oils, or the cross for the Chalice.

Victors staffs, tables for the meal, the crown, myrrh.

> The bearing out of the Chalice.

The beautiful meal of the Round Table, as large as the universe

We are invited to the transcendentally beautiful meal of the Round Table, as large as the universe. The sun of suns of the Father of pure love descends to its silver mother-of-pearl surface. And this is also the Grail of San Salvador Verdadero.

The master of the feast bows above me. The joy amongst us is greatest today. Victory! $12 \times 12 = 144$ prepared wreaths!!!

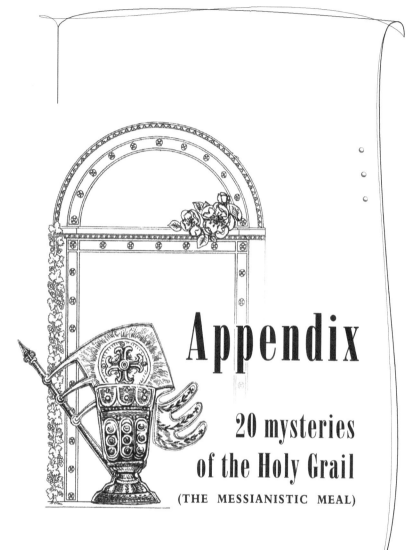

Appendix

20 mysteries
of the Holy Grail
(THE MESSIANISTIC MEAL)

$\mathscr{P}$reliminary remarks from on high

JUAN OF THE HOLY CHALICE:

t is not a liturgy, but a divine meal, the messianistic meal of Christ.

The disciples around the Round Table. The Bridal Supper, the mystery of mysteries of the Holy Grail, includes the following sequence of 10 (12) great and small mysteries.

*

Concept № 1: the meal of the Grail – transubstantiation:

1) Christ into humanity;

2) humanity into Christ,

3) the Blood into the Chalice;

4) the Blood into myrrh;

5) Christ's myrrh into the divinized, enriched human (theohuman) composition.

Without the perspective of transubstantiation, there is no admission into it or active realization.

The chimeras of the Chrysostom-Byzantine liturgy or the Roman mass are stolen from the Holy Grail.

NB!! There are no recollections 'in honour and memory', historical reminiscences, or magical rituals.

The Sang Real, the holy Blood of Christ (the Holy Grail) = the composition of the myrrh of the Lamb of God, the fullness of the Divinity.

The pleroma, being shed into the Chalice for the subsequent transubstantiation into the chose vessels (the knights and the wife-myrrhbearers of the Holy Chalice).

The Blood-myrrh of Christ is partaken of for the renewal of compositions. Thus,

transubstantiation passes into divinization,
the mystery of the Bridal Chamber.

I. EMBODIMENT

The embodiment of the Father in Theohumanity.

• Our Father the Sun of suns of pure love...

Embodiment as an act of the divinity becoming man.

The last drop of the Divinity as the pearl of the Holy Grail, melted at 3003°C.

The call signs of the Theocivilization, the entrance into the kingdom of the Holy Grail:

- Ave Maria, the Most Fragrant Virgin...

- Rejoice, Mary, in complete grace...

- God-bearer, Virgin of lights, rejoice!
  Blessed are You among His brides
  and blessed is the fruit of Your bosom,
  the Light of the immaculate conception.

- Original immaculateness,
  the immaculate origin,
  the immaculate conception –
  the three gifts of the Mother of God.

II. THE REGAL APPEARANCE OF THE HOLY CHALICE

Golgotha of Jerusalem (the crucifixion of the Lamb). The regal appearance of the Holy Chalice.

The Father sends it from the highest heavens and entrust it to the keeper of the Chalice, Saint Joseph of Arimathea.

With him are the apostles Andrew the First-Called and John the Theologian.

And with them are three wife-myrrhbearers.

The first motion around the Round Table with the prayer:

> The mystery of the renewal of compositions –
> Ave Father Ave.
> The blood of Christ is collected in the Chalice –
> the sweetest Lamb transubstantiates.
> O priceless treasure trove,
> found by the loving.

The ascent of the Chalice filled with the most restful wine, into which is stirred lemon, cinnamon, bread, and mixed with a spoonful of honey and a drop of hot water, symbolizing the heart warmed by love.

III. DIVINE EXISTENCE

Where is the meal held?

In divine existence, where there are no re-calling antiques, relics, external ritual, and so on.

The entrance into divine existence excludes 'friends in grey clothing' (the gospel words of Christ). Not one unworthy will dare to enter it, however hard he mimics, however hard he imitates.

However much you pray with the saints, the entrance into divine existence has been sealed if the seals of the anointed ones have not been laid on your brow.

> The meal of the Grail, Saint Juan de San Grial emphasises, occurs exclusively in divine existence.

Driven, slandered, and called to account by the servants of Lucifer, the Holy Grail is preserved in divine existence, carried from one castle to another. It is covered from above.

The form of life – deep catacombs, the control of the world, incredible (holy fool) manifestation of the Divinity in creation.

IV. EXORCISM IN THE HOLY GRAIL

Divine existence presupposes *entrances*; instant for the perfect ones, but for others gradual.

Melchizedek opens the twelve gates of divine existence,

the 12 entrances into the Kingdom, the 12 blessings, the 12 bridal beds, the 12 thrones...

Like the strings of the divine lyra, melchizedek runs his fingers over the Second Solovetsky, the Bridal Chamber, the gates of metanoia, universal, unified, ecclesiastical and personal (many great saints, having begun to shine in the scrolls of the Grail, have a golden throne, beneath which they gather a flock of many thousand)...

THE GATES (12x12=144)

– Euphrosinia of Pochaev

– Seraphim of Sarov

– the church of John

– the knights of the Holy Grail

– sunny entrances into the Theocivilization

– the Father of pure love

– Exceeding Wisdom

– Sacred Theogamites...

From 12 to 144 gates (at the great festive meals).

The opening of the gates creates incomparable joy for Melchizedek, holding the staff of blessing and of the opening of the heavenly gates (with the mention of the three great mountains) in his hands).[75]

V. GRADULATION

The entrances into divine existence foreordain the following mystery of the Holy Grail: gradular staffs, or prayers of direct entrance into the heavenly spheres and the control of global processes, including the prohibition of Luciferic gates, and the creation of the spheres of the Divinity, and with them the modelling of the divine man.

> The gates of the Kingdom have been opened.
> Enter, Theogamites,
>   Paracletes, Seraphites...
> The entrances to the Heavenly Kingdom have
>   been opened.
> enter, brides of Christ!
> Lay the meals of superabundance.
> Evdoksia, the ascent on newly-gained wings.

VI. PETITIONS FOR THE CONVERSION OF THE WORLD

Gradular entrances presuppose unified prayer petitions for the conversion of the world.

For the conversion of the world, salvation,
purification, divinization, ascent
to the thrones of the Father
       of the six billion prisoners of the earth,
for their liberation
from the hypnotic oppression of Rex Mundi;
San Salvador Verdadero,
the true Saviour,
bless us.

VII. EXORCISM IN THE HOLY GRAIL

Shield[+], patronage[+], sword[+] and heavenly blessings[+] are completed by exorcism, understood in the
Holy Grail as the renunciation of the machinations
of the prince of this world with the added gifts of
sobriety and of distinguishing the spirits.

VIII. THE HOLY EVDOKSIYA

The unworldly holy fool pilgrims, troubadours
driven from the world, virgins and poets are accompanied by the unearthly blessing called *evdok-
sia* or joy in the Holy Grail, otherwise unattainable
on earth, but only

       in the kingdom of the Holy Grail /
       in divine existence /
       in the bosom of Exceeding Wisdom /
       the mystery of the holy evdoksia.

There follows a sequence of blessings:
Blessed are, blessed are...

IX. ETERNAL VIRGINITY

The entrance to the eighth castle (the eighth mystery of the Holy Grail) is eternal virginity.

It is located after exorcism because virginal vestments, perfect purity, spotlessness are considered the most powerful weapon against the prince of this world and his diabolical army.

X. THE SACRED THEOGAMY

The Theogamic virgin is prepared for the joys of the Bridal Chamber.

The prayer of Sacred Theogamy:

> My Lady, God's Exceeding Wisdom,
> God-blessed and most immaculate,
> most pure Sacred Theogamy,
> Flawless Mirror and Queen of the universe,
> combine Your children
>   with the Heavenly Bridegroom,
> blessed to enter this world,
> and anoint us with the oils of uniting
>   with the Divinity,
> o myrrhic Virgin of conciliation.

The angels most restfully gaze at the virgins.

The second motion of the wise virgins around the Round table.

XI. SUPREME PEACE

PEACE is found through spiritual pilgrimage to the internal castles. In each is the imperishable treasure trove and regal altar with one of the 144 hypostases of Christ. The Great Church of Love opens them.

- Church of Love / approach, approach, approach... PEACE. The blessing of the Divinity.

  - I came to this world,
    in order to be the one with God
    through suffering humanity.
      PEACE, PEACE, PEACE
      Heavenly Peace. PEACE

XII. THE MOTION WITH THE CANDLES

O Sacred Minne,
Love, of a kind
not in heaven nor on earth...

O more and more!
O there is nothing higher.
The myrrh is shedding.

The wreath of ecstatic prayers.
The mystery of Sacred Minne revealed solely in

the Holy Grail and penetrating the immortal composition of immortal man.

XIII. THE MYSTERY OF THE UNRAVELLING OF THE WHITE SCROLLS

Reading from them is indeed a blessing for those that love the Father and reject the wretchedness of the historical chronicles and their false interpretation by the pillars of church history, liars, conformists and hypocrites, not permitted into the Holy Grail – the place of lovers of truth and endurers of the Holy Passions (the martyrs of love).

A reading from one of the heavenly treatises of the Mother of God or Christ.

XIV. THE BLESSED MOTION WITH EXTINGUISHED CANDLES

Prayer for the deceased.

• The burial vault stood,
  Millions passed
  by its sweetest / gates,
  whispered with their lips:
  We had not heard sweeter music.

Wilderness. Holy Passions. Golgotha in the Universum (as the mysteries of the Holy Grail)

Seven cries from the cross, from *'Forgive them, they know not what they do...'* to *'It is done!!!'*

XV. THE MOTHER OF GOD OF PIETY

Awaiting the Cross with the wife-myrrhbearers, with John the Theologian, as the personified Chalice of the Divinity – the personified Holy Grail.

Singing to the Most Holy God-bearer:

- God-bearer, the Life-giving Font.
- O blessed, O wonderful...
- *and others.*

XVI. THE SECOND SOLOVETSKAY GOLGOTHA

The Second Solovetskay Golgotha.

The candles begin to burn, symbolizing the lighting of the internal candle, turning into the bush, into fire in the divinized lungs.

XVII. THE SHEDDING OF THE LAST DROP

The meaning of the 17th mystery of the Holy Grail: the overflowing of the Chalice from the God-bearer into Christ (and from Christ into the God-bearer) and the shedding of the answering Last Drop during the kindling of the temperature of the heart.

The love for the divine Beloved is intensifying.

I am dying of love for You, Jesus...
My mad love, for Jesus the Lamb...

- The myrrh of the Last Drop is being shed⁺.
  The devotee transubstantiates into Christ⁺.
  The mystery is completed⁺...

XVIII. CHERUBIC

Movement with candles.
The credo of transubstantiation:

WHAT IS THIS?

I believe, my Father, that You sent me into the world, in order to compete the mystery of the Bridal Chamber and shed the Last Drop of answering love. And, having passed the path of the holy fool wanderer, a beggar on earth, to enter the Bridal Chamber as Your divinized bride and rest at the Bridal Supper of love in His eternal kingdom with the God-bearer, the Virgin Mary, and my holy brothers and sisters.

*

I came into this world,
in order to enter into marriage with God
through the suffering humanity
and to become a bride in His Kingdom.

XIX. THE PARTAKING OF THE SWEETEST LAMB

The highest and greatest of the mysteries in which Christ flawlessly, with all His fullness in several drops of myrrhic Blood (thrice transubstantiated[76]), turns into His disciple, becoming a l e s s e r c h r i s t after the mystical meal.

> After the great mysteries of the Grail, which comprise the liturgy just described, are t h e b e n e - d i c t i o n s (thanksgivings, hallelujahs, universal joy).

XX. THE KISS OF PEACE

The meal finished with brotherly embraces, kisses of peace and the rapture of heaven.

The knights of the Holy Chalice experienced the blessings.

The sweetest Lamb entered them.

They felt themselves lesser christs and god-bearers.

Through the entrance into the interior was accomplished the Kingdom of He whom the knights of the Holy Chalice worshipped in the most lofty fashion.

> The most powerful aromas of relics were smelt, as from the relics of Mother Euphrosinia in Gethsemane.

God's Messenger
of Love and Peace

Charles Mercieca, Ph.D.
President International Association
of Educators for World Peace
Dedicated to United Nations Goals
of Peace Education,
Environmental Protection,
Human Rights & Disarmament
Professor Emeritus, Alabama A&M University

From the early days of creation God tended to send messengers to bring among all of His children love and peace. Some of these messengers were angels, while others were carefully selected human beings, who were generally characterized by an angelic mind and heart. In the early centuries of recorded civilization most of these were known as prophets, who talked about the wonders of God and His plans for the future of our earthly community. They outlined for us God's plans, which were all geared toward our benefit.

These prophets were instrumental in inspiring many to change their bad habits and to embark upon a new life, where the practice of virtue becomes their top priority and primary concern. Some of them communicated directly with angels, that went by the name of Michael, Raphael and Gabriel. What has been of great importance may be viewed as the implementation of God's noble plans in the best interest of all of God's children without exception. God had always ways to look after His children properly and effectively.

Throughout history, people from every walk of life and profession in all the various cultures of the world always sought to elevate their mind and heart to a higher level of existence. They viewed such a higher level as a real powerful and genuinely caring Being that went by different names. They all felt that such a Divine entity could speak silently with clarity in the mind and heart of all those who search for Him. This developed in many the habit of prayer, that we use to talk with God and of meditation, where we listen to what God wishes to tell us.

Some of the most familiar names given to such a Supreme Being were Yahweh, God, and Allah in addition to others. His guidance was always needed, since human beings happen to be surrounded by the forces of evil in a number of instances. Among those names attributed to such evil forces we find such commonly heard names as Satan, Beelzebub, and Devil among others. This explains why the human life was described as pugna constans – a steady battle. What is important in life lies in overcoming the obstacles we encounter.

The great religious leaders of all time, from Buddha, Lao Tze down to Jesus of Nazareth, and all the way to Francis of Assisi, Mahatma Gandhi, Martin Luther King, Jr. and Mother Teresa in addition to numerous others, were all characterized by their great spirituality. They could all be described as the apple of God's eyes. Their mission was to bring good life to all of God's children and to alleviate them from their pain to the best of their ability. They all were altruistic, working always for the good of others while expecting nothing in return.

$\mathcal{G}$od's Messengers at Work

If we were to give a glance throughout history, we will discover that all those, who spent their lives working exclusively for the benefit of all people have all experienced inner joy and happiness on a habitual basis. Both Confucius and Jesus exhorted us to do to others, what we would like others to do to us. Most ascetical writers admonished us that the art of living is the art of giving. This means that we need to put ourselves constantly at the disposal of others and not the other way round.

This way we will give ourselves the opportunity to become God-like, that is, representatives of the real image of God. We will then merit becoming genuine messengers of God on earth imbued with great spiritual powers. At this stage of our life it would be wonderful, if we were to become familiar with all the teachings and exhortations of God's messengers of all time. It would help us immensely, if we were to become personally acquainted with one or more of these chosen messengers of His.

The purpose of this presentation was to present us with the unique opportunity to learn about one of God's great messengers of our time, with whom He constantly communicates through His Blessed Mother. In fact, for the past several years, the Virgin Mary has given to this great messenger several messages, which were then put in writing. I am referring here to Blessed John (Bereslavsky), Patriarch of the Mother of God Church Derjevnaya, who is from Moscow. He became soon the enlightenment of the New Holy Russia.

When the communists took over Russia in 1917, part of the Russian Orthodox Church went underground and became the Church of the Catacomb, while the other part remained in operation to the best it could. After the collapse of communism in 1987, the Church of the Catacomb emerged into the open and soon became known as the Mother of God Church Derjevnaya, with Blessed John as its Patriarch. Within a short time, this holy Marian Church was blessed with numerous vocations consisting of priests, brothers, nuns, sisters and laity. Many branches spread quickly across Russia and Eastern Europe.

The strength of Blessed John could be traced to his phenomenal love for the Virgin Mary, who has been his constant guide ever since. He has always tried, to the best of his ability, to imitate all the possible virtues he could detect in this Holy Woman, who is known by numerous titles including Queen of Heaven. One of the virtues of the Blessed Virgin that has fascinated this great servant of God was her virginity. He firmly believes that this great virtue of Blessed Mother was one of the basic reasons, why God was so much fascinated with her that He chose her to become the Mother of His Divine Son.

As a result of his tremendous dedication and love for the Virgin Mary, Father John has been blessed with the seven gifts of the Holy Spirit, which may be outlined as follows:

1. *Wisdom*: This consists of the ability to see things into true perspective, the way God sees them. It also reveals the ability to have one's priorities in life better organized and more properly managed.

2. *Understanding*: This helps one to visualize things from other people's perspective. This way there will be more harmony and peace in human relations, which would make life more pleasant.

3. *Council*: This enables us to give better advices to people from various walks of life and profession. As a result, we are enabled to develop better insights into what is eventually going on.

4. *Fortitude*: This explains well our strength and courage, when confronted with difficulties and problems of one kind or another. Through this gift many positive and constructive things are expected to follow.

5. *Knowledge*: This gives us the ability to learn properly and effectively and to bestow such ac-

quired knowledge successfully to others eventually. Besides, one becomes capable to apply such knowledge properly, when needed.

6. *Piety*: This fills us with the ability to exercise a spirit of compassion, when we come across unfortunate people, that may lack the vital needs of life. It enables us to be merciful same way as God has been merciful to us.

7. *Fear of God*: This involves the fear of offending God not because He has the power to punish us, but because He is a God of love and mercy, that is always ready to forgive us and to provide us with everything we need.

Blessed John was born in Moscow in 1946 one year after World War II was over. He studied music, foreign languages, philosophy and religion in addition to other subject areas. Later on, after he was ordained priest and then archbishop. Soon after, he embarked upon writing many books, that were deeply spiritual and highly inspirational. At the same time, he began to have several interlocutions with the Virgin Mary, from whom he was inspired to write more books. Those, who may wish to learn more about this great messenger of love and peace, may go on the internet, where there are quite a few websites on him.

In recent years, the Russian Orthodox Church emerged to become very touchy in seeing the Russian laity joining other Christian denominations. The authorities of this old traditional Russian Church made it clear that the Russian Orthodox Church should be viewed as the dominant religion of Russia and that other religions ought not to interfere, when "on Russian turf." Consequently, the Mother of God Church Derjevnaya found out it could no longer function in public without some kind of persecution. Of course, the adherents to this Church still function, but inside homes or monasteries instead of public places.

In view of this, Blessed John felt that the Virgin Mary was guiding him to establish branches of this great and noble Marian Church in other parts of the world. Consequently, branches were established in Ukraine, Turkey, Croatia, and Spain in addition to others. Nowadays, this valiant messenger of love and peace directs this fast growing Marian Church from Barcelona in Spain. At present, he is trying to establish branches in the United Kingdom, Canada and the United States. The liturgical functions of this Marian Church instill in participants an atmosphere of heaven.

One of such functions is known as the Sobor, that lasts for a whole day during which the hours pass like minutes and the minutes like split seconds. There were times, when it lasted from the middle of the morning till late in the evening. Participants get the feeling of an out-of-time experience with a good taste of heaven. During such a religious function one could really feel the presence of the Blessed Virgin Mary accompanied by numerous angels.

When you get this experience once, you keep on searching and waiting for the next Sobor. In the past, people came for such an event not only from all over Russia but from countries representing all the continents. The participants, who come from every walk of life and profession, are all saturated with joy and they receive plenty of energy during such a liturgical service. Every sermon of Blessed John reveals great love for the Blessed Mother and for one another.

As God's true messenger of love and peace, Blessed John has travelled very extensively across Asia, Europe and North America. He is very fluent in English, which is viewed today as the international language of communication. He has a pleasant and charming personality even though, at times, he suffers from great anguish due to the fact that so many children of God have conflicts with each other. However, he tends to view suffering as a means of becoming better united with the suffering of His Lord and Master, Jesus, the cherished and most beloved son of Mary, whom he loves so dearly and infinitely.

Mary Mother of all People

Blessed John views all people of all faiths simply as the most beloved children of the Virgin Mother. He feels all people across every continent are his genuine brothers and sisters. The liturgy that he presents in all the functions of the Mother of God Church Derjevnaya represents a combination of the enrichment of Eastern Orthodox, Catholic and Protestant Churches. Besides, he reveres the saints of all the world religions. When the Blessed Mother appeared in Medjugorje to the six children during the decades of the eighties, she stated:

"I am the Mother of all people, of those who know me and of those, who do not know me, of those who love me and of those, who do not care about me, of those who believe in me and of those, who do not believe in me." She also added saying that these were all God's children and that her only one and beloved Son Jesus has shed His life for them to save them from peril. Fortunately, most of the books of Archbishop John have been translated into English and other languages as well, including Spanish. His writings may as well serve as books for meditation that may help elevate the human mind to God.

In view of what has been stated it is obvious that God is guiding Blessed John through His Blessed Mother to help create a better world, that is characterized by love and peace. A careful study of the life and work of this valiant messenger of peace and love will enable us understand with clarity, how God really works in mysterious ways. Let us keep in mind that in a number of instances God's ways are not ours. Hence, we should not get discouraged, when things may go wrong. What is important for us all is that we do our very best and then God will take over and do the rest.

In other words, we need to start the work and then God will see to it that it will be finished, even at a time least expected. We need to keep Blessed John, along with his priests, brothers, nuns, sister and laity, in our prayers. Besides, let us not forget that in all the good work we perform, God sends us His Blessed Mother accompanied by many angels to be constantly with us.

<hr/>

Footnotes

[1] The mother Mary Orlovskaya and the great myrrh-pouring elderly nun Mother Euphrosinia.

[2] Investiture: the appointment of church dignitaries by secular authorities. Today the term has been used for a practice which spread during the Soviet period, when clergymen were appointed with the sanction of the KGB, and the Moscow patriarchate itself was established according to the direct order of Stalin.

[3] Christ-I – Jerusalem, Gospel;

Christ-II – parousia, transubstantiated into the Chalice in the two thousand year history of the true Church;

Christ-III – The King of the new universe, the Divinity of divinities among the divinized ones (in the Theocivilization).

[4] The Third Christ – see footnote 3.

[5] *Caduceus* (ancient Jewish, *kadosh:* holiness, staff of the high priest; Latin, *caduceus:* staff of the messenger, herald). In the Cathar understanding: a special mystical staff of the Exceeding Wisdom of God (it is possible to witness it in the world iconography of the Mother of God-Sophia). The caduceus of Exceeding Wisdom performs a threefold function: blessing, initiation into the Holy Passion (perforation), and anointing. The upper part is topped with a crown and

a cross (blessing). The lower part is a spear of divine love, for the eucharistic perforation of the heart of Christ. In the spiritual life of the anointed sovereign the action of the caduceus is connected with a sudden spiritual pain or blow, according to the judgement of Exceeding Wisdom by those performing the secret of sorrows or penitential suffering. The middle part (the shaft) is filled with myrrhic oils and unifying particles. During the mystical perforation by the caduceus, oils are inserted into the interior of the spiritual heart of the devotee through canals in the point, changing the composition of his spiritual particles on the path to divinization, transformation, and the revealing of the divine potential.

[6] Thus the Cathars scornfully named the Roman bishops. – Author.

[7] That is, 'Asses' jawbones' (from the Catalonian Mandibules d'ase), as the Cathars called the institutional priests.

[8] Cyprian's prayer – exorcism prayer of Russian ascetics.

[9] Nightingale Mountain – "My child, I will tell you about the origin of the Nightingale mountain. The Nightingale mountain was a spiritual centre of three immaculate civilizations, which hadn't disappeared but transubstantiated into another dimension, in higher and more beautiful worlds. Their grace dwells heavily on the Nightingale mountain. And the coming to it

communicant joins through the open gates the perfect sages of Atlantis, Ancient Egypt, Assyria, Babylon and of going into more distant past the divine civilizations." (From the revelation of the Mother of God). Located in Turkey near Ephesus.

[10] Eloi – Hebrew name of God, which displays His luminiferous essence.

[11] Mirron – one of the names of the sunny Divinity.

[12] The Mountain of Our Father: Padre Nuestro San Salvador Verdadero (Spanish). Our father, the true and holy Saviour (from the machinations of Rex Mundi).

[13] Seraphic compositions, seraphit – new man with new immaculate compositions, divinized, not mixed with the original sin.

[14] Adaptational reformation / remodelling – according to the revelation of the Cathars and the immortals, man being born in heaven as a divinity like an angel, was tempted by devil and underwent adaptational reformation, which means of acquiring by the man of an earthly flesh with incorporation of the perverse compositions. The purpose of the spiritual practices of the Cathars is the transforming of a spoiled earthly flesh into the sunny virgin essence.

[15] Kenosis (Greek) – descending of the Divinity into this world.

[16] Bridal Bed – mystical term, meaning a place of absolute uniting of man and God.

[17] Melhoramentum (Occitan): from the Latin 'meliorare', 'to transform, to make better'.

[18] The two most widespread forms of remission of sins during the Christian confession (in Catholicism and Orthodoxy respectively).

[19] See the teaching about the three traps of Lucifer in the books of the Blessed John: 'The Cathars. The Great Church of Love' and 'The Father of Pure Love'.

[20] Metanoia – the term of ancient Greek origin, meaning the spiritual practice of cleansing the heart of man from the sinful beginnings.

[21] Famous mentions in the prophesies of those who have seen God throughout all the world, about the great wonder of the last times.

[22] Locutio interno (Latin, 'internal hearing') – a special state, in which the devotee is able with heartfelt hearing to heed the divine voice. The majority of prophetic revelations and mystical inspirations occur in this way.

[23] Altisimo (Spanish) – one of the names of the Sunny Divinity.

[24] The institutional Christian church.

[25] The apocalyptic accounts which humanity, tormented, presents to its executioners, inquisitors and institutional priests in eternity (see Rev. 6:10: "Until when, Sovereign Lord, holy and true, are you restrain-

ing from judging and avenging our blood upon those who dwell on the earth?")

[26] Padre Nuestro San Salvador Verdadero (Spanish) – Our Father, our holy and true Saviour (from the machinations of Rex Mundi.

[27] Perderodes (distorted Saint Pierre de Roses, the Holy Peter of Roses) – a Catholic monastery and castle opposite San Salvador, near the settlement of Roses. The monks of Perderodes opposed the knights of San Salvador.

[28] The Seraphites (from homo seraphicus, 'the Seraphic man') – the Theohumanity of the future, whose composition, in contrast to the Adamites, is immaculate and woven from the particles and oils of the Divinity.

[29] The secret particle of man, which never abandons the heavens of Our Divinity. The perfect ones called this the regal particle. For more detail about this see chapter 8: 'The vows of eternal virginity and eternal brotherhood'.

[30] Te-el' – the highest part of the soul, inhabiting the heavens.

[31] Cosmic conception – depraved conception of the spirits from the dead planets.

[32] The ancient biblical name Elohim (Almighty) morphologically signifies heavenly powers *in plural*, sometimes translated as 'gods' (e.g. in Exodus 20:3).

[33] Κατακλυσμός (ancient Greek), chastisement: a notion used often in heavenly revelations of recent decades.

[34] Kibeho (Rwanda) and Medjugorje (Bosnia and Herzegovina) were the largest places of miraculous appearances of the Mother of God in the 1980s, having revealed the mission of the Most Holy Virgin as the Messenger of Peace. The denial of these appearances by the church and humanity led to heavy consequences: the Rwandan genocide in 1994 and the fratricidal Serbo-Croat war in the 1990s, which were predicted by the God-bearer as signs of the last times.

[35] Lucifer (the Day Star) in his different hypostases is considered to be the eldest son of the heavenly Father, having turned into His enemy and the enemy of His true sons after his fall.

[36] From the Italian sacerdote – 'priest'. Here the institutional priests, basing their spiritual service exclusively on ritual succession and legal status, distancing themselves from the common human norms of morality and the spiritual laws of the universum.

[37] The appearance of the God-bearer to Father John at the icon of Odigitriya in the Cathedral of the Assumption in Smolensk in autumn 1984 was the beginning of the Russian revelation of the Mother of God.

[38] Second Solovetsky Golgotha – Solovki is a place, where the second Calvary of Christ was implemented,

but in the face of all mankind. 100 million people died during the Red Terror.

[39] Embodiment, incorpulation (Latin incorpulatio), is a term from Cathar teaching, and signifies the arrival of the soul on earth in the divine spiritual body (corpus) attached to it. The opinion of Catharism in this is fundamentally different from the Eastern teaching about *reincarnation.* Reincarnation, from the Latin *re* (again) + *in* (in) + *carne* (flesh, meat) signifies the repeated residence of the soul within the limits of coarsely material earthly flesh.

[40] Bogomils – Slavic predecessors of the Cathars.

[41] From bon homme (Occitan.) – a good, kind man.

[42] So the pious and holy father-Theogamites called original sin.

[43] Solovki – an ancient monastery in the north of Russia. In the days of the Soviet power there was a concentration camp and the Virgin Lady often appeared to the prisoners of Solovki.

[44] Kitezh-grads – old Russian term for the divine city on earth.

[45] The Mother of Exceeding Wisdom (Spanish).

[46] We have in mind the highest part of the soul, the internal secret one.

[47] From the teaching of the Cathars: 'Man has been formed from divine compositions, from the pollen of

the sunny rays in the fiery vestments (Adam Cadmon). Divine radiances have been inserted into him: original immaculateness, the immaculate beginning and the never-ending divine potential in 144x12 caskets. The storerooms were to be opened after a thousand years...' (Blessed John, 'The Cathars: The Church of Love', M., 2006, p.318).

[48] 'Lamb of the 85 civilization' – the souls with the sign of Christ of the Second Coming, of the 85 new civilizations, going to replace the 84 modern civilization.

[49] 'Believers' (Latin).

[50] Garabandal – place of the great revelation of the Virgin Mary, where She talked about the coming transformations.

[51] In the record of the revelation a tentative period is indicated for the sign: 2009-2010. But it has been expressed that to rely on earthly chronology is not blessed: the period may change.

[52] Christ-III – see footnote 3.

[53] The revelations of the life of Jesus Christ and the Most Holy Virgin Mary, having been dictated in the beginning of the 19th century to the bed-ridden stigmatic Anne Catherine Emmerick. These revelations were recorded over several years and published by the German poet K. Bretano. They have been published in Russian under the name 'The Day by Day Gospel'.

[54] Christ came to Jerusalem at the age of thirty and

was, to begin with, received favourably by the Jews, having seriously accepted him as the Judaic prophet and messiah. But, when he revealed his origin from the Father of pure love, and not from Moses, and taught that the synagogue was the institution of Satan, the Jews considered Him the most evil heretic and their primary enemy. – Author.

[55] Tibetan cosmism – occult and magic practices from Tibet.

[56] Ammialies – special kind of angelic beings.

[57] Ruakh-Elohim in the translation from Hebrew means spirit. We have in mind one of the beginning verses of the Old Testament, translated as "and the spirit (of Elohim, the Omnipotent) soared above the water" (Genesis, 1:2). In Christian theology it was accepted to identify the Holy Spirit with the spirit of the biblical god Elohim, the creator of the material world.

[58] Compare 'the mirror of the kingdom' in the mysticism of the Eastern Church.

[59] According to the definition of the orthodox monk of Pskov, Filofei (sixteenth century), which became the official ideology of the tsars of Moscow, Byzantium became the second Rome (the heir to the Roman empire). Moscow is fit to be called the third, 'and there will be no fourth'.

[60] Anzer: an island of the Solovetsky archipelago, the great treasure trove of imperishable and myrrh-

pouring relics of the great martyrs from the time of Stalinism.

[61] Gastronom: the holy-fool name of the three-storey building on Bolshoy Solovetsky Island, every centimetre of which flowed with the blood of innocent victims. The main location of tortures in the years of the Gulag.

[62] In accordance with Cathar teaching, the so-called 'creation of man by the Creator', described in the Bible (Genesis 1-2), was in actually fact the illegitimate remodelling of divine man by the fallen one, Lucifer, for the sham adaptation to the conditions of this world.

[63] Pochaev: a place of the serving and witness of the mother Euphrosinia, loved by me, which Exceeding Wisdom, at the very height of the Soviets, laid as a fiery lamp of the Holy Spirit and presented with the imperishable fragrant relics. – Author.

[64] Disposins – race, coming from the mystical marriage of Christ and Mary Magdalene. Desposins gave rise to the royal dynasties of Europe

[65] So it is in the record of the revelation. According to historical witnesses, Simon de Montfor was killed long before the fall of Montségur. In all likelihood they are talking about the spirit which had prevailed over the crusaders.

[66] The gradula staff of the anointed ones (from gradula – the upper area in the towers of the Cathar

castles, from where the immortals mystically control the global proceedings).

⁶⁷ Agapic love – (old Greek) divine love.

⁶⁸ We have in mind the prayer 'Our Father'.

⁶⁹ We have in mind the internal treasure trove of the heart.

⁷⁰ Pneumatology – teaching about the acquisition of the Holy Spirit.

⁷¹ Genocide of the Holyminne – it means the destruction of the messengers of Minne – pure divine love – by the Catholic Inquisition.

⁷² From Occitan, 'bon homme': kind man; 'mal homme': evil man.

⁷³ Jehovah or Yahweh (Jewish יהוי) – 'I-am-who-am', is translated as 'the Existing One' is the Bible.

⁷⁴ From the Greek Deuteronomon (Jewish, Second Law, 'copied law') – one of the books of the Old Testament and the Judaic Pentateuch, which retells that which is contained in other books.

⁷⁵ Nightingale Mountain (the Bridal Chamber), Montségur (the control of the world, the original Grail) and San Salvador Verdadero (the throne of the Father of pure love in the Theocivilization III).

⁷⁶ Wine into Blood, Blood into myrrh, and myrrh into the internal compositions of man.